Renoir

THE MAN, THE PAINTER, AND HIS WORLD

Renoir

THE MAN, THE PAINTER, AND HIS WORLD

By LAWRENCE HANSON

ILLUSTRATED

DODD, MEAD & COMPANY

NEW YORK

Copyright © 1968 by Lawrence Hanson

No part of this book may be reproduced in any form
without permission in writing from the publisher

Library of Congress Catalog Card Number: 68-21898

Printed in the United States of America
by The Cornwall Press, Inc., Cornwall, N. Y.

To
Philip S. Tank

PREFACE

M<small>ANY YEARS AGO</small> I began to collect materials for a biography of Auguste Renoir. I had sketched out about one third of the book when I heard that the long-awaited memoir by Jean Renoir was at last to be published. I put my work aside. I had a definite aim, to provide the first full and documented account in English of the painter's life and work. If M. Jean Renoir had anticipated me, so much the better.

This thought, as it soon appeared, was to do M. Renoir less than justice. When his book was published some five years ago it placed itself at once in quite a different category. I have called it a memoir. That is how most reviewers described it. It is that, of course, but many feel that it chiefly owes its unusual importance and very considerable charm to the fact that it is much more than a distinguished son's recollections of his famous father.

Perhaps I should enlarge on this. Auguste Renoir was in his fifties when Jean was born. As a result, as Jean Renoir explains in his book, he did not know his father in any real sense of the word until they came together in Paris in the middle of the first World War. By that time the painter was old and ill, within a year or two of his death. During those months in a Paris apartment he spoke freely to his son. These conversations—listenings they might more exactly be called—form the basis of the Jean Renoir book.

In consequence, it might more justly be described as an auto-biography by the father written down by the son; certainly its most memorable passages are, as one would expect, those in which the elder Renoir speaks. As is the way with old men, Renoir's thoughts often dwelt during those months on the days of his youth; that is why his son's book gives us such a wonderful picture of the Renoir family and of Auguste as boy and youth. For his part, Jean Renoir naturally remembers his father in his sixties and seventies, when he himself was a schoolboy and young man, and he presents us with a moving account of those heroic last years.

Whether M. Renoir has also provided us with a professional biography of his father is another matter. In his book the years between youth and old age are naturally less detailed because his father had less to say about them and he himself was not then born. Yet these years form by far the most important period of Renoir's life, when he reached his height as man and painter.

So, having consulted those better fitted than myself to judge, I decided that my original intention should stand, that there was still need for the kind of biography I had planned—indeed, I felt, an even greater need, since it could now supplement Renoir's reminiscences with the kind of systematic information, drawn from responsible eyewitnesses, that readers of a serious biography have a right to expect, and which many of the readers of M. Renoir's book, anxious to know more about this delightful man, might be glad to consult.

We all have our heroes, and I have had many, but I cannot think of one who expresses my philosophy so consistently and triumphantly as Renoir. And as biography, after all, should be a profession of faith, I have written *con amore* this story of a man who was as admirable as his work. Renoir's life offers perpetual encouragement to the gifted who start from nothing; it shows how, given determination, anyone so endowed can win the world's acclaim. It also demonstrates the true drama of a man who time after time declared himself no fighter but who was nevertheless driven on by love of his work.

Unlike many good men whom we all know, Renoir was neither prig nor bore because his goodness was founded on a knowledge of and acceptance of life, not an avoidance of it. He did not understand the meaning of spite, he was naturally modest, and he had a pithy sense of humor. He could and did mix with every kind of person, treating all alike. He was a model son, a faithful husband, a fond father. He was nevertheless an artist and a very fine one, though unpretentious about the fact in an age notorious for its pretension.

It must be left to accredited critics to determine whether or no Renoir was a great painter. The men and women who may enjoy this book—men and women who love paintings without finding it necessary to dissect them and who can appreciate a man without demanding antisocial behavior from him—may think that to produce one happy picture after another, as Renoir did for nearly fifty years, is good enough to be going on with.

The biographer of Renoir is fortunate that he can draw on many contemporary records. Eyewitnesses fill out the picture of that vital period of the eighteen seventies, eighties and nineties when he was struggling to become the maker of paintings now so famous. In the references and notes of this book almost every statement of moment is related to its source.

I have been fortunate, too, in my places and friends. The Paris of my youth was in effect the Paris of Renoir's middle and later years—the places he knew and loved and lived in changed slowly in those days—and my home in the Midi was a mere mile or so from Cagnes, which had not changed at all, where Renoir was vividly and vocally remembered.

In Paris, thanks to my good friends, I have been able to reinforce these early memories of what I have always thought of as exclusively Renoir terrain by hearing much about him from those who knew him intimately. For example, I cannot adequately express my gratitude to Mme. R. de Goldschmidt-Rothschild; to her I owe many days of hospitality and a collection of pictures and rare documents opened to me without reserve; I owe introductions to the famous galleries of the Faubourg Saint-Honoré and elsewhere in which I met men who had known Renoir very well and were happy to talk about him; above all, I owe a most prized introduction, to Mme. Ernest Rouart, only child of Berthe Morisot, niece of Edouard Manet, cousin of Paul Valéry, godchild of Stéphane Mallarmé. Mme. Rouart knew Renoir as few living people have; from the moment when he painted her as a child to his final visits to Paris when she had become the wife of Ernest Rouart she saw a great deal of him, watched him, talked to him, listened to him.

I was first taken to meet Mme. Rouart by M. François Valéry, who had much to tell me of his father's friendship with Renoir. And in the Rouart house—that house where Berthe Morisot had made so many of her paintings—I was entertained by my hostess and her family, shown paintings, letters, and as time went on, was presented with a most valuable and wholly authentic picture of Renoir through the years from the eighteen-eighties onward. I cannot overstate the value of these conversations, nor can I sufficiently thank the charming and knowledgeable woman who was so kind to me.

More briefly, I must mention the countless kindnesses of M. and Mme. Roland de Margerie. At their luncheons I met men and women who helped me in more ways than I can say. Through them I met M. François Valéry. And their own wide knowledge of French art was put completely at my disposal.

I have also to thank most heartily: M. le Baron de Heeckeren who gave me the full benefit of his unrivaled learning in the history of nineteenth-century Paris; M. and Mme. Saltzman who lent me unobtainable books and shared freely with me their wide knowledge of nineteenth-century French painting; M. and Mme. Henri Alter who introduced me to an old Renoir model then retired at Nice; M. Jean Adhémar; M. Michel Monet; M. Bernard Dorival; M. Germain Bazin; M. François Chapon; M. Jean Loize; M. Henri Matarasso; M. Dominique Denis; M. Alfred Dupont; Mme. Marie Dornoy; Mme. Joly-Segalen; Ir. V. W. van Gogh; and all the curators and directors of museums and libraries in which I have worked over the years as well as the staff of the various mairies and hotels de ville in which I have examined documents.

My grateful thanks go to my wife, who has worked hard on this book, to friends who have read and commentated at various stages, and to Miss B. Carpenter who has typed and retyped so often.

For permission to quote from letters and to reproduce illustrations I wish to thank: U.S.A.: Barnes Foundation, Merion; Ford Foundation, Detroit; Fogg Art Museum, Cambridge; Metropolitan Museum, New York; Museum of Fine Arts, Boston; Phillips Collection, Washington; Institute of Arts, Minneapolis; Collection Caroll S. Tyson; Collection Stephen C. Clark. Brazil: Museum of Modern Art, São Paulo. France: The Louvre; Bibliothèque Nationale; Archives de la Seine; Bibliothèque Jacques Doucet; Bibliothèque d'Art et d'Archéologie; Mme. Ernest Rouart; Mme. la Baroness R. de Goldschmidt-Rothschild; M. and Mme. Roland de Margerie; M. François Valéry. Algeria: Musée des Beaux Arts, Algiers. England: National Gallery, Courtauld Institute, London. Sweden: National Museum, Stockholm. West Germany: Folkwang Museum, Essen; Wallraf–Richartz Museum, Cologne.

CONTENTS

xiii

ILLUSTRATIONS

Mère Anthony's Inn, 1864
Frédéric Bazille, 1867
Renoir, painted by Bazille in 1867
La Grenouillère, 1869
The Studio, painted by Bazille in 1870
Lise with Parasol, 1867
The Sisleys, 1868
The Henriot Family, 1871
Bather with Dog, 1870
The Box, 1874
Portrait of M. Chocquet, 1875
Claude Monet, 1875
The Cup of Chocolate, 1878
Mme. Charpentier and Her Children, 1878
Portrait of Cézanne, 1880
Le Moulin de la Galette, 1879
Mussel Gatherer at Berneval, 1879
The First Outing, 1880
Gondola on the Grand Canal, 1881
The Bathers, 1887
The Dance at Bougival, 1883
The Luncheon of the Boating Party, 1881

Renoir

THE MAN, THE PAINTER, AND HIS WORLD

CHAPTER I

THE RENOIRS

1841-1854

RENOIR USED TO TELL a story about his ancestry. He told it with a smile, for one of the many charming qualities about him was his lack of pretension. His grandmother had repeated the tale proudly to him, when he was a child, that his grandfather was nobly born of aristocratic parents guillotined during the Terror and had been rescued and adopted by a tailor named Renoir.[1]

Renoir's father also believed this story. His son, however, characteristically discounted it and made a joke of it. Unlike his father he was to have time and the money to make inquiries and, if the theory proved correct, to live up to his rank. In fact he ignored the subject. The inquiries have been left to present-day scholars, and this is what they have discovered.

On January 8 in the year 1773 a newly born male child was found abandoned in Limoges, France, and taken to the General Hospital. That same day he was baptized with the name of François; he could not be given a surname in the baptismal register because his parents were unknown.

Twenty-three years later François reappears in the records of Limoges; he was married on November 24, 1796, to Anne, daughter of the carpenter Joseph Régnier, and for the first time is officially credited with a surname: he is described as François Renoir, shoemaker, of rue du Colombier.

1

A clerical error gave him the name that has since become so famous. No one called Renoir lived in Limoges. There was, however, a Renouard in the town and he was a shoemaker. It has been assumed that this man adopted the foundling—a common occurrence when a craftsman wanted an apprentice who would cost only the food he ate. It has also been assumed that when François was asked his name at the marriage ceremony he said Renouard and that the registrar wrote down the phonetic Renoir—a mistake François could not correct because he could neither read nor write.[2]

This is a tempting theory, but as there was no family of that name in Limoges the registrar must have needed an additional incentive to write down the Renoir he did not know rather than the Renouard he did. By a curious coincidence this incentive existed; although there was no Renoir in the town, there was more than one Lenoir, and two of them were well known to the registrar: the priest who baptized François in 1773 was the Abbé Lenoir and the magistrate who married him in 1796 was also called Lenoir. Obviously it was easier to change one letter than to alter the complete ending of a name.

In this haphazard fashion Auguste Renoir's grandfather got his name. François presumably accepted it for the sake of his work, but he did not accept the mystery of his birth. When the Revolution collapsed he asserted that he was nobly born and entitled to estates and fortune, and the moment royalty was restored in 1815 he went off to Paris to try to convince the commission set up to deal with the claims of dispossessed aristocrats.[3]

So much for family tradition. François returned unheard and had to get what satisfaction he could from the knowledge that his wife and eldest son believed him. Who convinced him that he was the son of aristocrats guillotined during the Terror remains as mysterious as the story he told; it could have been his master Renouard, the Abbé Lenoir, or most probably one of the sisters at the hospital.

The story has an obvious flaw: François was born in 1773, the Terror was twenty years later. In 1773 the aristocrats of

France were not obliged to fly from danger and leave children behind. The one satisfactory suggestion, assuming that François was of noble blood as he believed, seems to be that his father was an aristocrat and that the child was the result of one of the liaisons, frequent in those days, with a servant of his household. There the mystery must be left. One man it was not to affect in the slightest degree was Auguste Renoir; he much preferred to think of himself as the grandson of a shoemaker, doing a useful job with his hands.

Auguste's father, Léonard, worked with his hands too. The eldest son of François, he was born July 7, 1799, and in due course was apprenticed to a journeyman tailor, a man who moved from town to town, putting up at each one as long as orders continued to come in. This wandering life lasted until 1828 when the twenty-nine-year-old Léonard, a tailor in his own right by that time, visited Saintes, one hundred miles west of his birthplace. There he met and on November 17 married a twenty-one-year-old seamstress, Marguerite Merlet.[4]

This young woman provided a model for the famous man who was to be her son. She was a delightfully no-nonsense person in those frivolous days; she believed that her sex would do better to rely on natural feminine attractions rather than try to improvise them; she preferred soap and water to cosmetics, and a plain costume and hairstyle to the much favored highly decorative ones. Her speech was in character; she said what she thought and not what she thought others wanted to hear.[5]

She also believed in the duty of children to their parents; soon after their marriage she and Léonard went back to Limoges, made a home for François and his wife (considered elderly in those days), and followed national tradition by helping to carry on the family business. There at 4 Boulevard Sainte-Catherine (now 35 in the tree-lined Boulevard Gambetta) six children were born. Two died young. The four who lived on were Henri, born 1830, Lisa two years later, Victor four years after Lisa, and finally, on February 25, 1841, nearly five years later than Victor, the subject of this biography, Pierre Auguste Renoir.

On May 29, 1845, François died, aged seventy-two, and Léonard decided to move to Paris. He did so, Renoir said later, "to make his fortune in the capital." [6] He was evidently a conscientious craftsman and may have felt that good work would be better rewarded in Paris than in Limoges—the wealth of the great city was admired and envied in every province of France. But his own prospects were unlikely to have provided the main stimulant for the adventurous change, adventurous because at that time it was a major operation, in expense and physical endurance, to convey an entire family with furniture the two hundred and fifty miles between the two cities. Henri, then fifteen, was already showing talent as an engraver. Limoges offered little to him; Paris would offer much. There was no question of sending him off on his own; the Renoir family was a devoted one in its restrained way, and both parents were determined to provide a home for their children until they had homes of their own and to give a fair chance of advancement to all. So later that year the Renoir family moved en bloc to Paris.

2

They settled into a small apartment in the center of Paris, in a street that no longer exists. At that time the Tuileries Palace completed the rectangle of buildings made by the Palais du Louvre and its two flanks. Cutting through this rectangle, roughly where there now is the Place du Carrousel, was a narrow street, rue d'Argenteuil, which ran from rue de Rivoli to the river and stood between the Palace and the Louvre. In this street was a block of sixteenth-century houses built for the Palace Guard. The Guard had disappeared, but the houses stayed on and, in the manner of that time, had disintegrated physically and socially into poor apartments. In one of these, barely a stone's throw from the King in his palace, Léonard Renoir set up his home and business. The young Auguste Renoir played in the courtyard of the Louvre with his friends—

his favorite game was marbles—and grew up accustomed to being overlooked from the windows of the Palace by the servants and courtiers of Louis Philippe.[7]

One wonders whether Léonard chose rue d'Argenteuil because of his belief in his aristocratic blood; certainly Auguste's first substantial impressions of life came from a place that revolved around royalty and traditional ceremony. His father and mother often took him to the Louvre as he grew older, and there he saw pictures that powerfully confirmed the atmosphere in which he was brought up.

In the apartment the last Renoir child, Edmond, was born in 1849. By that time Henri was a much esteemed apprentice of a silversmith in rue des Petits Champs, a M. David; Lisa was learning dressmaking; Victor was apprenticed to a fashionable tailor; and Auguste was attending a local church school. The Renoir home life was happy in its undemonstrative fashion, mother and father both hardworking, earnest, and frugal. Auguste was fond of everyone and everyone of him, but he inclined chiefly to his mother and sister. He was always to prefer women to men, for their decorativeness, their good sense and reliance on the affections, and he began early and at home. He was obviously attractive with his solemn little face, his lively moods and affectionate nature, and the two women somehow managed to favor without spoiling him.

Beside him, the other children seem obscure. Henri was hardworking like his father and tended to become absorbed into the life of his master's household as apprentices did in those days (he eventually married M. David's daughter). Victor seems to have grown into a fairly typical product of his time and trade, a dandy and flirt, though with all the Renoir good nature. Lisa grew into a rather bellicose girl, very much a child of her age. Of the three she evidently had the most character; she became a devotee of Fournier and St. Simon and their feminine disciples, George Sand and Flora Tristan, and was a most lovable if at times alarming idealist and a fervent hater of injustice. All seem to have inherited their father's application to work, which soon enabled him to rent a little shop in rue de la Bibliothèque

instead of receiving customers in his apartment. In their in-
conspicuous way all the members of the family were doing well,
and the troubles of 1848 apparently passed over their heads.
Louis Napoleon in due course took the place of Louis Philippe
in the overshadowing Palace, and the Renoirs worked stolidly
and unconcernedly on.

With both elder boys out of the apartment Auguste came in
for more attention and Edmond's birth made little difference,
for the youngest soon showed every sign of becoming a devoted
admirer of his amusing and happy-natured older brother. If
Auguste's career at school was undistinguished, as it seems to
have been, the explanation may be in his friend Rivière's description of him as "timid, reserved and with a horror of drawing attention to himself." [8] The first attribute was surely a
misreading of a much more interesting quality, but the second
and third were characteristics from birth; Auguste hated to
push himself forward, he loathed publicity. This does not make
for success in childhood, when the brash children shine, but it
indicated the kind of nature that would win good friends and
attract observant women. One has to look no further than the
small Renoir boy's unobtrusive love of life to find why he had
such a strong appeal to the women of the family. The Renoir
home, though affectionate, was inclined to the somber, and the
lively, loving yet self-effacing Auguste seemed like a ray of sunshine to his mother and sister.[9]

In those days and on that level of society a child was expected
to earn money as soon as he had received as much free educa-
tion as possible, and discussions about Auguste's future must
have begun early in the family. He was interested in drawing,
no doubt following the examples of Henri and, more particularly, of the young man who had fallen in love with Lisa, a
Charles Leray, who made his living by drawing for fashion
magazines. Leray gave him the odd half hour of basic hints and
the Louvre did the rest. There Auguste used his eyes to some
purpose and became so devoted to drawing that he spent many of
his school hours scribbling in his lesson books and, at home,
plied a piece of chalk on the floor, sketching anything that came

into his head and anyone who came into his range of vision.[10] His mother bought him pencils and scribbling pads, though the assumption that she did so because she thought him gifted has to be made with caution; she may merely have been humoring him to preserve her floors. His intention, as far as so young a boy can be said to have an intention, was to follow Leray into fashion designing.[11]

The discovery of another gift led to some heart-searching. The Renoir family worshipped at the church of St. Eustache in the middle of the district of Les Halles, the great Paris market and one of Auguste's joys. He loved the market men and women, the sound and the look of them, and he saw them again on Sundays in church, Rembrandtesque figures sitting, standing, kneeling. He had an excellent view of them on these occasions without being seen, because he was concealed by the organ casing.[12] The choirmaster and organist, Charles Gounod, discovered that Auguste possessed a promising voice, and he found himself in the church choir.

Gounod, then in his thirties, was the son of a distinguished painter and an equally distinguished musician and had followed his pianist mother into a career in music. He had already made a name for himself as a composer of religious music, but just about the time the young Renoir came into his choir his interest was turning toward opera—his first opera was produced when Auguste was ten.[13] He tended therefore to evaluate a good voice in terms of the stage. Impressed by the boy's possibilities, he gave him free lessons, wooed the family favor by the offer of a box at the opera, and eventually offered to train him as an opera singer and, in the meantime, to put him into the opera chorus. He tempted the boy with visions of a successful career as a singer of leading roles at high salaries. Obviously he thought very highly of him.

This story, which has been repeated by every writer on Renoir, presents a difficulty, for the Gounod offer is said by all to have coincided with another—from a manufacturer wanting to train a boy in the decoration of earthenware—and much has been made of Renoir's choice of the latter. The difficulty is this:

Renoir is said to have had a good baritone voice, and this is obviously what attracted Gounod, yet the boy was no more than fourteen (some accounts say thirteen) when the decorating job was offered, so his voice could scarcely have broken or, if it had, could not possibly have settled down into a recognizable baritone that would intrigue a good judge of the voice.[14]

So the story of an Auguste faced with these choices either cannot be true or Gounod possessed an uncanny gift for understanding how a boy's treble voice would develop. The probability is that Auguste continued to sing in the choir after he began work and that Gounod's suggestion came later. His exceptional dislike of public appearances no doubt played a part in his decision, but Gounod's offer must have tempted him enormously. Renoir was never to care for money in itself or for what it would give him. He loved to spend money on others but discovered very early that enjoyment of life must come from within. As a French boy, however, he was naturally thrifty, and having been brought up in near poverty, he saw money in its true light, as a purveyor of security. He also had the natural wish of every loving child who has watched his parents struggle to bring him up well fed and clothed, to help them in return. Yet he rejected the singing career. He also abandoned the once cherished plan to follow in Leray's footsteps. The occupation that he undertook was infinitely less promising than either.

"It's no use asking me about Limoges," Renoir often said in later years. "I was not more than four when I left it and I've never seen it again." [15] But Limoges had its effect on him just the same. It was then, as now, famed for the porcelain which could almost be said to be its raison d'être. In those days this porcelain was highly decorated—by hand, of course—and the most popular designs on plates and cups and saucers were copies of the nymphs and shepherdesses of the eighteenth-century painters as well as intricate floral patterns. It was impossible to live in Limoges without coming to know this china very well; it was used in the home, one saw it in the shops, saw it being made and decorated. Every other friend was employed in the workshops. Both the making and the decoration of the

Limoges porcelain were regarded there with great pride. Léonard Renoir, like most of his townsmen, thought of it as synonymous with art.

He remembered Limoges when he watched his young son covering his little books with drawings.[16] And when a friend of Henri's master, a M. Lévy, offered Auguste a job as apprentice in his earthenware works in rue Vielle du Temple, he must have thought what a happy conjunction of circumstances it was. It is doubtful if he ever wanted Auguste to go into tailoring, even if only for fear that he might become a dandy and womanizer such as Victor, whose master on the Boulevards thought more of smartness than solidity. Léonard was a serious workman. His fine face tells all. He was a man brought up the hard way, proud of his craft, fussy about his clients. It was not the face of a man who found laughter easy; he took life earnestly and no wonder, with the struggle it had been to bring up the children decently and to provide for old age. He was probably puritanical; he certainly looks it, and all that one knows of the Renoir home suggests it. If he disapproved of the way clothes were made on the Boulevards, how much more must he have disapproved of the stage as a career for a son of his. He believed in a man using his hands honestly so that he could feel the maximum self-respect, and he passed on this belief. He would obviously prefer the earthenware works to modern tailoring, the equally suspect fashion designing of Leray, and even more emphatically the opera of Gounod.

How much influence he had on his son we do not know; the likelihood is that in this instance it was not necessary. Auguste must have remembered Limoges too when he had M. Lévy's offer, for he seems to have thrown up the idea of fashion designing with less qualm than he was to dismiss singing as a career, and more or less cheerfully began his working life as a decorator of earthenware. He no doubt recalled the eighteenth-century designs painted on Limoges porcelain—the family meal table there and in Paris would surely boast a few pieces of this local work—so M. Lévy's workshop had a double attraction, as a place in which he could use his talent for drawing and use it to portray the kind of work that, unconsciously at Limoges and consciously during his visits to the Louvre, he had felt to be akin to his own sympathies.

The offer of M. Lévy virtually coincided with the decision of Louis Napoleon to pull down the houses in rue d'Argenteuil and extend the Louvre courtyard uninterruptedly to the Palace, and this decision may well have affected Auguste's acceptance. Louis, less royal than some of his predecessors there, probably wanted to enhance his dignity. Whatever the cause, in 1854 down the houses came and the Renoir family had to leave. They moved less than a mile, to more spacious quarters in another old house that had seen better days, this time in rue des Gravilliers, a narrow street connecting rue St. Martin and rue du Temple, a few hundred yards above the Hotel de Ville. This house was close to the earthenware works in rue Vielle du Temple (on the eastern side of rue du Temple) and Mme. Renoir must have been less reluctant to see Auguste go off early every morning when she knew he would not be going far. So sometime late in 1853 or in the early part of 1854 the boy began work.

CHAPTER II

EARNING A LIVING

1854-1862

THE EARTHENWARE made and decorated in M. Lévy's workshop was stamped "Sèvres" and sold to eastern countries. It had no more to do with the porcelain of Sèvres than with concrete, as Auguste soon discovered, and his ambition for some considerable time was "to become a maker of Sèvres porcelain." [1]

What he actually had to do six days a week—six long days—was "to paint little sprays of flowers on a white background which earned me five sous a dozen cups or plates or saucers. When the pieces to be decorated were larger the price went up a little—a very little. When I began to feel more confidence I was promoted from bouquets to portraits. The profile of Marie Antoinette, I remember, earned me eight sous." [2]

He was to tell his son that he received three sous apiece for the profiles of Marie Antoinette, Vollard that he received eight—an instance of the pitfalls awaiting the biographer who seeks exactitude—but he got neither eight nor even three sous when he began. All he brought home in these early days was the negligible wage of an apprentice. He liked the work and quickly showed himself deft; his touch with the brush was delicate, he learned precision and reveled in the use of bright colors. Lisa, now married to Leray but still living at home, heard how he was turning Marie Antoinettes out by the dozen for a pittance.

One of Lisa's anathemas was the exploitation of the masses, and here was her best loved brother a victim of capitalist cupidity. In no time at all she was off to confront M. Lévy in his lair. It is a scene one would have given much to see, particularly as it appears that the exploiter, a very small man, was physically as well as morally overborne. From that moment Auguste did piecework.

It is probable that M. Lévy was at least half genuine when he expressed horror at the idea of a small boy having it in his power to earn what was then considered a large wage—especially a boy so quick and so determined to get on. Some of Auguste's fellow workers, all much older than he, took even less kindly to the way he began to beat them at their own game. Their feelings are understandable if their actions are indefensible; they mocked him with the name Monsieur Rubens and often brought him to tears.[3]

But he stuck to it. In spite of a delicate appearance he had all the toughness, physical and moral, of a child accustomed to the hard knocks of the streets. He knew that his technique was improving. He was proud of the speed with which he was producing his decorations. He persuaded his master to let him vary his Marie Antoinettes (which had begun to bore him) with nudes which interested him much more—a significant pointer to the future. All were so efficiently and quickly done that in a year or two he was accumulating considerable savings. Far from being a burden on his parents, he was able to help them buy a country cottage for their retirement and still put by money for his own future.[4]

The future he had in his mind's eye remained the six francs a day—a substantial wage in those days—he could earn by decorating true porcelain selling at high prices instead of the crude earthenware of the rue Vielle du Temple workshop. He was always insistent, when talking of himself in later years, about the happy-go-lucky nature of his plans. He believed in being adaptable, in following his star of the moment. He found himself a decorator of poor quality china; he enjoyed the work and aimed logically to decorate the finest porcelain and to be the highest paid.

For a long time his ambition stopped there and he would not allow anyone or anything to distract him from it. He resisted one or two temptations. A conventional young painter called Laporte (possibly first encountered during visits to the Louvre, possibly introduced by Leray) urged him not only to study the old masters but to follow them literally. He tried to persuade him into a recognized studio and to take up painting as a career. Renoir would not listen. Nor would he allow himself to be led astray, as he saw it, by the even stronger appeals to the same end of an old china decorator who used to revisit the workshop and who offered to teach him to draw from a model and to use oils.[5] Renoir accepted the instruction gladly but kept his eyes firmly on porcelain decoration as a career.

This practicality was characteristic of him. Many in after years were to think of the young Renoir as the ideal figure of the artist. He must have looked the part with his thin and rather mournful face breaking occasionally into an attractive grin, his shy, nervous, abrupt manner, sharp movements, long silences, and above all his strange abstraction. For long periods he did not seem to be in or of this world at all but in some private one of his own. This outward appearance was not a lie—Renoir was incapable of subterfuge. But from the moment he was able to think he had two guiding principles, to enjoy life and to make enough money to live without the incessant and crippling anxieties of the poor. Not for one instant did he depart from these goals throughout a long life. To make money in the only acceptable way—he hated the shoddy and meretricious as much as his father—it was necessary to devote himself entirely to the work he was doing. He learned this lesson very early—from watching and listening to his father—and his ability to concentrate on one thing at a time became phenomenal. When he seemed to be rapt away from the world he was bound up at that moment with one part of it. This practical reason for the outwardly romantic appearance is essentially Renoir (Monet had similar characteristics) and must surely have accounted in some part for his fascination for women, a fascination that had already led to comical attempts by Mme. Lévy to half-vamp, half-pet him;[6] it undoubtedly ex-

plains all that can be explained of the success of the highly
gifted man.

The making of money had to come first—his whole short life
had been an object lesson in its importance—but the need for
enjoyment was not far behind. His idea of enjoyment was
simple and natural. As he grew up—and he grew up quickly—he
appreciated the pleasures of the senses but he understood their
limitations. Where this kind of pleasure ended another began,
and that, for him, consisted in the use of his hands and brain to
make the most of the gifts with which he had been born. He
said again and again that working creatively with the hands was
the greatest joy life had to offer, and he proved it in his own life,
though he was a man who liked many things. He detested idleness
as much as he despised luxury.

Feeling as he did, the life at the workshop gave him a great
deal of satisfaction, and he did not seriously think beyond it; he
was employed, helping his parents, and steadily improving himself as a craftsman.

Yet Auguste, in spite of his concentration on the work of
the moment, was endlessly curious. When Laporte went on and
on about the glories of the Louvre and the old workman
praised his first efforts on canvas, he was responsive; he had
nothing to lose and all to gain by looking more closely at free
pictures and spending evenings with an admirer who offered
him free models to copy.

It is not quite correct to say that he had nothing to lose, but
what he endangered—his lunch—meant little to a boy who
thought of one thing at a time. From about the age of fifteen
he fell into the habit of spending the lunch break in the Louvre.
He could not bear to waste a minute of any anticipated pleasure; he scarcely ever walked, he ran, arriving at the Louvre
breathless, a pencil in one hand, a drawing pad in the other.[7]

At first he went the rounds, taking in everything with those
sharp brown eyes, and drew from the antique as Laporte had
advised him; then he began to form his judgment. He was soon
to be seen riveted before the canvases of Delacroix, whose free
drawing and rich color pleased him, and the eighteenth-century

painters whose nymphs and sheperdesses and gaily dressed women reminded him nostalgically of Limoges china. He responded instinctively to reproductions of clothes emphasizing the feminine form. His love of women was thorough, like everything he did and felt. The look came first, then the feel, then the disposition, soft but eminently sensible too. He liked his women to look like women—he would have hated the contourless boyish fashions of later years—and thought a well-developed bosom one of the most satisfactory sights in life.

Back at the workshop, if he could not charm something out of Mme. Lévy he relied on being sent on errands in the afternoon so that he could call at one of the Halles wineshops, drink a cheap vin rouge with the market porters, and chew a quickly fried beefsteak.

On one of these excursions he made a momentous discovery, the sixteenth-century Fontaine des Innocents. "I stopped spellbound," [8] he said afterward. He was on the point of going to a wineshop to eat and drink but at once gave up the idea. Instead he bought a few centimeters of sausage at a nearby shop and returned to the fountain. He walked round and round it slowly, studying the group of statues from every angle, as he munched his sausage. From that moment he felt a particular affinity with the sculptor Jean Goujon; his work possessed everything he loved: grace, solidity and elegance, and with it the feeling of living flesh. "Goujon," he said, "gives you the texture of flesh and knew how to make drapery cling to the figure. Until then I hadn't realised how drapery brings out the form." [9]

Auguste could fairly be described as a very happy youth in his mid-teens; his work was getting quicker and more assured month by month, his savings were mounting, and his relations with the workmen had become good. Most men, like women, if for different reasons, responded to him in the long run. He earned his money in the workshop—the most envious could not deny that—and never crowed about it. He was always eager to learn from anyone who would teach him.

Besides, life was opening out in several directions: he reveled in his excursions to the Louvre and saw plainly the link between

a Goujon and a Boucher and himself; and he had discovered
other pleasures in the hours between the closing of the workshop and his tumble into bed. He had begun to feel a certain
power in his essays in oils, and by the time he was sixteen had
made his first portrait in this medium. He made it, of course,
at home, and the sitter was a woman.

There is a little mystery about this canvas. Renoir's biog-
raphers and those who have written on his work have always
assumed it to be a portrait of his grandmother. No doubt they
were led to this conclusion by the portrait, which certainly appears to represent the head of an old woman, and which enabled
them to place the work before April 23, 1857, when Anne
Renoir died—that is, shortly after Auguste's sixteenth birthday.
Jean Renoir believes the portrait to represent the mother, then
just fifty. This difficulty apart, the work is full of promise, is
indeed remarkably efficient for a boy of that age.

Whether Auguste saw the likeness to himself in his model's
face—the bright brown eyes, the good bone structure—one cannot know, but without doubt he saw with a painter's eye its
possibilities on canvas. All were pleased, the family, Laporte,
the retired china decorator; and great things were prophesied
for him, though in the vaguest of terms. Laporte and the old
teacher did not mince their words—the boy had talent, they said,
and should make use of it. To the Renoirs, Auguste included,
this was pleasant criticism but dangerous counsel. To praise was
one thing, to advise quite another. No notice was taken in
practical terms.

When the boy left the workman's apartment after an evening's lesson, he often used to go up the street instead of turning
off it toward his home. His destination was the Boulevard du
Temple at the top of the workshop street. Here he walked up
and down listening to the hawkers who filled the pavement
edges crying their wares. He loved their songs and he loved
them, too, and their shabby customers; to him the "noise and
bustle and good humor of the common people" [10] were a kind of
tonic; he did not think he would ever find their like in the
whole of France, and he had little time to spare for the richly

dressed people who passed in their carriages, and no envy, a feeling of which he remained absolutely innocent. If anything he felt pity for those bored people in the fiacres.

Having listened and looked to his satisfaction, he then went the length of the boulevard, examining the lurid placards outside the small theatres which lined the street. Melodramas predominated, with Alexandre Dumas the favorite, but there were comedies too, sophisticated and otherwise. After long study he would choose his play for the night and climb to the cheapest seat, at fifty centimes. He loved every moment of it but not uncritically. He much preferred Dumas père to Dumas fils. His great favorite into old age was *La Dame de Montsoreau* of the father; of the son he could only say, "I detest everything he's done, *La Dame aux Camélias* more than all the rest. I have always had an absolute horror of the sentimentalised prostitute." [11]

Victor Hugo was another matter; here the bombast offended the clearsighted and plainspoken young Auguste as he leaned over the gallery rail. "You would have to be out of your mind to say that Hugo has no genius; I can't stand the man because he has lured the French out of the way of speaking their language simply." [12]

In the comedies he had strong preferences. In his days of youthful theatre-going Mirbeau was all the rage and De Musset falling out of favor, but for Renoir the latter, however exaggerated and sentimental, at least did not try to cheapen human relationships. He acknowledged Mirbeau's sophistication but insisted that it was built on a foundation of untruth. And how boring this smart dialogue could be! Of the great favorite of those years, *Les Affaires sont les Affaires*, he said in his usual blunt way, "This thing may be very good but the conversation of businessmen doesn't interest me. I for one shan't be dining at their houses." [13]

These remarks were made to friends of his middle and later years, but they mirrored exactly the state of his mind in his teens. Indeed they could well be a repetition of the exact words he used at the time to Laporte and his family. One of the most refreshing aspects of Renoir is his changelessness; from boy to old man his likes and dislikes remained firm, and throughout his long life the dislikes were expressed in the same manner, with a quiet but devastating irony. His speech was always pithy and pungent; he called a spade a spade, like his father and mother, like his workshop companions, and laughed at refinements which he saw as evasions.[14]

2

So these years were predominantly happy ones, in the workshop, the Louvre, the friend's little studio, the home with its keen interest in the small daily doings of everybody, the streets with their life and bustle, and perhaps above all the hum and stuffy warmth of the theatre, the preliminary scrapings of the orchestra, if the theatre was lucky enough to possess such a thing, of the violin and piano if it did not, and the never failing thrill when the curtain rose and he threw off the life of a china decorator and lived with and in the characters on stage.

The shock must therefore have been severe when one day M. Lévy told his men that he was closing down the workshop. Several factories had begun to print colored designs on faïence and could produce the finished cup and saucer and plate much more cheaply than the hand-decorated earthenware turned out in rue Vielle du Temple. M. Lévy could not compete with his new rivals, so all his workers lost their jobs.[15]

Renoir felt as bitter as his happy temperament permitted; the enforced closure not only took away his livelihood and threatened all his future plans but demonstrated that in one important direction he had been born into the wrong century. He was then seventeen or eighteen (the exact date has not been recovered), and his feeling for Goujon, Rembrandt, and the eighteenth-century painters had already passed beyond a matter of taste to one of principle. He never wholly forgave his generation. "Progress and science," he was to say years later, "have killed the slow work of the hand that brings happiness." [16] Nor could he forgive the people of his time for the falling away of taste; as he soon discovered, the printed ware outsold the hand-painted, not merely because it was cheaper, which was understandable, but because it was preferred, which was pitiful.

At first he would not accept the abrupt end to the work he had been doing for so long with increasing pleasure and confidence, nor would he submit to the idea that all he had learned was to be thrown away. His reaction was prompt, characteristic in one sense, uncharacteristic in another. For once he took the lead. He did so because not one of his elders would move hand or foot; they faced calamity with the kind of apathy that drove reformers like Lisa to despair.

Renoir's lead was a proposal that all the workmen should form a pool, modeled on the popular cooperatives of the day, to buy, decorate, and sell china direct to Parisian retailers. "Monsieur Rubens" had his way, which illuminates how by sheer courage and a gritty humor he had transformed the sneers of early workshop days. Final honor, he seems to have been chosen unanimously to organize the entire plan.[17]

He invested in a set of plain cups and saucers, he and his associates decorated them carefully, and he took them off to the shops. He was turned away time after time to the refrain, "But that's done by hand! Our customers prefer the printed article, they say the design is much more regular." [18]

The disgusted Renoir finally bought more cups and saucers and, abandoning the stereotyped workshop designs, made his own decorations and proudly touted around the finished goods. Again he met refusal after refusal. Then, at last, he came across one man, still selling Sèvres porcelain, who offered to buy them, with some enthusiasm too.

The enthusiasm, so heady after so many failures, nearly wrecked the sale. Renoir, who was, after all, a mere boy, could not restrain his pride; he announced that the designs were his own. Immediately the shopkeeper changed his tone, pushed back the cups and saucers, accused Renoir of trying to trick him and said sternly that china decorators must follow the long established fashion.

The disconsolate Renoir retired. But he was not a city boy for nothing. He soon came back all smiles; he had only been joking, he explained; what he had done was strictly after the accepted Sèvres patterns. A smiling Renoir had a charm of face few people could resist: the dealer ordered a dozen.[19]

Renoir had disposed of the last batch of china but had also plunged into cynicism. He decided to give up the fight and look around for other work.

How little he thought at that time of painting as a career is shown by his present actions and later remarks on the closing down of the workshop. "This catastrophe," he said, "destroyed my dreams for the future—my vision of a magnificent career as a porcelain painter at six francs a day." [20]

He was serious; six francs a day then and for long afterward seemed the height of stability and riches. But he made no attempt to get a job as a decorator of genuine Sèvres ware; his faith in public taste had disintegrated and he could not believe that even Sèvres porcelain would remain hand-decorated much longer.

He was resourceful, few young men more so, and soon found new work, decorating fans. This drove him to the Louvre with a practical aim, to copy some of the pictures for use on the fans. His choice was automatic. "How many times I have copied the *Embarquement pour Cythère!*" he was to recall in his old age. "That's how the first painters I became familiar with were Watteau, Lancret, Boucher and Fragonard." [21] The work of these painters, already among his favorites, was the obvious choice for decorating fans, and it would be fascinating to know just how many fans now reposing in the dust and darkness of old second-hand shops were painted by the earnest young Renoir in the last years of the fifties; amazingly deft, he could turn out fans, like china, much more quickly than men with more than three times his experience.

This new bout of study at the Louvre did not produce only decorated fans. It led to a most emphatic declaration of taste, confirmed the direction he would take as painter in later years, and bolstered his belief in the interrelationship of art and craftsmanship. "Boucher's *Diane au bain* was the first picture to thrill me," he remembered, "and I've continued to love it all my life as one does love one's first loves." Then came a typical "I've been told many times since then that I ought not to like Boucher because 'he's only a decorator.' A decorator—as if that were a fault! In fact, Boucher understands the feminine body better than most men. He painted young buttocks, with their little dimples, exactly as they are." And he drove home his argument with the often quoted "A painter who has a feeling for breasts and buttocks is a saved man." [22]

From this belief he was never to move. It will not surprise many that the thin ascetic-looking youth of these years, with his serious face and shy manner, was at heart a born sensualist, reveling in the female body. Where he differed from almost all whose views he apparently shared was that so much of his pleasure rested in appreciation of the perfection of line and the fine texture of feminine flesh with its enchanting medley of soft colors.

He was a man, enjoying what a man enjoys and saying so (he had his usual blunt word for men who pretended they did not get a thrill out of a glimpse down a woman's bodice),[23] but whether he knew it or not he was also enjoying with the eye of a painter who was to become famous for his studies of women and his mastery in reproducing flesh. As a young man, he was not long in opening his account with the professionals; it seems that he had several mistresses in these early years, though details about them are naturally cloudy.[24] His attitude toward them, however, is clear enough; it was, as usual, sensible. He was to say again and again that he never experienced anything thoroughly or deeply unless or until he was able to touch it; for him the sensory test was decisive.[25] So unattached girls (he would never attempt married ones, believing in the sanctity of marriage [26]) were fair game for him, as he was for them. He was a natural poet in quest of natural pleasure. Women were a joy to him in themselves, a physical joy, but they were also a visual joy, a challenge to the craftsman he insisted that he was: could he reproduce them like Boucher, like Fragonard, like a dozen other masters?

He had not yet begun to put this question in the late eighteen-fifties; the lover, a little uncertain of himself at first, and the incipient painter remained a badly paid decorator of fans anxious to increase his income. He was helped by his brother Henri, who put in his way the occasional job of copying coats of arms. This work, too, Auguste cheerfully took on, but being Auguste, he was forever improving on his instructions and making a game out of a necessity. He tells one characteristic story: "I remember making a *Saint Georges tenant un bouclier*. On the shield I painted another Saint Georges with his shield, and on that shield another and so on until the last Saint Georges and his shield could only be seen with the aid of a magnifying glass." [27] This pleased his sense of humor and also gave him the kind of practice he loved, of painting with the utmost correctness even to the point where what he painted could no longer be seen with the naked eye. He did in fact paint it with the naked eye, it should be said, proof of his astonishing strength of sight.

The fans and the coats of arms together earned him the most paltry of incomes, and his precious savings had to be drawn upon. This depletion of his resources was a kind of agony, and he was always on the lookout for a means of getting more money. The chance came one day when he was walking down rue Dauphine. In his own words: "I saw a large glassed-in café at the bottom of a court leading out of the street, and I could see painters at work decorating the walls. Having ventured into the court, I found myself in the midst of a row; the owner was cursing and swearing at his 'loafers' of workmen; the paintings in his café, he cried, would never be done in time!" [28]

Renoir had long since been forced to do violence to his inveterate shyness, a luxury to the poor man. He conquered it again, realizing quickly that this was a heaven-sent chance for him. "I immediately offered to do the decorations myself."

The owner stared disparagingly at the small, thin youth with his peaky face, looking even less than his few years. "This job needs at least three workmen," he said. "Real ones!"

Renoir's answer was to snatch up a brush and continue one of the murals. "I showed him, to his intense satisfaction, that I could paint as fast as any three workmen." [29]

He got the job and enjoyed himself improving on his predecessors' design with a fairly sumptuous Venus. When every wall was blazing with color and he had collected his final payment, he looked about for similar assignments; they were fun and brought in more money than the fan decorations and the occasional coat of arms put together. Evidently he did find them; he was to tell his son that he decorated about twenty cafés.[30] He gave no details and one wonders whether by some miracle a Renoir mural, like the Renoir fans, exists to this day, disguised by darkness and dirt, in an old Paris lane or impasse. But this way of earning a living was very much hit or miss. There was no future in it. So he continued to walk the streets, keeping his eyes open, and at last, in rue St. Denis, came on a shop with a small sign pasted on the door: "Painter for window shades wanted." He went in, spoke to the owner, and was at once faced with the question, "Where have you worked?" His mind was quick; he foresaw a demand for references if he gave the name of a Parisian shop, and this would at once reveal that he had never painted a window blind in his life. He replied, "At Bordeaux." The owner told him to bring a sample of what he could do.[31]

So far, so good, but he had only the haziest notion of what was required. On the way out he saw a young man actually painting a blind and asked him for a few tips. The young man was so taken with him that he invited him to his home the next Sunday. Renoir went, and discovered with relief that the painting of blinds did not differ radically from anything he had learned so far; the chief difference was the addition of turps to the color.

He also learned all about the destination of these window blinds. They were for the use of missionaries and were therefore made to look like stained glass; the missionaries hung them in the huts where they preached to give their congregation the illusion of worshipping in a real church. Luckily for him his instructor turned out to be a relation of the owner of the shop as well as an obliging friend.[32] Renoir tried his hand at a Virgin with Magi and Cherubim, having been told beforehand that the clouds surrounding these personages could be made with fair ease by rubbing the canvas circularwise with a cloth. The young man coupled this with a warning, "Mind the color doesn't run down your sleeve," but Renoir was too quick a worker to be caught out; he "dashed off a superb one" and left his instructor speechless with admiration. He was then given the more difficult job of making another standard design, a St. Vincent, more difficult because in place of the clouds the painter had to show St. Vincent in the regulation pose, at a church door bestowing alms to the worthy. Renoir was new at painting buildings but gaily made a stab at them, and his air of insouciance and his natural skill combined to leave this new friend with the impression that he was entertaining genius.[33]

Renoir was taken on right away the next day and soon had the pleasure of hearing his employer say that he had never known such a clever painter. But the employer's satisfaction soon soured. Like M. Lévy, he had a rooted objection to seeing too much money going into his workmen's pockets. It was a senseless objection because he paid his men by piecework, and the more they earned the more his own profits mounted. Nevertheless, he had an obscure feeling that he was somehow being cheated, and nothing would drive it from his mind. He watched the new employee at work and his initial triumph at the thought of what he was denying his competitors degenerated into alarm and despondency; Renoir was turning out Virgins and St. Vincents with almost indecent speed and earning what seemed to the horrified man to be a small fortune. He did what he could to discourage the frightful flow of work; he noticed that Renoir had begun to dispense with the careful preparation made by the other workmen before embarking on a finished sketch—particularly the ruling of the space into penciled squares—and warned him against unseemly haste to make money. "In the end," he said, "you'll fall trying to be too clever."

Renoir took no notice, and the unhappy employer had to confess that his spontaneous sketches were better than the labored efforts of the others. He then tried to reduce the price for each blind but was betrayed by his relation. "Don't listen," he told Renoir. "He can't do without you." Renoir did not listen and his savings began to mount as never before.[34]

The blinds earned Renoir much more money than cups and saucers, coats of arms or fans, and provided a steadier income than café decorating, but he did not care for the work when the exhilaration of mastering a new trade passed off and the satisfaction of quick savings grew monotonous. His life's principle, to enjoy his work or give it up, was soon tested and, as always, the principle won. He did not try to deceive himself; he did not like painting blinds for missionaries, and for more than one reason. The first difficulties surmounted, the work could not advance his technique; it was mostly a question of being slick and dishonest. Besides, it was boring, and if there was one thing Renoir would not endure, it was boredom.

For the first time he began to listen seriously to the men who were still advising him to take up painting as a career. His mother and father followed the French custom of holding open house every Saturday evening for the family friends.[35] All kinds of people shared the simple meal, and it seems that more than one painter dropped in, Lisa and Leray having aspirations as well as kind hearts. Jean Renoir tells us something of one of these men, a now forgotten painter named Oullevé, who also perceived the promise in Auguste and urged him to copy the old masters in the Louvre—a good turn that Renoir never forgot.[36] It is probable that he, Laporte, and the workman-instructor all tried to convince Renoir during and after these meals, for if they knew the family at all well, they would think that the mother and father must be convinced first.

Laporte eventually developed an argument calculated to appeal as much to Léonard Renoir as to his son; he insisted that Auguste follow him to the Beaux-Arts because there alone could he learn his trade from A to Z and there alone win the cachet which led to lucrative commissions and the favorable notice of Salon juries. As further inducement to the thrifty, he pointed out that Gleyre's studio, attached to the Beaux-Arts, though not actually of it, provided just what Auguste was looking for—teaching by a Beaux-Arts professor on Beaux-Arts lines and with admission to Beaux-Arts lectures and examinations, all for a fee kept low precisely to encourage talent like Auguste's.

Renoir listened and weighed the matter. In his few spare hours of daylight at home he was as busy as ever experimenting in oils. After a year of blind-painting his savings had grown so handsomely that he felt able to take a chance without jeopardizing his parents' position. Beyond all this, he had, one cannot doubt, the beginnings of a wish to express himself outside the limits of fans, blinds, and china decorations, though he would put this wish no higher than "I wanted to draw from the life." [37]

Even so he was strongly tempted to stay where he was; when he told his employer that he thought of leaving he was promptly offered a partnership. His final word on the subject was: "I might have remained with the firm if Laporte had not begged me so often to join him." [38]

Some may find this hesitation unromantic, but Renoir was not romantic in the conventional sense of an artist who counts the world well lost for his art. He knew that poverty is the most unromantic of all sufferings, and also he was extraordinarily modest. He considered that he was quick and clever with the brush but never once regarded himself as a neglected genius. If one had mentioned the word genius to him he would have laughed. He thought of himself as talented, a good craftsman, and this view was to survive until his dying day. He was, it cannot be too often stressed, delightfully frank about his gifts; and even when he finally decided to take up painting—"serious painting," he said with a grin [39]—it was with the common-sense view that money was there to be made too, and in the most attractive of all ways, in one's own time and painting what one chose to paint.

Eventually and typically he consulted his parents. They had been good to him and he repaid generosity with generosity; if he gave up the blind-painting and failed in his "serious painting," they would suffer, mildly but definitely, because he would not be able to contribute further to the family funds until he had returned to business. More important, if he failed he would have failed them too.

It was agreed, after a discussion in which as usual the whole available family took part, that the decision should be left to someone whom all felt to be the last word in true art. Whether this was Oullevé, the old workman, or Laporte is not definitely known, but the evidence suggests that the arbiter was the workman. Renoir was given a subject to paint, and when he had finished the work the workman came along to the family apartment to pronounce judgment.

The scene was afterward described by Renoir's young brother Edmond (apprenticed to a trade but already dreaming of earning a living with the pen), whose passionate admiration for Auguste was proof enough that the prophet could, if he were a Renoir, find honor in his own country. The day of judgment had, of course, to be a Sunday, when Renoir was not at work. The Renoir apartment had been littered with sketches ever since the early days when Auguste, "armed with a piece of cardboard bigger than himself," had arrived home to "continue his free drawing lessons." [40] On the walls hung the portrait of the Renoir mother or grandmother, a splendid likeness of the father—the very image of a tightly principled self-made man— painted in 1859, and other oils including one just finished, his *Femme Endormie*. Now, on an easel, rested the test picture, and the entire family was awaiting the decision with mixed feelings, for the father and mother were divided between pride in their talented son and fear for him if he passed the test. Léonard Renoir did not care for the idea of a career as professional painter; it was uncertain and unrespectable. His wife's similar views were mitigated by pride in Auguste, who, she probably felt, would do anything well. [41]

Edmond recalled: "at last the first 'master' of the painter of *Lise* and *Moulin de la Galette* was announced. I remember it as if it were yesterday. Though still a youngster I knew quite well that momentous events were taking place. The easel holding the famous picture had been placed in the middle of the largest room of our humble home, everybody was restless and impatient and I had been smartened up and told to behave myself. The atmosphere was extremely solemn. The 'master' arrived, and I can tell you that the Renoir family felt itself in a tight corner. At a sign, I pushed a chair forward for him in front of the easel, he sat himself down and studied 'the great work.' It was—I can see it to this day—an 'Eve': behind her the serpent twined round the branches of an oak, its open mouth thrust forward as if to bewitch her.

"The examination lasted a good quarter of an hour; after which, without beating about the bush, the poor good old man walked over to our father and mother and said these simple words to them: 'You must let your son take up painting as an art; in our trade he would end at the very most by earning twelve to fifteen francs a day. I predict a brilliant future for him in the arts; make sure that you do what I say.'

"That evening we dined sadly; the joy caused by Auguste's triumph disappeared before the terrible prospect of his leaving the work, which would give him a safe living income, for the arts which could lead him straight into wretchedness. However, everyone resigned themselves and the École des Beaux-Arts gained another student. Auguste entered Gleyre's studio." [42]

CHAPTER III

THE REBEL

1862-1863

THIS WAS IN APRIL, 1862. Renoir was just twenty-one, almost
as small and quite as thin as when he had left the workshop
four years earlier. Out of the peaky face, with its forehead
marked by the furrows of the child worker, eyes sparkled under
thin dark eyebrows, eyes that were gradually lightening to an
attractive hazel. The rough hair, darker than his eyes, had
already begun to retreat from his forehead—a fine forehead,
perhaps his best feature, broad and white—leaving a widow's
peak. His nose was straight and firm, thin like the rest of him,
and ended close to the narrow upper lip. On this a small dark
mustache grew which counteracted the prominently out-thrust
lower lip. In repose it was a somber face and truthfully told the
story of his life to that time; no feeling child brought up on the
skirts of poverty and put to work in his early teens could regard
life as a picnic, and a more realistic young man than Renoir
would have been hard to find. Nonetheless, his face belied the
spirit behind it; gaiety was never far away; he had the city
child's sharp sense of humor. More rare, his special gift of discovering charm in most people's commonplace had never been
knocked out of him by hard living or his many disillusioning
experiences. The world remained fresh and beautiful to him,
and the nature that could find it so was shown at once when

he smiled and still more when he laughed his rare laugh. His face changed magically.

At that time the curriculum of the Beaux-Arts proper consisted of a series of lectures by appointed professors. To supplement this, some of the professors, Gleyre among them, opened studios in which students could work all day under personal guidance. That, at least, was the theory; in fact, as Renoir discovered at once, the students were usually left to their own devices. These devices had little to do with drawing and painting; more than half Gleyre's large class had no greater ambition than to while away tedious hours, which they did by community singing and the roughest kind of horseplay.[1] "Gleyre," said Renoir later, "was a much respected painter but did not help his students." He added whimsically, "He had the merit, though, of leaving them to themselves." [2] Renoir was left to himself literally; Laporte, who had importuned him into Gleyre's studio, quickly abandoned the frivolous study of painting for the serious study of pretty young women,[3] and Auguste retreated to the least noisy spot and drew and painted as best he could.

It was as well that he had already punctured the illusion of worldly justice, for he received none in Gleyre's studio. He was one of the few hard workers: "Whilst other students smashed windows, teased the life out of the models and made the teacher's life a misery, I stayed quietly in my corner, very attentive, very quiet, studying the model and giving all my attention to the lecturer." All, it seemed, to no purpose: "I was the one who was treated as the rebel." [4]

This, though exasperating, was not really surprising. "That estimable Swiss painter," [5] as Renoir was generously to describe Gleyre, had been in nominal charge of the studio for nearly twenty years. He was a skilled but conventional painter, personally timid, and troubled by failing eyesight. He had grown cynical over the years, and by the time Renoir joined his studio had all but given up the fight; he would appear usually on a Monday, pass from easel to easel commenting on the work of the past week, then leave the class to please itself for one week more.[6] He expected his students to be silly young men, to make a racket and behave like children; all he asked was lip service to his standards of drawing and painting.

These standards must have strained Renoir's easygoing nature. "He would only admit the reproduction of everyday life as worthy of the art of painting," one of Gleyre's students wrote, "on the understanding that the nude was not permissible." He dismissed the realistic art of Courbet and Manet: "He loathed ugliness and would never forgive contemporary realism for what he called 'the systematic exhibition of vulgarity by which public taste is being defiled.'" To sum up, "Gleyre's essential— he would willingly have said only—aim in painting was to reproduce beauty."[7]

His students, even the silliest, honored the unspoken pact; they humored him and he humored them. But Renoir had given up a profitable job to pay for full-time instruction; he wanted to learn, not to listen to platitudes. It did not occur to him to humor Gleyre, and he was astonished and dismayed when he first saw the master making his rounds, heard his banal comments and the grave agreements of the students, followed by sniggers when he had passed on.

When Gleyre reached him there was bound to be misunderstanding. Unlike most students in the studio, Renoir had done what he wanted to do, not what he thought Gleyre wanted to see. Gleyre was by that time too old, too bored, and too kind to make a scene. Renoir's study contained plenty of what he called "devilish color"[8] and none of the correct and lifeless drawing he admired. Gleyre's aim was, in fact, a colored drawing and Renoir had not obliged. After a long inspection, he said, "You are playing at painting to amuse yourself, no doubt?"

Renoir's reply—the exchange is vouched for by Baudelaire— was a cool and honest, "If it didn't amuse me to paint, I wouldn't be doing it."[9]

At the time Gleyre might have thought this simply cheek from a new student. It is to his credit that within the next few months he realized, however incredulously, that Renoir meant what he said and that he was hard-working and serious. Gleyre still could not approve; he did, however, encourage Renoir to persevere, hoping that he would see the error of his ways.

From Renoir's point of view this was small comfort; he saw his hard-earned savings dwindling and not much to show for them but a master's incomprehension. Nor was his position any better at the École classes in drawing and anatomy which he attended from eight to ten every evening. He ran into trouble at the very first lecture—by the diehard Signol—when he showed an oil he had brought with him. He was then for the most part painting very darkly, using bitumen in large quantities as Laporte had counseled him, but had introduced into this particular study what he afterward described as "a very dirty red." Signol overlooked the black and concentrated on the red; he was, said Renoir, "quite beside himself" at the sight of it. "Be careful," he said sharply, "that you don't become a second Delacroix." [10]

As Delacroix was already one of Renoir's gods, the remark came like a dash of cold water. When, a little later, he tried his hand at drawing, the response was no happier. Signol stared at the drawing—Renoir had painstakingly copied the cast used as a model—and said repressively, "Can't you understand the big toe of Germanicus ought to have more majesty than the big toe of the local coal merchant?" [11]

These remarks opened the student's eyes. He loved Delacroix's colors and believed that a draftsman should draw what he saw. Within a few weeks of entering the Beaux-Arts and Gleyre's, he understood that he could expect no help from the professors and would have to rely on himself. In this first lonely period as student it seemed to him that he was paying the fees simply for the privilege of drawing and painting from the life and plaster casts.[12] He could not convince himself that his progress was marked; he was nothing if not honest and was soon disgusted by an apparent inability to master the technique of line. "I thought I should never learn how to draw a head, it seemed so difficult," he was to say.[13]

With some difficulty he wrested Laporte from his preoccupation with young women, only to find that his trouble had been for nothing, because Laporte followed Gleyre slavishly and held up David as the great exemplar. He urged Renoir to apply himself and pay as much attention to drawing as to painting. "You must *make* yourself draw." After which Renoir, to Laporte's incomprehension, replied: "I'm like a cork thrown into a stream; when I paint I have to let myself go completely." [14]

There was no more to be said after that, but his friend's backsliding failed to amuse Renoir. There was he, spending hard-earned money and getting next to nothing for it, not even enjoyment; most of the students jeered at his workaday appearance and insistence on living up to it, and all the masters disapproved of this disturbing young man who dissipated such rare energy in the wrong direction.

The nonconformist must often have wished to throw the whole thing up and go back to the maker of window blinds. He did not, however. No doubt his pride was touched; he had told his worried parents that he would get on in this new pursuit. Besides, he had paid his fees. But the deciding factor was surely the attitude of one or two young men in the studio. Not everybody played the fool at Gleyre's, and he soon became friendly with one of those who did not.

Alfred Sisley was much of an age—eighteen months older— and just as hard-working and determined to succeed, but this apart, no two men could have been more unalike. Perhaps that explained the friendship which did so much to keep Renoir in the studio. Sisley was English but born in Paris. His father, who lived in one of the fashionable mansions in Avenue de Neuilly, was a prosperous manufacturer of artificial flowers. He had sent Alfred (who preferred to be called Henri) [15] to London to learn the business, only to find that the boy spent his time drawing and painting the flowers instead of learning how to make and sell them. The Sisleys humored him. They put him into an English studio; then, when he disliked that and asked to be allowed to join the Beaux-Arts, they agreed to this too.[16]

By the time he met Renoir, Sisley was a small, handsome young man with fine eyes, dark hair and beard. He was intense, quiet, determined, and rather shy but, like Renoir, devoted to women. Unlike Renoir, his sense of humor was not his strong point; he listened unsmiling to his new friend exaggerating his accent to the point of caricature as a gesture of defiance to the many Gleyre snobs, but admired his application—Renoir was in the studio at eight every morning—his moral courage (Sisley had heard about the reply to Gleyre), and perhaps above all his gaiety in the midst of what must have seemed to him a dreary existence. Possibly Sisley happened one evening to catch sight of Renoir, who always stayed until the studio closed, going the rounds of the floor, picking up discarded tubes of paint in the hope of squeezing half an inch of color from them.[17] In any case Renoir's clothes, his meals, his conversation and his thin, lined face all shouted poverty to the compassionate, and Sisley had a heart. But Renoir's spirit and his taste chiefly won Sisley, that and the pleasure Renoir took in his work whenever he was allowed to use a brush; this was half pathetic, half inspiring.

Both students intended to try for the Prix de Rome—Renoir because he needed the free study that this would bring, Sisley because he wanted to excel in whatever he took up—and both took the first step toward the prize by passing the first Beaux-Arts examination in August.[18] They worked together, visited each other's houses occasionally, ate together, spent many hours at the Louvre studying and sketching, and discussed what they had seen and done over a drink at one of the neighboring cafés—the Closerie des Lilas was their favorite.[19] Both were united in opposition to Ingres' slogan "well drawn is well painted," which all the Beaux-Arts professors taught; but this apart, their likings were not the same. Sisley worshipped Corot, Renoir the eighteenth-century painters, Delacroix, and, of the moderns, the dramatic landscape painter Diaz. But their differences merely made their arguments the more interesting. During these talks their characters came out clearly: Sisley would scarcely budge an inch, Renoir was prepared to try anything once. When Sisley offered to help his friend, another facet of character emerged, for Renoir would take whatever came with an unself-conscious cheerfulness and absence of false pride that Sisley envied.

In the new year of 1863 the little band of two more than doubled. A few weeks earlier, in November, a tall, thin, elegant young man appeared at Gleyre's. He was fair-haired, with a wisp of beard, and blue-eyed, he had charm and was very lively. He was seen only in the mornings, and it was soon learned that he was studying medicine in the afternoons.

This young man (six months Renoir's junior) was Frédéric Bazille, who came from a well-to-do family in the southern town of Montpellier. He added to the gaiety of any party—one could not be downcast when he was around—if he did not always add to its sense of purpose. He was suffering from "indigestion of walls and streets," [20] as he pithily described the effect of Paris on a countryman; he was wavering between medicine, which his parents preferred, and painting, which came more easily to him. He was beginning to revel at the same time in the advantages of those walls and streets—the concerts which he adored, the parties at the house of his uncle, Commandant Lejosne, and, very soon, the amateur dramatics which Gleyre's students were getting up for the New Year. Delightful though he was and capable of quick enthusiasm, he was not a stabilizing influence, since his first great need was to be stabilized himself.

No doubt this was why he attached himself to a fellow Montpellierian five years his senior, Louise-Émile Villa, and to a Norman who had joined Gleyre's at the same time, Claude Monet. By the next month Bazille was writing home, "Villa and Monet are the only students I see a lot of. They are very fond of me and I return the feeling. They are charming fellows." [21]

Monet was more than charming; he was strong and knew where he was going. Like Renoir, his first encounter with Gleyre proved his mettle. Gleyre looked critically at his study of a male model. "Not bad," he said, "not bad at all. But it is too much like the model. He's a stocky man, you make him stocky. He has enormous feet, you make them enormous. That kind of thing is very ugly."

"I draw what I see," replied Monet in the tone Renoir was to know so well, a blend of assurance and defiance.

Gleyre corrected him. "Remember, young man, when one draws from the figure one must always think of the antique. Nature is very beautiful, my friend, as an element of study but has nothing of interest to offer in itself. Style, you understand— that's what counts." [22]

At this, Monet's black brows contracted, and had it not been for Bazille he might have left the studio that day. But his stand led to a rapprochement with Bazille, who loved spirit and high principles, a Bazille with money, a Bazille ready and eager to be led. Monet's experience with Gleyre matched Renoir's with Signol, but it was some time before the two groups of friends merged into a huddle of disgusted sympathy. Renoir, who missed little, had of course noted Monet's arrival in class—the dark, heavily built, carefully dressed young man of twenty-two was much too impressive a figure to be overlooked—but did not speak to him and was not spoken to.

It seems that Renoir at first regarded Monet with a certain amusement,[23] into which a touch of awe might have entered, because of the clothes he wore, beautifully cut clothes which the son of a tailor could place as the work of an exclusive cutter in Faubourg Saint-Honoré and which contrasted picturesquely with the spattered blue porcelain-painter's overall which Renoir had thriftily and proudly used ever since the days of M. Lévy's workshop. Monet was by no means the only well-dressed student— Renoir had long since accustomed himself to supercilious stares from various dandies—but Monet wore lace-edged shirt-sleeves which no doubt temporarily obscured the man who was wearing them. It was not long before Renoir learned that the newcomer scarcely had a sou to his name and lived on credit; then he felt much more at home with him.

The gregarious Bazille finally brought all the friends together and did so typically. One day he asked Renoir if he would care to go for a stroll. Jean Renoir tells us that Bazille explained the invitation by saying that he had admired a Renoir drawing. The compliment must have surprised as well as flattered Renoir, for he believed his drawing to be the weakest part of his equipment. And however much Bazille might have meant what he said—and his wish to be friendly and polite sometimes distorted his judgment—what was occupying his mind most at that moment was the approaching New Year theatrical show *La Tour de Nesle* the students were putting on before a distinguished audience, including the famous Gérôme.[24] He wanted more actors and fixed on Renoir, Sisley, and another young man, Franc-Lamy, who attached himself to them from time to time.[25]

2

From then on there was a single group. The size of the group seems to have varied—in addition to Villa and Lamy other young men came and went—but for all practical purposes was fixed at four, the four who were to make history: Monet, Renoir, Sisley, Bazille.

Somewhat to the surprise of three out of the four it quickly became a group of rebels. Monet was the sole instigator of the rebellion; he disliked Gleyre's classical teaching, thought it retrograde and said so. Temperamentally inclined to leadership, he assumed that all thought as he did. He was for walking out there and then.[26] Gleyre, he said bluntly, had nothing to teach them; he could only corrupt their vision. The man had actually described landscape painting as "a decadent art"; [27] he failed to understand that the decadence was in the painters and not in the art.

Practical defiance of this kind shocked the other three. Renoir intended to get value for his hard-earned money; Sisley and Bazille were accustomed to working off their feelings in words. But Monet, they found, was not an easy person to overrule. Although he could not claim any special authority by way of age, he could claim it in almost every other way. At fifteen he had been earning twenty francs apiece for caricature portraits, a performance that made Renoir's feats with his Marie Antoinettes very small. He had become a kind of boy wonder in Le Havre, where his father had a grocery store. Boudin had heard of him and offered to teach him. He had been tutored for months by Jongkind. All one winter and spring he had been an habitué, even if rather a countrified one, of the Brasserie des Martyrs, headquarters of the venerated rebel, Courbet. He had made a painting expedition along the Marne with Pissarro, whom he had met in the well-known Académie Suisse. Monet had come to the Beaux-Arts only because his father had refused further supplies unless he made some concession to conformity. He had made the gesture but, he assured his new friends, he knew his way and would follow it. It was the way of Boudin, of Jongkind, of Pissarro—to paint nature out of doors.[28]

All this alarmed Renoir, Bazille, and Sisley, however hard they tried to disguise it. They dug their heels in on the question of leaving Gleyre's forthwith: Renoir was not prepared to throw up his hope of the profitable career which only a fully fledged Beaux-Arts student could expect; Sisley's mind was inelastic and he took time to change; Bazille was possibly more concerned with the play they were rehearsing—how could he walk out of Gleyre's at such a moment?

Their resistance stopped at this point. Monet offered them all a creed and a rallying point. Criticism of a method of teaching was a poor incentive to action; Monet presented a positive program. He proposed that all should try their hand at landscape painting as soon as the weather made it practicable.

In their various ways one and all soon came round to his way of thinking. Sisley, admiring Corot as he did, needed little persuasion to landscape, though he frowned at the thought of painting out of doors. Bazille, charmed by Monet's bluntness as he was charmed by everything, welcomed the opportunity to get into the country. Renoir, who had never thought seriously of landscape in his life, was quickly enthusiastic, wooed by the prospect of variety; if the experiment did nothing else, it promised a few carefree days in good company and might even improve his technique. He could be guaranteed to enjoy himself wherever he was if left free to paint as he felt inclined.

So opposition was feeble or nonexistent, and it was agreed that the four should make a painting expedition outside Paris. Renoir, anything but overawed, insisted that as quid pro quo

Monet come with them to the Louvre during the winter days. Renoir's own view of the study of the masters was already fixed. "It's in the galleries that one learns to paint," he was to remark. "When I say one learns at the Louvre I don't mean that one scrapes away the old varnish, pinches the tricks of the trade, and blossoms out as a new Rubens or Rembrandt. Everyone sings his own song if he has a voice. One must make the painting of one's time. But it's at the Louvre that one gets the taste for painting that nature on its own can't give us." [29]

To Monet this was a kind of blasphemy; he was no friend to frowsting in picture galleries and believed that the study of nature would teach the painter all he needed to know. No doubt Renoir, who had long since learned in a hard school the value of silence, did not press his argument, and Monet soon left the studiers to themselves.[30] He encouraged Bazille, who had time and money to spare, to make weekend trips with him into the country around Paris and let Renoir and Sisley take their sketching pads to the Louvre. There Renoir, who had the gift of making acquaintance with the most unlikely people, had already gathered a body of friends in passing, among them Fantin-Latour, an admirer of Delacroix and renowned in a limited circle for his flower studies. Fantin promised to introduce Renoir to his friends and get him some commissions.[31]

Léonard Renoir had retired to a cottage at Ville d'Avray just outside Paris.[32] This left his son to fend for himself. As it turned out, nothing could have been more convenient, for at much the same moment Bazille, who had been staying with relatives, began to look around for a studio. Renoir found him one, in rue de la Condamine in the Batignolles, and ended by sharing it with him; Bazille was excellent company but was out many evenings of the week, so that Renoir could make good use of the free studio space.

Nor was this the end of it, for the generous Bazille helped the needy Renoir practically by introducing him to the Lejosne evenings. Here he met a variety of the advanced men of their day: Baudelaire, Manet,[33] Gambetta, Carjat, Sylvestre, Banville, Gautier, Arsène Houssaye.[34] Renoir, never at a loss in any society, was soon accepted and was promised one or two portrait commissions. One of the most valuable patrons he made in this distinguished set was Prince Bibesco, well known at court and a young man of considerable influence. Bazille first brought him along to meet the group at the Closerie des Lilas; he was interested in painting and was quickly attracted to the unaffected Renoir.[35]

There is no indication that Renoir played any notable part in the conversation at the Avenue Trudaine evenings, revolutionary in the arts as in politics. He was a believer in a social revolution but not in an artistic one, and must in any case have regarded these armchair revolutionaries with some amusement. He had, however, the priceless gift of enjoying every experience, including the homely ones of leaning back on a sofa and stretching hands to a warm fire. To the others, who had never been uncomfortable or cold, the young man's delight was charming. Although Renoir did not care for theoretical discussions and would take no part in them, when pressed he would give his views on music, painting, the theatre, and life in general. They stimulated discussion, and in the Lejosne house, as in many other salons, he more than earned the cost of his wine and food; cynicism could not live with him, and every man felt younger and less blasé. He neither minced words nor criticized captiously; he was constructive even when crude by the decidedly precious standards of the time.[36]

He was not, of course, a prominent or regular member of the gatherings, simply a young *copain* of Bazille's, who himself was regarded for some time as little more than the host's nephew. Renoir would sit for long periods in what appeared to be a state of dream, his eyes shut. But his comments often put the rest of the supposedly brilliant talk to shame. His penetrating judgment on Zola the novelist—"Zola thinks he has described people when he says they smell" [37]—was an example of his inspired common sense. His views were usually fresh and always sensible.

He was more at home with two men whom Bazille brought back to the studio one day with a preliminary shout from the staircase of "I've brought you two fine recruits!" [38] Bazille meant, in his delightfully haphazard way, painters he had persuaded to join Monet's *plein air* group. He was doubly wide of the mark, for one of the "recruits" was Camille Pissarro, who had been making landscapes when the rebels were scarcely out of their cradles, and the other was Paul Cézanne, who had never made a serious landscape in his life and at that time had no intention of making any. But nobody took any notice of Bazille's vagueness. Pissarro, the most modest of men, had been overcome with pleasure when he heard of the proposed trip to Fontainebleau, as if he had never painted landscape before; he recalled his short painting trip with Monet a few years earlier and was altogether helpful and encouraging.[39]

Renoir liked him at once; Pissarro was a son of the people like himself, innocent of airs and graces, who said what he thought with a robust earnestness which made the Lejosne gatherings appear the trivial and pretentious affairs they so often were. His knowledge of painting was considerable, and his researches into the new painting he was trying to make were fascinating to a Renoir always on the lookout for technical tips. Pissarro was also a rabid socialist, and Renoir, in so far as he bothered himself with politics, was at one with him here too; both believed the common man and woman to be the salt of the earth. Pissarro's emphasis, violent to the point of absurdity, must have reminded Renoir of Lisa, and that alone would ensure an affection for this lovable man with the friendly brown eyes and heavy beard already graying. Pissarro had a warm heart, like Lisa, and Renoir was at a loss only with the cold-hearted.

He loved Pissarro; he was impressed by Cézanne. Cézanne was then twenty-four but, with thinning black hair and glowing black eyes, looked much older. No one could have guessed that he was the son of a wealthy banker; he did not look like it—his clothes were fantastically worn and dirty—and did not behave like it. The first fact to strike Renoir was Cézanne's approach to his work; not even Monet felt more strongly about his painting. Renoir was to comment with awe on Cézanne's "passionate love

of his art," [40] yet (and this must have puzzled Renoir) Cézanne
was almost indifferent to the fate of his pictures once he had
painted them. At first the answer seemed simple: Cézanne was
the son of a rich man. But Renoir soon discovered that this
explanation was too simple; Cézanne's standards were excep-
tionally high, and he was living on a very small allowance. He
valued money as much as Renoir but had long since made his
choice between money and art when he threw up a position in
his father's bank to paint. He despised the men who were
making money hand over fist, the bourgeois, and he did not
hide it. Renoir felt an unholy joy in discovering that this
rugged southerner, even more than the kindhearted Pissarro,
said exactly what he thought. His language was often coarse,
always pungent, and delivered in a thick Provençal accent
which made Renoir's homely speech appear mild. Cézanne declared that he was of peasant stock and proud of it, and that the
peasants of Aix were his best models and his best friends. [41]

This attitude appealed to Renoir, occasionally overcome by
the gentility of Bazille and Sisley, good friends though they had
become. Renoir relished this passionate plain speaking and felt
as drawn to Cézanne as to Monet, men who might have been
expected to be antipathetic to him. Beneath his apparent light-
heartedness, Renoir's experience of life had given him a certain
somberness of disposition, which none but the most intimate
friend suspected.

Cézanne, constitutionally suspicious, was a difficult man to
reach, but he responded to Renoir's sincere admiration. Renoir
knew at once that he was in the presence of genius and showed
it. A comradeship which was to have a long and varied history
was cemented by the discovery that they shared, together with
a love of bright and even violent color, a passion for Delacroix.

These meetings did more than give pleasure to Renoir. It is
not possible to overestimate the moral effect of these two men—
the generous, encouraging, experienced Pissarro; Cézanne with
his fiery genius—on a young man whose theory of life was being
severely tested at the Beaux-Arts. Renoir was getting little satisfaction from his work and could not convince himself that he

possessed the necessary talent to make a success of painting.

Before the projected Monet plan for a joint assault on *plein air* painting could be carried out at Easter, 1863, another dismal possibility was raising its head. Just before they left for Fontainebleau, Bazille reported to his parents that Gleyre's eyes were giving him a lot of trouble; [42] everyone expected that the master would soon be driven to close the studio. Nevertheless, Renoir went off with his three friends in fairly good heart. He had just been cheered by passing his second examination,[43] and he responded to action and change of scene. He had made some good friends and some acquaintances who might become patrons if judiciously handled; he had found a corner in Bazille's studio to sleep and work, and he had a country nook in the Renoir cottage at Ville d'Avray.

All the same, judged by practical standards—and he never judged by anything else—his first year outside business had been far from a success. Though he lived simply, his savings were draining away and he had far to go. Despite the many promises at Lejosne's, he had not actually been given a firm commission to paint a picture, and the canvases he had attempted on his own were, he feared, far from salable. His drawing did not seem to have advanced, and his frequent though somewhat reluctant use of bitumen in large quantities (the result, now, of pressure by Fantin-Latour) darkened many of his canvases so much that a good deal of their original charm was lost.[44]

His fears were justified. He could not sell this early work except to a patron-friend like Bibesco, though one wonders how the dealers he visited could have been so blind; many of these canvases are genuine Renoir with obvious hints of the later mastery. But they were left on his hands and he had many moments as black as his pictures, doubting whether he had done rightly to leave his job and squander his savings. If he had been dowered with greater vanity at birth, he might have sailed on regardless, confident in his genius; being genuinely modest, he suffered, destroyed some canvases, gave away others, and stuffed the rest into corners. He may well have wondered whether the Monet excursion, with all its promised joys, would be worth the francs he would have to lay out on it. However, he went, and it was well that he did so, even though he was still a year from his first unmistakable stride forward.

By 1863 the Barbizon painters (called after the village) had been working in the forest of Fontainebleau for the better part of twenty years. Diaz, Théodore Rousseau, Millet, Jules Dupré, and Daubigny were leading members of the group which had won a certain amount of public favor and many disciples among the younger painters. Rousseau and Millet had settled in Barbizon, and Corot painted there too; the dealer Jean Durand-Ruel, father of the more famous Paul, had backed all of them for years past and had found many buyers for their pictures. Their view of landscape was both dramatic and romantic—Vlaminck is an obvious inheritor in this century.

It stood to reason, then, that all young men studying in Paris who considered themselves advanced and wished to attempt landscape followed literally in the footsteps of their elders; in summer and at Easter every tiny inn for miles around Barbizon was stuffed with aspiring landscapists. In April, 1863, Monet and his friends could not find room there and moved a mile or two farther, packs on back, to Chailly. There they settled in Père Paillard's Cheval Blanc, one of the two village inns, and were fed and lodged for the modest price of forty sous per head per day.[45] The Cheval Blanc was a typical country inn frequented by painters; the walls were all but invisible for paintings of the forest, of the painters themselves, and of fellow travelers, some left in gratitude, some in disgust, but most because, when the pinch came, even forty sous was found to be beyond the painter and he offered a would-be masterpiece to settle the bill. This the amiable Père Paillard accepted with a sigh—there was little he could do about it—just as he accepted the racket after dinner when popular Paris songs were howled out by the young men crowded round the long table.[46]

The four friends thus broke no new ground by settling themselves in the middle of the forest, but Monet had the air of an innovator and of one who intended that the other three should follow him. The Barbizon painters, though making landscapes, did not paint them wholly or even mainly on the spot; they usually made a sketch out of doors, then finished the canvas at their leisure in the studio or the inn where they lodged. Naturally, the finished work differed considerably from the actual scene: the colors were changed; technical "improvements" [47] altered the position of rocks, trees, and bushes. The light under which the painters first saw the motif was not considered by them as particularly important; they would jot down a few notes, that was all.[48]

This procedure was condemned by Monet, who said, following Boudin, Jongkind, and Pissarro, that the true landscape painter must paint what he saw where he saw it. He went further, asserting that the painter must either paint his chosen scene in a few hours or at the same time of day and in approximately the same conditions of light if he was to reproduce nature truthfully, and he explained his reason for this—that he believed the key to landscape painting was depiction of light.[49]

The four set to work the next morning, choosing their own parts of the forest round Chailly. Bazille, carried away by Monet's strong personality, launched enthusiastically into a series of *plein air* landscapes, Sisley copied as well as he could the delicate poetry of Corot,[50] and Renoir did exactly as he pleased. He sniffed mistrustfully at anything that smelled of dogma, even of the most progressive kind. Monet knew even less than Pissarro how to paint light; he was still experimenting. Renoir, young in years, old in experience, knew that the most earnest men were often those who were trying to convince themselves. He liked and respected Monet but had no intention of following him for the sake of a theory. *Plein air* painting as such was another matter. Willing to try anything, he tried *plein air* painting and liked it, not for any reason Monet had advanced, but because it enabled him to work quickly and without much thought for anything but the sheer pleasure of manipulating a brush.

Pleasure: that was his criterion. He attached himself stubbornly to the principle from which nothing was to dislodge him throughout a long life: he painted only for pleasure, his own and others. "For me, a picture should be a pleasant thing, joyful and pretty—yes, pretty! There are quite enough unpleasant things in life without the need for us to manufacture more." And he added the Renoiresque "I know very well that it is difficult to make anyone admit that a picture can be very great if it is joyful. No one ever takes cheerful people seriously." [51]

So Monet, with all his force of character, could not dominate Renoir; his friend went along with him for the reasons he had given, reasons he did not think it necessary to repeat. And his first salutary lesson did not come from Monet, as in a logical world it would have done, but from a man who met him in the forest in curious circumstances when he and Sisley returned to Chailly the following year.

CHAPTER IV

THE PAINTER APPEARS

1863-1865

THE YEAR BETWEEN the two visits to the forest is quickly described. It was, for Renoir, a year of almost constant anxiety. He passed his Beaux-Arts examinations in August and October, 1863, and again in April, 1864,[1] only to find himself without a studio, without money and, what was worse, without the will to continue the academic treadmill. Early in 1864 Gleyre decided to close the studio, thus ending Renoir's cheap tuition. Gleyre had nothing to say to Monet, who had virtually abandoned studio work long before, or to Bazille, whom he did not take seriously; he did, however, counsel Renoir and Sisley to work hard, telling them that they had a future in painting if they applied themselves.[2]

Both young men had decided by this time that even with the glittering Prix de Rome in view, they could not continue to attend the Beaux-Arts; the disappearance of Gleyre was merely the last straw; they contrasted the futilities of academic painting with the courage of a man like Manet, who after the scandalous treatment of *Déjeuner sur l'herbe* at the Salon des Refusés of 1863 had become the hero of all young painters determined to paint life as it was and not as clients or convention wished it to be seen.

For Renoir the decision posed a serious problem. His savings had gone. He had learned something about drawing and paint-

ing in spite of the professors but did not feel sufficiently well
equipped to stand on his own feet. There was no sign that he
could live off his work; he did not even know how he wanted
to paint, and his only hope of survival until he did know was
an occasional commission for a portrait from a wealthy acquaintance like Bibesco. The immediate future seemed gloomy.
There was no family home in Paris to fall back on even if he
could have brought himself to live off his parents or brothers.

Of course he was used to austerity—his lunches in the past
two years had been sketchy [3]—but the life of pinching and scrap-
ing he now saw ahead of him if he stuck to painting was very
different; then he had economized voluntarily, now he was
likely to be forced into semistarvation. He had the healthy respect for security of all who know the borderline between want
and sufficiency.

Nor was this all. The Renoir family was flourishing in a mild
way. His father had been able to retire, Henri and Victor were
well established, Edmond was showing promise of a successful
journalistic career, Leray and Lisa were living comfortably with
the parents at Ville d'Avray.[4] Auguste was the only failure,
monetarily speaking. To any man with a spark of pride this was
galling and must have been much more so when it became clear
that all but one of his family viewed his continuance as a
painter with misgiving. They apparently had little doubt about
his ability but thought the competition too fierce for a half-
taught young man without influence or money.[5] Even Lisa
seemed to think the game not worth the candle, which must
have been most disquieting to Auguste. Edmond alone stood
out. He still admired his brother unreservedly and believed that
he would succeed in whatever he took up.

The decision must have been difficult to make. A year earlier
Renoir might have gone back into business. That he did not do
so in 1864 must be set down to Bazille who gave him a home, to
Monet who was the living image of the artistic conscience, to
one of Bazille's friends who commissioned a picture at a crucial
moment, and, more than all these tangible reasons put together,
to an intangible feeling that had grown in him. Being what he

was, he would have described this, no doubt, as nothing more mysterious or significant than the fact that he had discovered how enjoyable it was to paint pictures, any picture that occurred to him and could be painted in his own time and way.

His belief in the workings of fate must have played its part, too. The entry into Gleyre's studio had been one of his few definite acts, but the meetings with Sisley, Bazille, and Monet were pure chance, the kind of chance by which he allowed himself to be guided. He might smile wryly at the idea of himself as a hot rebel, he the lover of eighteenth-century painting, still obediently piling on the bitumen.[6] Yet Monet could be right. Certainly the conventional painters of the day—and the bulk of the Gleyre students who firmly trod in their footsteps—had nothing to recommend them but cowardly or lazy conformism, and insofar as Monet tried to improve on them he should be followed.

Renoir was always a poor partisan. He had been born with one of the smallest bumps of intolerance ever known in a famous man. He thought everyone should worship, play at politics, paint, work, love, live as they pleased as long as they gave others the same freedom.[7] His fancy at that moment led him to experiment with landscape painting on the spot. So far he obeyed Monet, but no further.

So off he went with Sisley to Chailly in the spring of 1864, leaving behind him for consideration by that year's Salon jury a vast and very black canvas which must have discouraged Monet considerably. It depicted Hugo's Esmeralda dancing with a goat in the light of a campfire, surrounded by admiring followers and backed by a flame-lit cathedral, a canvas he was to remember and chuckle at to the end of his life.[8]

He had no plan. He returned to the forest simply because he had enjoyed the first country excursion and could remember many motifs he would have liked to paint if he had had time. Monet and Bazille, after keeping them company for a few days, moved on—Monet to paint at Le Havre,[9] Bazille to take his medicals in Paris [10]—and when they had gone, Renoir made an important acquaintance. He was painting that day in a forest

glade some way from Sisley, as usual in his old blue overall.
"This time," he told Vollard, "I had a row with some passers-by
who began to make fun of my outfit. This got my back up and
things began to look ugly." [11]

The teen-age problem was present in the eighteen-sixties as
now and took much the same form—cruel, infantile humor
directed whenever possible at a solitary person by a gang. The
gang who decided to torment Renoir consisted of Paris shopgirls
and youths on a Sunday outing. The fun opened with derisive
remarks about the painter's overall. When Renoir refused to
respond and it was clear that he was peaceably inclined, one
youth was sufficiently daring to kick his palette out of his hand.
This roused the painter, and he went on the attack. His canvas
would obviously be the next target.

He was in a poor position, likely to get himself knocked down
and kicked and, what really mattered to him, his precious painting mauled. But fortune was with him: "At that moment a man
appeared who, in spite of having a wooden leg, managed to put
my aggressors to flight, thanks to a stick which he wielded with
great dexterity. When I thanked him, he said 'I'm a painter too;
my name is Diaz.' "

They talked; and it transpired that Renoir owed his rescue
to his old workshop overall. Diaz had also spent part of his
youth in a china workshop, and the familiar sight of a blue
overall through the trees had made him curious to see who was
working there.

Renoir's reaction to this extraordinary piece of good luck was
in character; he took his chance and, after telling Diaz how
much he admired his work, asked if he would look at the canvas
he was then painting. He asked "timidly," but he asked.

Diaz studied the unfinished forest scene; it was the kind of
subject in which he specialized. His first remark was, "It's not
badly drawn," a remark that astonished Renoir and gave him a
good story for the rest of his life. "That was about the only time
I ever heard my drawing praised," he used to say with a twinkle
in after years. [12]

Diaz' next remark was blunt enough; he was a man of few

words and those to the point. "Why the devil do you paint so black?" he demanded.[13]

From that moment bitumen was finished for Renoir, and the final restraint on a natural love of bright color fell away. But before he could begin a new canvas with bitumen restricted to the minimum—and he could scarcely wait—he had further and most satisfactory talk with the great man.

Like so many men, Diaz took an immediate liking to him. In a few minutes he had extracted enough information to show him that the young man was very poor and did not know how to make ends meet. Before they parted he told Renoir that he could get some colors and canvases at his dealer's and mark them down to him.[14]

Elated by this generous gesture,[15] Renoir set to work the moment Diaz stumped off, and he changed his style and color so successfully that Sisley, staring at the canvas put in front of him triumphantly that evening in the Cheval Blanc, exclaimed, "You're out of your mind! What's the idea of painting trees blue and earth lilac?" [16]

No amount of protest by the horrified Sisley, who had not departed one inch from his efforts to follow Corot,[17] could move his friend, and when Renoir went back to Paris he demonstrated his denial of bitumen in dramatic fashion, a fashion few young men of any age could rival.

On arrival he was greeted with the exciting news that *La Esmeralda* had been accepted by the Salon. He was then just twenty-three. At his first attempt he had managed to storm the Salon jury, noted for its dislike of youth and novelty. Admittedly the novelty of *La Esmeralda* was not conspicuous, but the youth and anonymity of its maker were undeniable; nobody knew Auguste Renoir, he was entirely without the influence that so often persuaded the jury to admit canvases. Neither Bazille, Monet, nor Sisley had even thought of daring to submit a canvas. His triumph was complete; two years earlier a painter of blinds without a scrap of technical experience, he had managed to get himself into the one exhibition in France that was seen by all the collectors, all the people interested in painting. His family were immensely gratified and proud.

Most young people would have been beside themselves with pleasure and would have shown it, as young people do, by a display of vanity. Renoir, when the canvas was returned to him, destroyed it. His reasons for this astonishing act of abnegation were simplicity itself: he had formed a distaste for black pictures since meeting Diaz, and he thought the canvas too big to house comfortably in the tiny Bazille studio; it would hinder him in painting freely. So with a last lingering look at the red flicker of flames on the cathedral—which he much preferred to his attempt at Esmeralda—he put an end to it.

The finale is pure Renoir, and one can see the wry grin: "My luck was not in. That very day an Englishman called; he wanted to buy the picture!" [18]

The remainder of the year he devoted to the production of pictures for the 1865 Salon. The intimacy with Bazille and the evenings in the Avenue Trudaine house of Commandant Lejosne were at last bearing fruit. He had two commissions that year, one the portrait of a man who preferred to remain anonymous, the other of a young daughter of Judge Lascaux, a fervent Wagnerite. This was the first of Renoir's many child portraits, and the study of Romaine Lascaux was to compare favorably with many of its successors.

Being Renoir, he painted as he pleased. The canvases of an ordinary young man who had met Diaz and incontinently abandoned the use of black in large masses would be expected to betray a fairly comprehensive imitation of the master. But not those of Renoir. In the course of that year he made a flower study, of lilies with greenhouse plants, and the canvas resembled one of the old Dutch paintings, highly finished, with every leaf clearly painted, the whole given a dull green background shading into near black. He went back to Chailly and painted *Soirée d'été*; he stayed with his parents, he stayed with Sisley, he made canvas after canvas and scraped off what he had done. He was not satisfied with his work and could see no future for himself.

The next year, 1865, he had another artistic success; the Salon showed—hung virtually out of sight—his *Arums et plantes de serre* and his commissioned portrait of Monsieur W.S. He did not make one sou out of the showings, but he was cheered despite the fact, and once more joined his friends at Fontaine-bleau. He no longer had a pied-à-terre in Paris. Bazille, who had a changeable nature, had moved in January to another studio which he offered to share with Monet.[19] Renoir did not resent the change. Monet was short of money too, and Renoir did not grudge him the chance of a bed and a place in which to work; on the contrary, Renoir called often and made the most of the varied company he found there, including Cézanne and his friend Solari the sculptor; Carjat, poet and a sort of genius as a photographer who was a friend of Nadar, famed for a very different kind of photography, society portraits; and the notorious Courbet.

The net result of Bazille's change of companions was the kind of pilgrimage known only too well to the young artists of the day, and which had been immortalized by a man Renoir was soon to meet. The attic life reads romantically, on the surface at least, in Murger's *Scènes de la Vie de Bohème,* and looks it in Puccini's opera; in practice, as Renoir soon discovered, it was spirit-breaking. The everlasting tramp from one wretched lodging to another, the begging of loans, the cold, the hunger, the attempts to paint with stiff fingers, the monotony— all this reduced the pursuit of art to a kind of martyrdom. And Renoir was not, at this point in his life, of the stuff of which martyrs are made. He could not tell himself that the world was well lost for his art. He loved painting but he did not love his own paintings. He said again and again that he was a craftsman who could not find his way.[20] He had many miserable moments.

For all that, when he went down to Chailly for the third year running, in 1865, having just been paid for one of his commissioned pictures, he was the life and soul of the party. Monet, impressed by Renoir's Salon showing the previous year, had submitted two seascapes that spring. Like his friend he was admitted; unlike him Monet got an unusually good press for an unknown man and was spoken of by some critics as a coming painter.[21] Immensely cheered, he set to work at a vast landscape with figures.[22] Perhaps Renoir and Sisley sensed that the despotic Monet [23] would soon be demanding their services to pose and that their own painting would dwindle to nothing; perhaps Renoir could not find the money for the much sought after Cheval Blanc. Whatever the reason, both moved to the nearby but less fashionable Marlotte, leaving the good-natured Bazille to pose for all Monet's male figures. At Marlotte they put up at the inn of Mère Anthony, famous to young painters. The life in the forest painting day after day was near idyllic, and Renoir quickly forgot the troubles awaiting him when summer drew away. He had the great gift of living in the present, and this present he found most agreeable. He had not found his style; he was painting as every mood took him, but he kept cheerful in the sun.

There were distractions, too, though Renoir deliberately stayed on the fringe of them. He was painting nearby when Bazille made his study of Monet sitting under a tree in a forest glade, with his model and mistress Camille at his side while Sisley and his fiancée, another model, lay on the grass reading. Renoir probably thought Monet unwise to have launched into such an intimacy so early, for Renoir had strong principles. He had made up his mind early that he would not marry unless or until he could afford to keep a wife and home in tolerable comfort and without pressing anxiety—the sight of his parents' worried faces through the years had never left him. He had no criticism of Sisley, the wealthy one, except for a doubt whether his engagement might not hinder his development as a painter. For himself, though he adored women, he was determined not to involve them in a life of poverty.

He was at his ease in Mère Anthony's inn. This was "the true village auberge," [24] he said, and there he quickly became the favorite of the patronne, a grim-faced woman who always wore a kerchief over her head but whose sour looks masked a soft heart for young painters with more talent than money. Her servant Nana—that "superb girl" [25]—would do anything for

Renoir because, unlike most of the youthful habitués, he treated her as a human being instead of a creature to fetch and carry and to feel honored if asked to share a bed. The white poodle Toto, who had lost one paw (which Renoir tried unsuccessfully to reproduce artificially),[26] was forever trying to follow him in his walks through the forest. He was at home with most of the visiting painters (who included an old acquaintance in Lamy) and became intimate with a Jules Lecoeur, who used to drop into the inn of an evening for a glass of wine and a chat. Lecoeur lived in the village and soon attached himself to Renoir as a painting companion. The excursions led to an introduction to the Lecoeur home. Finally, encouraged by his family's approval of this new friend, Lecoeur made a proposal which lightened Renoir's heart; he offered to share his Paris studio with him that winter.

So this early summer excursion turned out very much more successful than Renoir could have hoped; and back in Paris with Sisley, he at once expressed his feelings by organizing a river outing. To organize meant in practice to persuade Sisley to make it possible. Like so many city-bred men, Renoir loved water and hankered for a yacht to sail or, since that was obviously out of the question, even a boat to row. In fact he had nothing, not even a skiff, and he used to listen to Monet on boats and boating with a kind of anguish. At Ville d'Avray one of his chief joys was to walk along the river and watch the happy boatloads passing by, making his pleasure theirs.

Monet, who was to say on his deathbed, "I wish I could die on a buoy," was always talking of the ships he had known and loved from his earliest days. His father now owned a small yacht at Sainte-Adresse, and the past summer Monet had made an attractive picture of the regatta at Le Havre, one of the best canvases he had painted to date.

When Renoir saw this canvas nothing would satisfy him but that he and Sisley visit the next regatta, and this was what he now planned to do, by water. He arranged to hire a small yacht, persuaded the captain of the *Paris et Londres* to give them a tow as far as Rouen, then wrote to Bazille to invite him to join the party. Renoir was not a great letter writer, and few survive of the letters he felt himself obliged to write; but the letter to Bazille is true Renoir in its blend of friendliness, candor, and independence—as much like him as were the arrangements he had made instinctively to ensure pleasure every foot of the way from Paris. He regarded his dwindling stock of francs jealously; every one spent had to buy good business or good pleasure.

"We intend to stay at Le Havre about ten days," he explained, "and the total cost will be about fifty francs. If you want to come it will give me pleasure. There is still a seat in our boat. I am taking my box of colors so as to make a sketch of the parts that please me. I think this could be charming. There's nothing to prevent you from leaving a place that doesn't please you and nothing to prevent you from staying on in a place which amuses you. Very frugal meals."

Such was the invitation and such was Renoir's care not to give a friend the kind of embarrassment he himself would detest that he added: "You have no need to worry if you feel like refusing. It's true that I should be very happy to have you with us, but take this invitation as acceptable only if it appeals to you. As you have already been there I believed you might be pleased to see once more a place you considered beautiful. That's why I thought of you. But I say again, don't worry, you aren't committed to anything. Just reply, that's all." [27]

Bazille did not come on the trip. He was still posing endlessly and writing apologetically home, "I'm at Chailly simply and solely to help Monet." [28] Life at Chailly was not without incident. While the yacht was carrying Sisley, Renoir, and party to Le Havre, Bazille suddenly found himself acting as male nurse. Some English painters foolishly threw a heavy bronze disc about outside the inn and let it slip. It would have struck a child if Monet had not jumped in front of it. He was hit on the knee and carried to bed in great pain. Whatever his first thoughts, Bazille was handsomely recompensed for being cooped up in an inn, for the patient unexpectedly had two distinguished visitors, the great Courbet and Corot.[29]

CHAPTER V

MEETING COURBET

1865-1866

THE FOLLOWING YEAR, in 1866, Courbet was to move Renoir a further step in his career as the result of an encounter that again took place in the forest of Fontainebleau.

The winter between Renoir's painting trip to Le Havre regatta and this meeting is best passed over quickly. He had shelter in Lecoeur's studio [1] and that was all. Once more he was put to the most demoralizing shifts to keep himself alive and in good heart. His two Salon exhibits, like *La Esmeralda* of the previous year, brought him precisely nothing; they were hung too high to be seen [2]—the usual treatment meted out to unknown men—and did not receive a single critical note. He had already spent the small sums paid for his two commissioned canvases (even the supposedly enlightened members of the Lejosne gatherings had taken the chance to beat down the price with a young man plainly desperate). For weeks on end he did not know where the next meal was coming from, had no change of clothes, and was given no excuse for hope. He tramped the dealers with the few canvases he had made; all laughed at them. He had not even the essential belief in himself; he was both clearsighted and absurdly modest. He did not think he could draw, he was uncertain about his colors, he wondered incessantly whether he had not made a mistake in ever attempting to paint outside a workshop.

Renoir was to say of himself in later years that he was no fighter.[3] He certainly had many self-doubts. Yet none but a fighter could have gone on at that moment in 1865. There was nothing to prevent him resuming the work he had done before joining the Beaux-Arts; a man of his speed and certainty with the brush would have been welcome in a dozen commercial enterprises. Instead he went hungry, physically wretched in the cold (which he detested) and the abundant rain of that winter.[4]

In March of 1866 he was back in Marlotte with Sisley and hard at work on two pictures for the Salon, a portrait of Lecoeur and his dogs in a forest glade done with the knife, Courbet style, and a canvas in which he had more faith, *Paysage avec deux figures.*

Both canvases were finished in the Lecoeur house; Sisley went back to Paris ahead of him, and he did not need much persuasion to leave the inn for a comfortable home. As always Renoir repaid the hospitality handsomely; his cheerfulness and unpretentious manner quickly made him like another son. Never was there an easier guest or a more helpful one when he was not in a state of dream, and he gave great pleasure by tactfully asking Mme. Lecoeur whether she would sit for him.

What Lecoeur's young sister thought of him can be seen from a letter she wrote toward the end of March, a letter revealing a comedy absolutely typical of Renoir. "When he had finished his pictures for the exhibition the poor boy was like a body without a soul because he didn't know what he wanted to do next. The day before yesterday he and Jules decided to go to Paris, then he thought he would stay on a little and finish mother's portrait while his friend Sisley found a room for him to go to. Ever since finishing his exhibition pictures he had been tormented by this friend Sisley on the one hand, and Jules on the other. But yesterday morning he at last began to work, saying that now he would never leave us. This morning he was still saying he wouldn't leave us, then he walked to the railway station to see Jules off and at the last moment got in the train himself. He had taken nothing with him so he'll have to come back to get his things. I am sure he is now regretting having given way." [5]

He did come back for the summer after the Salon opening in May and, after announcing good news—the great success of Monet's portrait of Camille, which he had painted almost at the last moment [6]—gave the Lecoeur family a humorously wry account of the way in which he had heard the Salon jury's decision about his own favored canvas. He waited for a long time, he said, outside the Palais de l'Industrie, the building in which the jury examined the entries, and at last saw Corot and Daubigny coming down the steps. He knew that both were on that year's jury, but at the last moment as he walked toward them his courage failed and he hastily pretended to be a friend of himself.

Daubigny, always sympathetic to young and progressive painters, said he well remembered *Paysage avec deux figures* and was very sorry to say that it had been rejected. His next words cheered the immediately disconsolate Renoir. "We did everything we possibly could to stop it being rejected," he said kindly (perhaps he suspected that he was talking to the painter of the picture but was too tactful to say so). "We demanded a viewing of it ten times but could not persuade a majority of the jury to agree with us. What can you expect; we were six in favor against all the others." Nor was this all; Daubigny added, "Tell your friend not to be downhearted. His picture has great qualities." [7]

Renoir told this story with panache; by that time his disappointment was weeks old and he could see only the hopeful side. Like his three fellow painters from Gleyre's he would a thousand times prefer a good word from Corot or Daubigny to the favorable decision of a hopelessly academic jury, and his volatile nature rose to those magical words "great qualities." He did not meet Daubigny in the forest; by this time Daubigny had settled at Auvers and did not often leave his garden or the river Oise which ran close to it. He did see Corot working in a glade, but the great man was far from being alone; and Renoir, who disliked toadies, "admired from a distance. He was always surrounded by a group of idiots and I had no wish to be taken for one." [8] When he did at last meet Corot and said how difficult he found *plein air* painting, he was dumbfounded by the master's "One can never be certain what one has done in the open air. One must touch it up in the studio." [9]

This glimpse of Corot at work and the single short interview had no immediate effect on Renoir; by that time he was already following another star, the bulky and supremely confident star of Courbet. Courbet had been brought down to Fontainebleau forest the previous year by news of Monet's great outdoor canvas. He liked the young Norman right away, helped him with money, poured advice on him, and ended by persuading him to make changes at the last moment which made it impossible for Monet to submit the canvas to the 1866 Salon. [10] Oblivious of the harm he had done, Courbet was back in the forest the next year, and there Renoir found him when he walked across to see what Monet and Bazille were doing.

Courbet was, of course, known to him as the most famous revolutionary painter of the day. In the circle in which Renoir moved, Courbet was considered less advanced as well as less realistic than Manet, whom Cézanne, for one, spoke of with positive awe, [11] but this was not yet the general view. Courbet possessed the advantages of seniority, a recognized following, a name known throughout the country and, not least, a genius for self-advertisement. He had been demanding for years, in stentorian tones, that the painter abandon academic futilities and take as subject what he saw before his eyes, the scene and people of his own time. [12] At a moment when radicalism was all the rage with the rising generation, this had become a popular rallying call to the many frustrated painters who were unable to obtain a viewing in the Salon and who despised the unreal subjects, lifelessly painted, which the Beaux-Arts taught and the Salon juries rewarded. Courbet had brought a breath of hope to young men and had become a sort of god in the school generally called naturalist.

Courbet's command, echoed in all the youthful studios and cafés, "Paint what you see," ran directly counter to Renoir's early loves and, indeed, to his inmost nature. It was not for nothing that he had been drawn from childhood to the eighteenth-century painters. Yet never was there a less hidebound man than Renoir nor one who delighted more in all the ordinary manifestations of his age—the clothes, the cafés, the theatres, the shops, the crowded streets, the lines of stalls with their naphtha lamps and the shrill cries of their owners, the street dances on fete days, the circus, the midinette. He was, for all his eighteenth-century preconceptions, a true son of his time, and Courbet merely confirmed his own common-sense deduction that these nineteenth-century scenes and people afforded magnificent subjects for the painter. Courbet also suggested what he, naturally shrewd, must believe true, that buyers of pictures would prefer present-day scenes to the ancient battles, classical anecdotes, great moments in French history, moral reflections, and all the rest of the academic repertoire put before the Salon audience year after year.

Renoir had a strong sense of the ludicrous, and this second important meeting in the forest must have taxed his self-control. Courbet played the great man beyond its credible limits; he was greater than any great man could possibly be.[13] Displays of self-importance were given short shrift in Renoir's down-to-earth world, and it was as well for his immediate development as painter that he was sharp enough to see that Courbet, for all his theatrical poses and ridiculous demonstrations of vanity, was a kind man. And when Renoir actually saw the painter at work, slashing a canvas into shape with strong, sure strokes of the brush and palette knife, he forgot criticism and simply admired. He admired the strength and the certainty, the broad treatment and the interesting use of color; he also felt reassured by the sense that the work was based firmly on traditional methods.

He was one of the last to succumb to Courbet's influence. Monet had been painting broadly after Courbet for the best part of a year; Cézanne and Pissarro both altered their technique for a time to approximate to that of the master; Bazille was bowled over immediately; and even Sisley tentatively experimented once or twice in the Courbet manner. But though last, Renoir was the most wholehearted when he did meet Courbet; he let himself go completely and began a series of paintings which, though they could have been painted by no one but himself, could not have been made at all if Courbet had never existed. He began a nude on a very large canvas, he made a number of forest studies, and he did a study of Mère Anthony's inn when he moved there for a time later in the summer.

All these canvases were strongly and very quickly made, and it could be argued that they were better than any other Courbet-inspired work from any other man—this for the good reason that Renoir had no fear, as his friends had, of his particular sensation as painter being submerged by another influence. Renoir did not think in these terms at all. He knew that he had far to go and was willing and even eager to go another man's way. He was quite sure that if he had anything in him—which he took leave to doubt often enough—it would assert itself in time. Meanwhile, to paint was the thing. All he asked of life when he had food inside him, a coat on his back, and a bed at night was to get his hands on a paintbrush and to be set down in front of an empty canvas; the mere act of painting was enough to make him whistle and sing.[14]

He did plenty of whistling and singing this summer of 1866, and one, at least, of the pictures he made, of the room in the inn where the painters ate and talked and sang, was, though decidedly Courbetesque, definitely the best thing he had yet done. The canvas shows the attractive Nana clearing away the dishes, Lecoeur standing behind the table, Lamy and Sisley sitting at it, Toto close by it, Mère Anthony in the background, and along the back wall the frescoes contributed by visiting painters, including the latest addition, by Renoir, a satirical view of Murger, whom he had met there. "This study of the inn's habitués," he said later, "though unpretentious, was quite successful in some ways." [15] From Renoir, this was high self-praise.

As if in reward for his courage, a slight amelioration in the immediate future showed itself. The joint tenancy of a studio shared by Bazille and Monet had come to a hurried end early in the year. They had given a noisy fancy dress "ball" and were turned out.[16] After the summer of painting, Monet, having asked Renoir's advice, went to Ville d'Avray, rented a cottage, installed Camille in it, and prepared to get to work on the second of his big *plein air* canvases—this time in the cottage garden.

Bazille was not happy about Monet's decision to live with Camille [17] (one of the prominent dancers at their disastrous dance) and, after a short spell on his own, invited Renoir to share with him again. Bazille had missed the perky cheerfulness of his friend more than he cared to confess. He took a new studio in rue Visconti [18] on the Left Bank, and Renoir found himself settled for the winter and spring. He at once dismissed all thought of the future; Bazille was well off as Lecoeur was not; a man would not starve in his studio and had a reasonable chance of keeping warm. Besides, Bazille usually went home to Montpellier for some part of the winter, and the man who shared his studio had it to himself.

So it turned out. Bazille went off, not without leaving a generous loan behind him, and Renoir set to a perfect frenzy of work, though with him the word frenzy must be taken in its old meaning, to be carried out of oneself with enthusiasm.

As one would expect, he did not confine himself to Courbetesque canvases; as always he painted just what he felt like painting at the moment and in the style that he felt suited the subject. Again he painted a flower piece, his *Grand Bouquet,* in which he applied the paint smoothly and with great care, displaying a feeling for textures that was rare in the men painting at that time; even Fantin-Latour, whom Renoir was no doubt trying to emulate, could not convey the delicate life of flowers so well as his young imitator.

During the winter Renoir also began to pay some attention to street scenes. It was perhaps surprising that he had not tried his hand at this before, since more than most men he knew and loved the sight of the "bricks" that the countryman Bazille regarded so often with distaste.[19] Now he got to work. He made a

sparkling sketch of the Champs-Élysées; he painted a strictly
realistic view of the Pont des Arts with the Louvre in the background. Then, after the turn of the year, he joined forces with
Monet to make cityscapes, a Monet up from Ville d'Avray to try
to sell a canvas to a dealer and whom Renoir, in the absence of
Bazille, gladly put up in his studio.

Renoir's view of Monet was mixed. Monet's artistic rectitude
half-appalled, half-swept him off his feet. The long fight against
unsympathetic parents, typical philistines, astonished him; yet
Monet went on calmly, disregarding their displeasure and
somehow managing to exist without their help. As for Monet's
view of painting, this was practically beyond Renoir's compre-
hension. Monet refused even to think of accepting commissions;
he went on painting as he felt he must paint, making landscapes and figure studies out of doors. Every other form of art
left him uninterested; he knew what he was intended to do and
was prepared to do it whether he starved or not.

To Renoir this was a sort of glorious insanity. Monet's technique and experience, so much greater than his own, could have
earned him enough to live on if he were willing to conform
until he became better established. Renoir would not have
hesitated; he would have earned the money. He felt at times
irritated with this fantastically obstinate man. He thought that
Monet was even more foolish to have broken with his parents
in order to live with Camille, of whom they disapproved, than
he was to paint outside the Beaux-Arts. Yet mingled strongly
with this criticism was a kind of envy; Monet at least knew
where he was going and had the strength of mind to refuse to
look in any other direction. Renoir noticed that even though
his friend had burdened himself with Camille he did not allow
this to interfere with his principles; she too would have to face
starvation if he could not live off the pictures he wished to
paint. To Renoir, this was as much inhuman as superhuman—
one powerful reason that made him vow not to marry while
poor was his horror of causing a woman to suffer—but it was
also undeniably impressive.[20]

On the whole this period of street painting gave Renoir much more pleasure than otherwise; one might find Monet's purpose-fulness occasionally boring, as he did, but to work side by side with such a man was inspiring too. And more than this; Renoir kept his eyes open—never were there sharper eyes—and noticed that Monet was trying out a new technique. When Monet sat on the balcony at the eastern end of the Louvre to make a picture of the Princess's garden, he painted the leaves on the trees with small brushstrokes to give the effect of fragility, and he used pure yellows, reds, and blues to give the effect of light.[21] This, the beginnings of Impressionism long before such a term was ever thought of, remained in Renoir's mind. He too had used such colors after the meeting with Courbet. He did not change his technique then, but made a note of the fact for the right moment.

Accompanying himself and Monet was one who had become practically Renoir's shadow. This was his young brother Edmond. From his earliest years Edmond had worshipped his middle brother and insisted on regarding him as a great artist. Nothing that Renoir could say would alter this faith. At last, in a kind of humorous despair, Renoir took him down to the forest. This was when he met Courbet, and his brother's awe at this encounter sent Renoir into fits of secret laughter. After that, Edmond's belief in Auguste was indestructible.[22]

So when Renoir began to paint in the Paris streets Edmond was there, insisting on carrying his canvas, his colors, anything with which he could possibly burden himself to save this be-loved brother from tiring exercise which would interfere with his work. And when, as often happened, Renoir wanted a model, in the street or out of it, there was Edmond, ready to stand motionless as long as necessary.[23]

But Edmond was not entirely unobjective about his brother. Afterward he wrote of this time, describing Renoir as he was seen by others. "His everyday manner was pensive, dreamy and rather distrait and gloomy, with an eye that did not appear to see anything or anyone. When he went to fetch something he would always run. When he got there he would come back, once, twice, as many as ten times, having forgotten what it was he went for. In the street he walked hurriedly, oblivious of everything and everybody. In the home or his studio he was exactly the opposite; he used to sit for hours without moving or speaking. Where were his thoughts? I used to wonder; was he thinking of the picture he was going to make? If so, he never talked about it; painting was the last subject he would embark on. All the same, if you wanted to see his face alight, to hear him sing a cheerful song, there was no point in looking for him at the meal table or in places of amusement, the theatre or café; try to come on him just when he's beginning to paint!" [24]

That, then, was the twenty-six-year-old Renoir according to his brother. It is a true portrait—many have confirmed it—yet only half true; behind that dreamy manner ran the keen brain, the brain of one trained from infancy to look for opportunities and take advantage of them. But at this moment early in 1867 some other force seemed to control him, for the subject singled out for submission to the Salon that year was none other than the vast nude he had begun months earlier. This was made very much in the Courbet style, with great use of the palette knife. Yet for all its technical weaknesses Courbet could scarcely have rendered the voluptuous nature of the pose and the texture of the skin.

The voluptuousness struck most people first, and before the time for submission came round, Renoir was advised that it would be hopeless to send it; the Salon jury would instantly reject it as improper.

The artist's reaction to this was unique. Not for him hurt or angry protests that it was nothing of the kind, that he had painted it as a painter, that he was following a time-honored tradition and had not a lustful thought in his head, being absorbed by the problem of conveying the naked body as it appeared to him. None of this. Instead, as he described it with amused contempt, "I put a bow in the hand of my nude and a dead doe at her feet and I painted an animal skin across her crotch to cover what these purists consider nakedness to mean. Then I renamed it *Diana!*" [25]

Even this did not save the picture; the jury rejected it, leaving

Renoir for the first time without an exhibit and with an unsalable picture. "One day a prospective purchaser turned up,"
he said with a twinkle, "but we couldn't come to terms because
he wanted to buy the doe only!" [26]

CHAPTER VI

―――

TRADITION OR NEW ERA?

―――

1867-1869

THE MODEL FOR HIS DIANA was a girl called Lise. Her parents, like his, lived at Ville d'Avray,[1] and it seems probable that Renoir was the first painter to use her as model. She afterward posed for a number of his friends but evidently preferred him and Lecoeur; both of them stayed with her at her parents' house during a summer of painting.

The effect of this summer of 1867 was expressed in two of the most promising pictures Renoir had made, his *Lise* and *Lise à l'ombrelle*. They too show the influence of Courbet—in the treatment of the tree trunk in the latter picture and the dull green background—but the painting of the white dress, the flesh of the arm seen through the muslin, and the detail on the little black parasol are pure Renoir, as are the arrangement and execution of the great sweep of black sash to the very hem of the dress. He has already begun to use light and shadow to give unity of style to his figure, and the principle of irregularity which he was to emphasize in later years is already put into action; he was not painting a goddess but a human being.

Personally, Renoir was turning against Courbet. In Paris that year the two great rebels Courbet and Manet had been rejected at the Salon, and each had decided to build an exhibition hall for himself in the grounds of the World's Fair then being held in the capital. Courbet's exhibition was a huge success, Manet's not so, but Renoir found his hero's vanity hard to take. Courbet had built over his wooden shed a small attic in which he used to sleep—acting as a kind of watchman over his pictures—and the attic window opened on to a balcony which commanded a view of the front door of the exhibition hall. From this balcony he would watch and comment loudly on the number of people visiting the hall and their behavior. On the first morning, and maybe other mornings too, he decided to set the tone. He awakened a little late, found visitors already approaching, and hurried down in his shirt, carrying his trousers and coat over one arm. When the first arrivals walked in, a moment later they found him, still undressed, standing rigid with admiration before his pictures. "How beautiful they are!" he exclaimed in a loud voice. "How magnificent! They are incredible! They take one's breath away!" And to make doubly sure that all had heard, he continued to repeat, never taking his eyes from his work, "Incredible! Incredible!" [2]

Renoir used to tell the story with a smile, but he added, not so humorously, "Of course he kept that kind of admiration for his own work." [3] Behind this remark was perhaps a little pique. It was true enough that Courbet thought himself the greatest of all painters and that he took considerable liberties in criticism of the pictures of other men, including some outrageous remarks about Manet. He was nevertheless a generous man when in the mood to be so, and he had praised Monet, whom he liked instinctively, quite fulsomely. For Renoir he never had a good word, and Renoir was not one to miss the irony of the situation, since he more than all his friends had responded to Courbet's influence.

It is possible to see the Courbet-Manet exhibitions as the high watermark of this influence. Later, discussing the strength for which Courbet was always praised, Renoir said bluntly, "I'd much prefer a plate costing one sou and painted in three pretty colors than kilometres of super-powerful—and boring—painting." [4] He exaggerated, of course, but even in 1867 he was tiring of a style which did not truly suit him any more than the bull-like Courbet as a man commended himself to the quick-

witted city boy. He saw both exhibitions several times, as did
all his friends, and his final comment was a penetrating one.
"Courbet," he said, "is still in the tradition. Manet is a new
era." [5]

Among the Gleyre studio friends there was almost perpetual
discussion of the best way of selling their work. Dealers would
not look at their paintings, had never heard of them and said
so. The Salon had done nothing for them and seemed likely to
do nothing. They still tried to exhibit there because there was
nowhere else to exhibit, and since all were young and the young
are resilient, they still hoped to be accepted, well hung and
highly praised. The young are impatient too, and Renoir and
Monet were more than that: they were desperate, dependent on
sales for the food they ate. It was Monet who this year suggested
that they, their friends, and elder supporters put on an exhibition
of their own the following year. Courbet was proposing to rent
out his hall when he had done with it; he would charge little
for a group headed by Monet. And Monet said they ought to
take it and try their luck.

Bazille explained to his parents that twelve of them had
decided "to rent each year a big studio where we can show as
many pictures as we please"; he was thinking, here, of the Salon
limitation of three pictures per painter. He continued, "We
shall also invite painters we admire to send canvases. Courbet,
Corot, Diaz, Daubigny, and many others you have not heard of
have promised to send us pictures and think our idea is a good
one. With these men and Monet, who is better than any of us,
we shall be sure to succeed. You will see how we shall be talked
about." [6]

Bazille's "twelve young painters" were the four of Gleyre's
plus Cézanne and Pissarro (thirty-seven at that time but eternally young at heart) and their friends. Renoir agreed to this
first attempt at a group exhibition because he could not afford
to refuse; that he liked the idea is doubtful. He did not want
to appear before the public as a member of a rebel, modernist
clique; he wanted to be free to paint what he liked and to show
where he liked. However, he dared not refuse this first chance

of showing his pictures. Good fellowship insisted that he go along with his friends; necessity demanded it. As it happened, nothing came of the plan. Bazille announced its demise: "By mulcting ourselves we have scraped together 2,500 francs but this is not enough. We shall be forced to go back to the maternal lap of the Salon." [7]

The question remained for Renoir—was he in the tradition or should he take his place in the new era of Manet and his friends? This was a turning point. He refused as ever to be too solemn about himself and his future, but he knew well enough that the choice was there. And from this time a change is seen. The change can be described as a recognition that he was living in the eighteen-sixties and not a century earlier. Much in him continued to prefer the earlier century, but he had to admit the anomaly of trying to live in it after the political revolution, followed by the beginnings of the industrial revolution, had promoted a new France, a new way of living, a new type of people. Was it possible to deny that these people and this world must lead to a new kind of art? Manet had shown the way; he had in fact done what Courbet had talked about: he had painted the people of his own day in the milieu of the age; he had attacked in the most practical way the legend that only the aristocrat was worthy to sit for his portrait and that the peasant, the city worker, and everything plain or ugly were not worthy of art, which should be confined to morally elevating scenes or distinguished persons.

Renoir was a man of his time, none more so if his taste for eighteenth-century art and his belief in craftsmanship are excepted. He liked the workingman, had no envy of riches, no wish to live any way but simply. He knew that he would find warmer hearts and stouter souls in the cheap cafés and restaurants than in the expensive ones, that he would get more amusement on the pavements than in a fiacre, in the theatre gallery than in the fauteuils. He was proud of his position and did not want it changed.

Almost everything, in fact, and not least his business sense, pulled him toward the modernity in subject and treatment that

his friends were preaching, and Maître was soon writing appre-
hensively about him to Bazille.[8] Edmond Maître, a young
Bordelais leisurely studying law, was the leading musical spirit
in the Lejosne set. He had seen a lot of Renoir since Bazille
once more set up house with him, for it was his habit to call in
and play piano duets with Bazille and to talk music till the
small hours.

The Lejosne set was very intellectual and inevitably radical.
Some of the men Renoir met there were truly great and advanced in their ideas; most of them were very much like the
people (indeed, some of them were the same) whom the young
Rimbaud was to meet and castigate in Paris a few years later.
Renoir was not a Rimbaud; he lacked the wit and the single-
mindedness, but like Rimbaud he knew a phony when he saw
one and he knew a man who was being progressive because it
was the thing to be progressive. He had his own way of dealing
with the type. In place of Rimbaud's moral courage, expressed
by jeers and *"merdes,"* he either paid no attention (an effective
damper to those wanting an audience) or smiled his charming
smile and punctured pretension by an apparently naïve judgment with a sting in its tail. Apart from ridicule or neglect there
is nothing the poseur dislikes quite so much as plain speech;
he calls it vulgar, childish, ignorant, but it hurts all the same.
And in this last year or two Renoir's reputation at Lejosne's had
been changing. At first his occasional comment had been regarded as a rather piquant juvenility; now these talkative rebels
muttered elegantly that they were harboring a rebel of quite
another kind, one who thought and spoke honestly; they said
crude, they did not use the word honest, but that was what they
meant. Renoir's commissions dwindled. What, for instance, was
one to do with a young man who said of Flaubert, then all the
rage in advanced circles, "He looks like a retired captain who
has become a traveler in wines," and who dismissed the much-
acclaimed and daringly realistic *Madame Bovary* as "The story
of an idiot whose wife wanted to become somebody," with a
final "When one has read these three hundred pages one can't

help thinking, 'I can't be bothered with any of these crea-
tures' "? [9]

In music Wagner was, of course, the god, and the high priest
was Maître. He had introduced Renoir to the work of the
master, and Renoir, up to a point, had reacted satisfactorily; he
liked what he heard at the Pasdeloup "very well." But what he
heard were overtures and arias. When he realized how long a
Wagner opera lasted he was appalled and said so in his own
way: "The cries of the Valkyries are all very well for a time, but
this kind of thing going on for six hours would be enough to
drive one mad." [10]

Before Maître could recover, Renoir was adding, apologetically perhaps but nonetheless decidedly, "I much prefer Italian
music; it's less schoolmastery than German music. Even Beetho-
ven has at times a professorial side which makes my flesh
creep." [11]

Then came the gaffe of gaffes in this circle which prided
itself on steadfastly looking forward without a backward glance.
"In any case," said Renoir, "there's nothing to beat a little air
by Couperin or Grétry or whoever you care to choose of the old
French composers. Now *their* music is really well designed." [12]

Maître, then, was on the qui vive for the unexpected from
Renoir and told Bazille this summer of 1867, with strong dis-
approval: "The last time I was in Paris I saw some very strange
pictures the painter Renoir had made. He had changed his
turpentine for that dreadful sulphate and has given up his
knife for the little syringe you know all about." [13]

Renoir, in short, was experimenting and, incidentally, was
providing an object lesson in contentment when he had very
little, in the world's view, to be contented about. He had been
painting for five years and had next to nothing to show for it
except many happy hours before the easel. But these happy
hours, to a man who lived in the present, were worth all the
dreams of an uncertain future. He loved to paint; he was
realizing that he must come to heel and paint contemporary
scenes and portraits and had no difficulty at all in seeing beauty
wherever he looked, no matter how commonplace the scene

might be to the bored or unperceptive. The supreme gift of the painter, like the poet and musician, is not in his technical mastery, which lesser men can rival by sheer application, but in his unspoiled nature. He sees the miraculous in the ordinary. Renoir had begun to show this in his studies of Lise. The canvases can be seen as splendid paintings of a woman's dress. They can also and more importantly be seen as studies of a type of woman, the everyday girl of the boulevards, who would have been thought unsuitable as a model before Renoir's day unless she posed in the nude or in clothes of previous centuries. They were Renoir's response to Courbet's call, Manet's example, and Zola's propaganda to revitalize art by expressing present-day life.

When Bazille came back in the fall of 1867, Renoir progressed further. They decided to make portraits of each other to save the cost of models. Bazille painted Renoir in a familiar and very characteristic pose, sitting bunched in a chair, his feet on the seat, knees up to chin, arms round legs. Although this portrait was little more than a sketch, Bazille caught the likeness very well; there is the tuft of hair above the wide forehead, the bright eyes over the long straight nose, the serious expression. Renoir had allowed a little growth of beard to run along his chin, which was the only change in the years since Gleyre's; his face was as thin as ever.

In return he painted Bazille at his easel. This picture has since become famous. It was Renoir's first serious portrait, and one of his most successful early works of this kind, very softly painted and, for all his self-criticism, beautifully drawn. It was Bazille to the life. When Manet saw it he admired it so much that Renoir at once begged him to take it. Needless to say, he was in no state to make gifts; he scarcely knew where the next meal was coming from unless Bazille, inclined to be overlavish with his allowance, had enough left over, after he had bought his latest concert tickets, music or clothes, to stand him a dinner.

Manet, understanding the code, gratefully accepted. It was, curiously enough, one of the few pictures by Renoir of which Manet was to approve, and perhaps the painter, sensing this, thought the unique moment had best be celebrated. Besides, Manet was a great man and a wealthy one, and Renoir's pride and pleasure both insisted on the gesture.

Before Bazille's return to Paris, poor Monet, in extremis, had been forced to leave the pregnant Camille in a room near the Bazille studio and to stay with his family, who refused to acknowledge her. He was without money except for the few francs he left with Camille—francs earned by the sale of two small canvases to a cutthroat dealer Pissarro had discovered, Père Martin. His appeals to Bazille were heartrending.[14]

For a time both Bazille in Montpellier and Renoir in Paris thought that Monet would be better off without Camille. Bazille believed that she would interfere with the development of his genius and was in any case too flighty to make a good mother. Renoir could see no good in a menage crippled by poverty. Bazille was unable to send Monet the money he begged for to be with Camille when the child was born, but Renoir, though he had no money to give, forgot all criticism when he called to see Camille. He did what he could, tried to keep her cheerful, and was a tower of strength when the child was born. Lise was there often. The Sisleys—married a few weeks and who had seen Monet during their honeymoon at Le Havre—helped by gifts of food and clothing.[15]

As the weeks went by, Renoir began to change his mind. Camille came through the ordeal of loneliness and fear and deprivation with touching courage and showed every sign of being a devoted mother. Her struggle to make do and her anguish at the enforced absence of Monet at Le Havre helped to convince Renoir that he was right to remain unattached, and if Lise had unexpressed hopes of him, they were doomed by the time fall was out. But his view of Camille quite altered, and ever after he was one of her strongest supporters. When Bazille came back from his vacation in the south, Renoir made sure that he too did the girl justice.

When at last Monet arrived in Paris—released by an aunt who could no longer endure his suffering—Bazille welcomed him with open arms. "Monet has just dropped on me from the blue with a collection of magnificent paintings," he told his family. "He'll be sleeping here till the end of the month. With Renoir, that makes two hard-pressed painters I'm putting up. It's a real workhouse. I'm delighted. We have enough room and both of them are in fine spirits." [16]

Their talk was mostly of the next year's Salon. Few things are more moving than the faith these young men expressed year by year in this academically dominated exhibition. No amount of failure could daunt them for long, nor would they knuckle under to the ominous lesson of Monet's experience that a few good critical notices were powerless to shift or soften the widespread hostility to advanced work.

Most aspiring painters looked in those days to the collectors, the rich men who patronized the Salon and on whom the dealers lived, but these men remained blind to progress. Since the revolution, wealth had changed hands. Many collectors of the eighteen-sixties were parvenus who bought pictures as they bought jewels for their wives, to advertise their wealth and flaunt a culture they did not possess. They judged a picture by the academic distinction of its painter. They were not interested in men without famous names, they felt the need to be able to wave an arm as they escorted guests round their pictures and to say, "A nice Cormon, don't you think?" "Bonnat has caught my wife's expression rather well I must say," or "Not a bad Couture I picked up"—these being three men of the moment.

Young painters with fresh ideas were therefore peculiarly unlucky in the régime of Louis Napoleon, when vulgarity flourished and the old aristocratic patron of taste had virtually disappeared. But Renoir, Bazille, Monet, and Sisley all dreamed of fame just the same. Each year they imagined that it must come, and by way of the Salon. And the fame, Bazille, Renoir, and Sisley were unselfishly agreed, would first be won by Monet; they looked up to him as their strong painter, the painter of the future.

Before the Salon jury met, Bazille had changed studios once more. Monet joined Camille in her Paris room.[17] Renoir continued with Bazille when he went back across the river to rue de

la Paix in the Batignolles, and this move by the restless man
was of some importance to Renoir's future.

2

The studio was the most spacious Bazille had occupied, with an
upper floor for the beds. It was also close to the Café Guerbois
at 11 de la Grand-Rue des Batignolles (now Avenue de Clichy)
where Manet held court. The gregarious Bazille loved to walk
along the street into the steamy little place where he was sure
to find friends and acquaintances after five o'clock on any
weekday and on Sunday evenings. He was by this time, thanks
to his Lejosne connections, on dining terms with Manet (married to a pianist of whom Maître thought highly). He respected
Degas rather fearfully, like many others. More importantly, he
held a sort of balance between these Guerbois leaders and the
landscape group of Pissarro and Monet, who, with a not too
happy Renoir, usually sat pointedly apart at one of the two
marble-topped tables by the window reserved for Manet and
his followers.

These informal Guerbois evenings,[18] with visitors drifting in
and out, were regarded with suspicion by the powerful academic
critics. They chose to see Manet as a dangerous rebel preaching
heresy. In accordance with the times, if men met to discuss art
they would sooner or later be given a name, and the Guerbois
gatherings were quickly christened from outside. The conventional critics began to write of and fulminate against what they
called the Batignolles group.[19]

In truth, more than half the men who came to the café were
not painters, and those who were had only the loosest kind of
attachment based on admiration for the work and personality of
Manet. They considered him the eventual legitimate successor
to Courbet. But this by no means indicated that they followed
him slavishly or at all; there are those who admire moral courage without possessing it, and the Guerbois was full of such.

Much the same could be said of the so-called advanced critics to be seen and heard there. Zola, Duranty, Sylvestre, Castagnary, Burty, and Duret were all regulars but had little in common except a belief that art should be related to modern times, and in this they were merely extending the campaign Baudelaire had been waging for years past, not to speak of Courbet. Nor were they concerned with painting only or even mainly. They claimed that the modern man and woman provided better material for painting and writing than people of times past. They insisted, in varying degrees of intensity, that the duty of the artist was to draw inspiration from what he saw before his eyes and that this included every aspect of modernity, the railway engine, the factory, the shop, the circus, the music hall, the ballet, the café. They demanded that painting, poetry, the novel, and music should draw its strength from truth rather than imagination. They preached that beauty lay in truthful representation.

Men of every art and craft dropped into the Guerbois, from Bellot the engraver to Guys the draftsman and Nadar the photographer. There were poets, journalists, musicians, dilettantes, farceurs, and the kind of man drawn simply by rumors that the conversation there was unusual and amusing, as it often was. Like the company it was mixed; it ranged from fairly scabrous gossip and much talk of food and wine to earnest discussion about art and, especially when Pissarro could make himself heard, of ways and means. In this matter of ways and means a sharp division showed itself between the few and the many. The many were tolerably well to do; the few downright poor, and of these Pissarro, Monet, and Renoir stood out.

It was no chance that they received dusty answers time and again. The bulk of the men in the café were good-natured and willing to help comrades in distress, but they balked at the landscape painters because they could not reconcile themselves to the kind of painting taught by Pissarro with the support of Monet. Manet had laughed at Monet's attempts at *plein air* painting with "As if the ancients wouldn't have done it if it were practicable!" Degas did not care for landscape of any kind. The rest of the company followed their lead.

Pissarro's suggestion of a separate exhibition of the "have-nots" was therefore pooh-poohed. Most of the painters there had no wish to be publicly bracketed with a man who was an anarchist in politics and seemed likely to become as dangerous an anarchist in painting. They did not agree with his theories and had not his need of money.

Renoir, then, found himself classed with Monet and Pissarro (Sisley rarely came to the café) as the wild men of the gatherings, which made him uneasy. After some hesitation he had made up his mind to follow his rule of floating with the tide of the moment, which happened to be, in the vaguest of terms, modernist. Like Monet and Pissarro he was very poor; unlike them he had no ideals in painting. He could by no means be described as a landscape painter, yet found himself firmly linked to them. In addition Degas disliked him and his work and made no secret of it, and Manet, in spite of his admiration for the portrait of Bazille, was socially his superior and did not take much trouble to hide his sense of this.

Renoir's answer to a problem of this kind was to avoid it if possible. He was not often seen at the Guerbois and rarely heard. He deplored equally the grand seigneur attitude of the leaders and the fulminations of Pissarro. He did not like argument, he did not like taking sides.[20] However, he had trained himself to be an opportunist, or life had trained him, and though he shied at the questions of ways, he listened intently to any discussion of means. How was the painter to live if he defied the academic call for polished paintings depicting scenes of the past? That was vital and he knew it. If he and his friends managed to get into the Salon, they were not fairly shown and never noticed. If they did not attempt to get in, their only hope of sales was a commission. And how many wealthy men would commission painters regarded by all respected authorities as tasteless rebels who did not know how to paint?

Renoir did not wholly abandon the Guerbois but tried to make the best of whatever it might have to offer. This was not nothing. To a man with Renoir's sense of humor, Pissarro could be a joy when he launched into a denunciation of capitalism, property, the church, and demanded the destruction of all art galleries—this to an audience, most of them well born and well provided with money and, for all their genuine interest in new art forms, essentially conventional and in no way interested in changing the face of society. The struggle between Cézanne— another infrequent visitor—and Manet also silently convulsed Renoir: Cézanne, purposefully dirty and talking like the lowest of peasants; Manet, the dandy, trying to ignore this living embodiment of *mauvais gout*.[21]

It was as well that Renoir got some amusement out of the Guerbois because he got nothing else. Plans abounded for putting the poor painter on his feet, but not one was practical or commanded general support. He soon realized that what most of the men there really wanted was good gossip about art and the personalities in art. They paid lip service to the struggling but did nothing about them.

These new acquaintances neither did nor could save him and Monet when the 1868 jury's decision was made. Monet suffered a heavy blow; his best painting was rejected, and he was publicly described in the jury room as a maker of the kind of work that was not to be encouraged.[22] Renoir's *Lise à l'ombrelle* was taken, together with Monet's lesser offering, but only after a long fight by Daubigny on the jury. The championship of this good friend to talented young painters could not penetrate to the hanging committee; as the previous year, both canvases were "relegated to the dump in the roof." [23] Visitors to the Salon could scarcely make out what the pictures were like at the height at which they were hung. Nothing sold.[24] Monet retired with Camille and the baby to Fécamp, where he hoped to live more cheaply than in Paris; Bazille went off to his parents at Montpellier, and Renoir, deprived of the occasional meal at his friend's expense which kept him going, was at his last financial gasp when he managed to get a commission.

This was the final commission to come out of the Lejosne evenings, and a very good one it was—to decorate the ceiling of the main room in the Paris mansion of Prince Bibesco. Renoir was by this time experienced in the making of frescoes—he had done several since the year of the rue Dauphine café [25]—and his work pleased the new patron. He pleased him as a man too, for one notable feature of Renoir was his ability to get on with all strata of society. He was as much at home in the great house as in the workmen's bistro, and a man like Bibesco, expecting either servility or insolence, found the artist's unspoken unawareness of class differences extremely refreshing. The Prince also appreciated Renoir's common-sense attitude toward his work; there was no fuss, no attitude of the great artist forced to turn his hand to something faintly disgusting, but simply unmistakable enjoyment in a job of work and a rather touching thankfulness to be able to earn some money pleasantly. This kind of painter was new to Bibesco, accustomed to the long-bearded variety who talked much and did little. He and Renoir parted good friends.

Just about this time, toward the end of June, Renoir had a very pleasant surprise, nothing less than a favorable Salon notice. After all, someone had taken the trouble to strain his eyes peering up into "the roof" to see what the young hopefuls were doing. The man who took the trouble was Zacharie Astruc. This poet, sculptor, and critic already had a fine record of courageous championship of progressive painters. As far back as 1859 his had been the sole voice raised in favor of a Pissarro landscape in the Salon. Four years later he acclaimed the much reviled *Le Déjeuner* of Manet in the Salon des Refusés and hailed the painter as "one of the greatest artistic figures of this age." [26] Now, in 1868, he was the first man to express in print the view that yet another "painter of the future" was on his way. In an article in *L'Étendard* he said of *Lise à l'ombrelle,* "The figure is well done and the painting has great charm—accuracy of effects, gem-like delicacy, unity, and sharpness of impression, excellent distribution of light. Though it appears simple, the art used is in fact very unusual and very interesting; it would not be possible to present more freshly a theme in which the whole charm rests in the use of the light. . . . It must be said that at the Salon, in the midst of this collection of commercial work, such a canvas shines out as a work of art and of taste by an exceptional talent which demands attention and careful study."

With money in his purse and a copy of *L'Étendard* under his arm, Renoir went happily down to Ville d'Avray to enjoy his summer. He popped back to Paris from time to time to look at the studio—Bazille wanted an eye kept on the landlord, who had not been paid up to date—but most of the summer and early fall was spent by the river.

He had no thought in his head but to make the most of the sun and the river, painting when he felt like it. In fact, this summer was to lead to a method of painting which in course of time became famous as Impressionism. Anything further from such an idea could scarcely be imagined than the happy-go-lucky Renoir taking his ease after the Bibesco windfall. But happy-go-lucky only described the more obvious part of him at such a time; he remained enviably curious and observant even when not particularly interested. That was as true then as it had been true when he sat not too happily in the midst of the squabbles at the Guerbois. When Pissarro expatiated on landscape painting as he saw it and Manet and Degas deplored his conceptions, Renoir, almost despite himself, took notice, much though he disliked academic discussion away from the easel. He thought his friends talked rather too earnestly about landscape painting as it should be, but one of the kernels of their proposition, to paint scenes and people of their own day, people at work and play in their milieu, was after his own heart. Courbet had trumpeted as much, but Renoir preferred to listen to his own friends. All that was needed to set him to work along their lines was the right spot. That he discovered by chance this summer.

Ville d'Avray stands at a neck of the Seine just before it bends in a long and narrow loop. At the far end of the neck, no more than a mile or so from Ville d'Avray, is the village of Bougival. And between Bougival and the railway bridge at Chatou is the tiny island of Croissy. Recognizing that these natural features offered the restaurateur a chance to attract the holiday crowds, Père Fournaise provided the island with amusement, food and drink, making it a favorite spot for weekenders from Paris. From the island he floated the Restaurant Fournaise and a dancing floor alongside built on piles driven into the river bed.

Guy de Maupassant, a frequent visitor, described La Grenouillère, as the floating pleasure garden was named: "The huge raft, covered with a tarpaulin roof supported by wooden columns, is connected with the charming Isle of Croissy by two footbridges, the first leading to the centre of the aquatic establishment, the other leading from the end of it to a miniature islet planted with a tree and called 'the flower pot.' From here one reaches land close to the bathing ticket office." [27]

At La Grenouillère one could eat, dance, swim, hire a skiff, or simply drink and watch the fun. There was plenty of this last, for all through the summer season the place was jammed. This is how De Maupassant saw the visitors: "At the entrance to La Grenouillère a crowd of people stroll under the great trees which make this corner of the island the most delightful park imaginable. Yellow-haired girls with large rounded breasts, their contours highly exaggerated, with heavily rouged faces, made-up eyes and excessively red lips, have their bodies laced suffocatingly tight in extravagant dresses which trail on the fresh turf. The bad taste of their toilette cries aloud. By their side young men preen themselves in clothes which ape the mode—white gloves, polished boots, large canes—and wear monocles which punctuate the inanity of their smiles." [28]

This was all on the Island of Croissy. De Maupassant then crosses over the main footbridge leading to the center of La Grenouillère: "In the floating establishment is a wild, howling scene. The wooden tables on which drinks are placed are wet with thin, sticky streams, covered with half-empty glasses and surrounded by half-tipsy people. The whole crowd cries, sings, shouts. The men, red-faced, hats on the back of their heads, have the shining eyes of drunkards; they talk vociferously, moved by the raffish desire for noise. The women, seeking their prey for the night, make the men pay for drinks while waiting. The free spaces between the tables are occupied by the ordinary customers, a battalion of rowdy oarsmen with their female companions in short flannel skirts." [29]

One day Renoir strolled across the neck of the river loop from Ville d'Avray to Bougival, walked up to the island and was instantly enchanted. He did not see La Grenouillère with the eyes of Maupassant: "The restaurant Fournaise was so amusing, a kind of perpetual fete. And what a mixture of people!" [30]

Never was the difference between painter and writer more clearly exemplified. Each man saw what he was looking for, and how different that thing was! The moral judgments of Maupassant's mind contrast powerfully with Renoir's healthy approach and visual preoccupation. Renoir was not to forget this first summer at La Grenouillère; in his old age he was still talking of how he went over day after day, taking his painting gear with him: "I was constantly at the Fournaises. Above all, I found there the most superb girls to paint I could ever have wished to see. One wasn't forced, as nowadays, to follow a little model for an hour and risk being treated like a dirty old man!" [31]

Whenever he found a good thing he liked to pass it on. His good nature was handsomely repaid: "I took several friends and recommended others to Père Fournaise. In gratitude he commissioned me to paint his portrait for two hundred francs as well as a portrait of his daughter at the same price. I painted him in his white bar-keeper's jacket just when he was taking his absinthe." [32]

This portrait, Renoir noted with a smile in the prosperous days to come, was in the time of his poverty "regarded as the height of vulgarity." When he became famous, the portrait mysteriously changed character in the eyes of critics and collectors and was described as "extremely distinguished." [33] But in 1868 there was no fame and little money. Renoir's chief dislike of the unfavorable criticisms was the fact that they threatened to send him hungry to bed; when fame came, he was to treat it with the supreme good sense he applied to every aspect of life, as an experience to enjoy if possible, to keep in proportion at all costs.

The real interest of the portraits and studies of midinettes on holiday is that they are vulgar in the true sense of the word. Renoir did not think of himself as making history at La Grenouillère that summer; he did not even remember that he was doing exactly what the few progressive painters and critics said must be done if French painting were to regain its soul and purpose. Nothing of this occurred; still less ruffled him for one instant. His discovery, he prided himself, was Père and Mère Fournaise and their La Grenouillère, and what he made of them was simply his expression of pleasure.

And what pleasure he had! That was his final and lasting thought. "How one laughed in those days!" recollected the Renoir of old age. "Life hadn't become mechanical then; one had time to amuse oneself and it wasn't held up to one as a grave fault to be light-hearted." [34]

3

At Fécamp, Monet had fallen once more into misery. He was painting well—better, he thought, than ever before—but could sell nothing. His money dwindled rapidly—there had not been much in the first place—and by the end of June he could not pay his bill at the inn. The outcome was hurriedly told to Bazille at Montpellier: "I write two words in haste to ask if you can help me quickly. I was certainly born under an unlucky star. I've just been thrown out of the inn without being allowed to take a stitch of clothing with me. I have stowed away my Camille and my poor little Jean under cover in the country for a few days. Tonight I am going to Le Havre to try to arrange something with my patron. My family refuses to do anything for me. I don't know where I shall sleep tomorrow. Your very tormented friend."

He added a postscript which, from him, must have shocked Bazille. "I was so upset yesterday that I was stupid enough to throw myself into the water. Luckily nothing fatal came of it." [35]

Yet whatever Bazille may have felt when he read this confession, the effect wore off only too soon. Writing to Renoir toward the end of the summer to ask him to attend to certain matters in the studio, he passed on the news with a certain weariness—even faith in Monet was not proof against irritation with a constant borrower—and a criticism of men who saddled themselves with a family they were unable to support.

Renoir had spent all his money at La Grenouillère by this time and was living quietly at his parents. He was quite used to being treated by Bazille as a handyman; it is a fate common to those who have to rely on others and one that Renoir knew especially well, for he did all the fetching and carrying with such obvious lack of hurt pride that even the kindest people tended to ask still more. He now told his friend what he had done, and pointed out, "I'm at Ville d'Avray and only go very rarely to Batignolles and then only to find odds and ends. What you ask me to do will be done and if you have any money you had better send it to me right away; this to one end only, so that you can't blow it all down there." [36]

His reaction to Bazille's complaints about Monet was simply, "You can rest easy about me, seeing that I have neither wife nor child and am not likely to have either the one or the other." [37] His final word about one favor Bazille asked of him, a job of carpentry which he particularly disliked, was the nearest thing he could get to a complaint, a plaintive "Tell me if I must do it immediately. It would put me out quite a bit, first because I'm working, second because I've nothing to buy food with in Paris and finally because I'm acquitting myself very well down here." [38]

He ended with a characteristic "I'll write at greater length another time because I'm hungry and in front of me there's a brill in white sauce. I won't stamp this, I have only a dozen sous in my pocket and these are to take me to Paris if it's necessary." [39]

Despite the attraction of La Grenouillère he managed to make two of his best canvases at Ville d'Avray before going back to Paris in the fall and a third which is interesting for his bold use of color. This last was a gypsy girl painted in very bright colors. The first two were of the Sisleys, who had taken a cottage at the nearby village of Louveciennes for the summer so that Sisley could continue his landscapes. Renoir made a portrait of him, then a double portrait. Both were an advance on anything he had done so far. The second, for all its hints of Courbet, is rich in color created as only Renoir could create it and with a gift for the treatment of clothes. His modeling also shows increasing confidence; yet perhaps the most notable feature of the canvas is its humanity. The studies of Lise had already shown how far he had progressed—she is not merely an excuse for color and design but a real Paris girl—but here he infuses into his character sketch of young husband and wife the feeling between them, conveyed without emphasis or sentimentality.

Back in Paris in time to escape the short and chilly evenings in the country, he made one *plein air* picture—a lively view of the skaters in the Bois de Boulogne which has something of the air of a Brueghel and a suggestion of Manet—then enclosed himself with Bazille in the heated studio determined never again to paint outdoors in winter. His discomfort produced an irreverent provocation of the millions who think of snow as one of the miracles of nature. Renoir was fearless when he knew his mind, and he knew it then. "I have never been able to bear the cold, but even if I could, why should I paint snow, that illness of nature?" [40]

His most satisfactory canvas that winter was a study of a nude boy caressing a cat; it is tenderly painted and drawn, and set against a gorgeous backcloth. But neither this nor any of his best work managed to please the 1869 Salon jury; one picture only was accepted, his gypsy study.[41]

His friends suffered even worse treatment; neither Sisley nor Monet had a single picture accepted. The blame for this "carnage" [42] was placed by Bazille on the head of Gérôme, one of the leading members of the jury: "He treats us like a band of madmen and declares he believes it his duty to do everything he can to prevent our pictures from being seen." [43] To Sisley the snub was a bitter disappointment, to Monet a disaster; the latter was left without money, and the assurance of some of his friends that he was head and shoulders above them as a painter must have seemed as much irony as comfort. Renoir was more practical; he advised Monet to settle close to Paris in the hope of selling a picture or two to a small dealer or advanced collector, and recommended Bougival where, he insisted, Monet would find motifs that exactly suited him.

Monet saw the point of this, was intrigued by Renoir's description of La Grenouillère, and took his advice. He managed to get another small advance from his enthusiast at Le Havre (who had rescued him from destitution the previous summer) and rented a cottage at Bougival.[44] Neither could have foreseen the result of this decision; to both it seemed merely common sense, with the added advantage to Renoir of an admired fellow painter nearby throughout the summer. The move was to provide the first impetus which led to Impressionism.

CHAPTER VII

———

THE BEGINNING OF IMPRESSIONISM

———

1869-1870

At the beginning of that summer of 1869 Renoir once more went down to Ville d'Avray when Bazille left for Montpellier and once again divided his time between the house of his parents and Lise. Lise posed twice for him. The first picture was a study of summer against a background of leaves and with one of the cheap striped skirts of the day Renoir painted so well. The second was *Baigneuse au griffon,* a study from the nude. In this Renoir had in mind prolonged examinations of pictures and sculpture at the Louvre; the pose was after a Roman copy of the Aphrodite of Cnidus he had drawn many times but with the significant difference that he imparted a sense of relaxation absent in the marble.

This, his second notable nude, eloquently expresses his enjoyment in this kind of subject and demonstrates that he was beginning to understand how to paint flesh. The result of careful observation and imaginative use of his palette is also clear. He made no attempt to beautify his model. It was to be a criticism of some of his later studies that he gave way too readily to his penchant for prettiness and to a wish not to be hurtful. He had no such feelings about Lise; though his attention was given mainly to the nude body, he kept to realism throughout; it was a woman's body he painted, not that of a goddess, and a woman's face, a face that might be seen every hundred yards on any of the great Paris boulevards.

In July he celebrated his father's seventieth birthday with a portrait, then virtually threw up Ville d'Avray for La Grenouillère. By that time he had visited Monet and Camille often in their cottage at Bougival and had introduced his friend to Père Fournaise, making sure that he was given a place for his easel on the restaurant balcony. But he had never stayed long with them as he was anxious to get on with his work at Ville d'Avray. Soon after he had finished his father's portrait came the flight, as it almost was, to the Monets.

There were several reasons for the change. This was the first time Renoir had seen much of the Monet household, and he liked what he saw very much. He had not changed his views about Monet; he had an enormous respect for him as a strong-willed and strong-principled man, but still found his implacability disconcerting. Renoir was impatient to get on to the next thing, and Monet's earnestness sometimes seemed dull to him, rather like going to school again. But Camille was a revelation; she had blossomed into a good housewife and mother without losing her charm and high spirits. She and Renoir made a fine lighthearted pair, Renoir playing with the small Jean while she made the lunch or dinner. He saw that her determined gaiety was a challenge to the conditions under which she had to live, in debt to the landlord, the butcher, the baker, and without hope of a break in their bad luck. This struck a chord, for Renoir often had to conjure cheerfulness out of nothing.

In every home under constant strain of poverty, dissension from time to time is unavoidable. If Renoir caught signs of it between the Monets he would not be surprised and was certainly not deterred. Drawn to women as he was he might imagine more clearly than Monet the heroism he lived with every day, but what seems to have brought him over to Bougival day after day was the charm of the domesticity he had denied himself until he felt financially safe. Besides, in mid-July the vacations began in earnest, the crowds rushed out from Paris, and La Grenouillère was as he had known and loved it the previous year, packed with gaily dressed and lighthearted, chattering people.

Yet the Monet home life and the holiday-makers, attractive though they were, were not the only reasons why Renoir abandoned Ville d'Avray for Bougival and became practically part of the Monet family. There was a third, more powerful reason, and this was Monet the painter. Renoir protested day in, day out, that he wished to enjoy life first and foremost. He was sincere but did himself less than justice. He also was a painter as bound in his way to his brush and palette as Monet himself. He could not leave them alone. He was forever trying to find new approaches to his art, willing to experiment in any way, likely to succeed or not. This explains his attitude when this same month he found Monet sitting before the bathing pool at La Grenouillère making a canvas of a kind he had never seen before. Monet was building it up entirely by the use of small brushstrokes and tiny dabs of pure colors; bounding lines had disappeared, black had gone, and the shadows were no longer dark but colored, a pale reflection of the colors surrounding them.

Renoir was fascinated. Monet explained what he was doing. Renoir at once recognized it as a logical conclusion drawn from those first experiments when he and Monet ranged the Paris streets a few years earlier and Monet had painted the Princess' garden. But what a conclusion and how far Monet had gone! He was now successfully reproducing the vibrations of light in the air which gave life to everything on the canvas—people, water, trees.

Renoir took one look and got to work on the same scene. It was a view of the balcony projecting into the water, the little artificial island beyond, and the stretch of river bounded by lines of trees.

As the days passed and the canvases neared completion they appeared at a quick glance two versions of the same scene, both painted with the little dots and dashes of pure color which were to become the Impressionist manner. At a second and third glance differences appeared, interesting differences since they

revealed both painters not only as artists but men. Monet concerned himself almost wholly with the view as pure landscape
and made his figures subordinate to nature, little more indeed
than blobs of color; Renoir was enthralled by the men and
women and employed nature to set them off as a corporate
expression of happiness under the sun. Monet was content to
stop short at his theory; he used it in masterly fashion to present
nature as seen by him at the particular moment of painting, and
seen truthfully because he had discovered the source of truth to
nature—the light. Renoir used Monet's theory as a stepping-
stone; for him the sparkling water, the bright rustling trees, the
reflections of light, however truthfully painted, were no more
than symbols of the high spirits of the people frolicking in the
water and under the trees. Monet's work was more rigid than
Renoir's, his colors more opaque, his touch heavier; it would
scarcely be an exaggeration to say that he made this sunlit scene
in some degree somber, like his life. His friend had typically
overhauled him at a bound; enthusiastic about this new method
of painting, Renoir used brighter colors, in which he reveled,
and his touch was more delicate, partly because he painted at
far greater speed, impatient to see the result of his work. *La
Grenouillère* is one of the sunniest and happiest pictures he was
ever to paint; it radiates joy in life because painted by a man
who liked nothing so well as to see others enjoying themselves.

Two months passed. They painted on, one canvas after
another. Not one discordant note entered into the canvases of
either, canvases that ever after were to mark one of the great
advances in painting. The one showed nature at her fairest, the
other people at their gayest. Who would believe that the makers
of these pictures were facing destitution, selling nothing, without discernible future? The growing desperation of Monet and
the humorous resignation of his friend were not permitted to
impinge on their work; when they sat before their easels they
were dedicated men, oblivious of time, of trouble, of everything
but the scene in front of them.

Renoir's morale was the first to crack. They seemed to him to
be painting in a vacuum, unseen, unheard. The utter disinterest

of all dealers, of every supposedly advanced collector was shattering. He began to suggest as lightly as he could that they had best give up and get a job, any job that brought in steady money and a certainty of regular meals. In July he was telling Bazille, "I've scarcely done anything lately because I have practically no paints left." [1] He had no need to add, no money left to buy them and no dealer who would give him credit; Bazille knew all about that. So he thought of the blind manufacturer with affection; he even wished he were back in the china workshop painting flowers and heads of Marie Antoinette for the few sous apiece they brought him.

Monet, strong, heavy, indomitable, tightened his belt and painted on. He treated Renoir's half-hearted motions of surrender as an aberration from which his friend would recover. How, he asked, could they think of giving up just when they (he kindly used the plural) had found the truth about *plein air* painting? They must push on; their luck was bound to turn. He felt sure of it. Any month must see the beginnings of recognition. And if not, if the world was so stupid, so criminally blind? The large shoulders would shrug, and Renoir knew what he meant: rather die than compromise. Large, stolid, the last word in the unromantic, his friend stood there, the living embodiment of the ideal. Renoir was ashamed of himself. He took up the brush again. "If I remained a painter," he was to say, "it is thanks to Monet. But for him I should have given up." [2]

Monet was writing to everyone he knew. Bazille was his chief hope, but Bazille was becoming hardened as most lenders do. The tone of his replies, and his lack of response, can be deduced from Monet's desperate appeal early in August: "Have you any idea of the way we've been living in the week since I last wrote? Just ask Renoir, who brings us bread from his home so that we don't die of starvation. All this last week we've had no bread in the house, no light, no wine, no fuel for the kitchen. It's really frightful, and it's too bad of you to forget me. After my last letter it was impossible not to see what would happen. And when you've read this, you won't be able to avoid seeing what is facing us. I haven't the heart to say another word to you." [3]

Bazille sent fifty francs. He had overdrawn his allowance before leaving Paris; he had pawned his watch, was in debt to his landlord and was forever writing to Renoir to ask him to make sure that his furniture was not spirited away as a surety. He refused to ask his parents for extra money nor would he approach his brother, who had just become engaged to a wealthy Parisienne.[4]

By the time the fifty francs arrived it was no more than a drop in an ocean; debts, food, fuel, painting materials whisked it away. If Père Fournaise had not given Renoir and Monet the occasional luncheon and not turned a blind eye to the scraps they put in a piece of paper to carry back to the Monet cottage, the ménage would have collapsed.

As September drew on and the colder weather began to set in, their state became even more precarious. "Here am I, brought to a halt for want of paints!" Monet wrote furiously to Bazille, who had sent advice but no more money. "This year I—and only I—shall have done nothing. This makes me hate everyone. I grow jealous, mean, practically out of my mind. I'm sure that if only I could go on working everything would come out as I hope. I'm sure of it. You say that fifty or a hundred francs won't get me out of this jam. Maybe you're right. But if I allow myself to think in that strain, I might as well go and knock my head against the nearest wall, for there's no hope of a fortune suddenly descending on me from the clouds." [5]

Renoir found himself in a peculiarly awkward position. He could get a square meal at his parents' cottage if he deserted Monet and his painting. Sometimes he did have the square meal, but more often he sidestepped the quandary by rushing over to Ville d'Avray, bolting half the lunch set before him, slipping the other half in his pocket and hurrying back to the Monet cottage.[6]

More embarrassingly, he remained spreadeagled between Bazille, who had housed and often fed him through hard and crucial winter months and who would no doubt do it again— he banked on it—and the splendid Monets, Camille bravely dealing with an empty cupboard and a hungry child, Monet stubbornly insisting that they go on painting. On the one side was admiration and affection, on the other side affection of a different kind (in lightness of tone and manner Bazille was much closer to him than Monet) and what was not far from necessity.

He dealt with the problem in his own way. One letter to Bazille reveals the man. "Your Salon picture is in the studio. I have put everything in order as well as I could and have given the key to the landlord, though I've looked in now and then to see that he hasn't made a mess of the place. For the rest, every time I've gone there I've told him I'm coming back that evening—this with the idea of keeping him within bounds if he suddenly takes a fancy to our beds and carts them off." [7]

Having attended to Bazille's interests, he turned with a jest— "I await your masterpieces, I have half a mind to slash them to pieces when they turn up"—to the facts of life as they faced him then. "I haven't seen anyone. I am at my parents' home but am almost always at Monet's where, incidentally, one tends to feel older than one is. There one doesn't eat every day. All the same I'm happy enough there because Monet is fine company while painting. I'm doing practically nothing at the moment because I scarcely have any paints left. But this may get better next month. If it does I'll write you." [8]

He ended this skillful letter sandwich fashion. Having inserted the meat, he finished off with another layer of the nonsense Bazille expected from him, for Renoir was yet another of those denominated clowns despite themselves and expected to be light whatever his feelings. So: "I send you greetings on behalf of all the girls. They aren't for you, these greetings, you'll understand, but for your bank roll. You'll be embraced in strict proportion to the amount of cash in your till." [9]

Neither Renoir's meaningful fun nor Monet's blunt appeals bore fruit. Bazille was in trouble too—the kind of trouble known only to those who can afford an overdraft at the bank— and could not help. By October the Monet home at Bougival was utterly without resources, and the friends were forced to split up. Monet abandoned the cottage and most of his belongings and struggled down to Le Havre to try yet again to soften his parents' hearts and beg another loan from his patron. Renoir, beginning to feel the chill of fall evenings by the river, went back to the Bazille studio.

There he had a pleasant surprise. Although his pictures at the Salon had been neither sold nor commented on, they had been noted favorably by two influential men, Théophile Gautier (a painter in his youth) and Arsène Houssaye, the editor of *L'Artiste*, one of the leading art magazines. Between them they prevailed on the Charpentier Gallery, one of the few private galleries that put on exhibitions independent of the Salon, to show *Lise* and *Portrait de Sisley*.

It is possible that Houssaye and Gautier had no need to argue strenuously to obtain this favor. According to Marie Samary, Renoir had met the Charpentier brothers—the art dealer and the modernist publisher—that summer at La Grenouillère, which they often visited in the company of Georges Samary.[10] The meeting was evidently no more than a casual holiday encounter, but Renoir's personality was so unusual and so delightful (he did not mince his words and the words were wittily chosen) that a remembrance of it may well have clinched the proposed showing at the gallery. Jean Renoir claims that his father was commissioned that same year to paint a portrait of the Charpentier mother. If this is so, it would demonstrate the effect on the brothers Charpentier of one chance meeting with the painter, an effect that was to have a considerable bearing on Renoir's future in later years.

For the moment, in 1869, the showing of the two Salon pictures and the painting of the portrait (if painted then)[11] put some money in his pocket and fresh hope in his heart. Protected from immediate want, he put worry aside and settled to work. He made a superb flower study, once again rivaling the experienced Fantin, and persuaded the obliging Lise to pose in Algerian costume for his *Femme d'Alger*, a work in which he gave his love of color its head.

It has often been said that Delacroix was the origin of this canvas. In color this is obvious, in treatment less so. Clearly Renoir had been reveling yet again in the Delacroix Algerian canvases in the Louvre and decided to try his hand at the gorgeous clothes worn by the women in this new French colony in which Monet had done his military service and about which he had often talked.

Renoir also posed this winter with Monet, Bazille, and Maître for a new *Hommage* picture by Fantin-Latour. This time Fantin moved from tributes to abstract ideas or the recent dead—his previous canvases had been in honor of "La Vérité" and of Baudelaire—to the man he considered the new great living leader, Manet. The large picture was named *L'Atelier des Batignolles* and showed Manet at his easel surrounded by disciples. "Christ in the midst of his disciples," was the response of the academic critics who were not renowned for good taste or originality.[12] Nevertheless the Batignolles school that winter became firmly established in men's minds as a formidable rebel group of painters—a good deal more firmly established in their minds than in fact, for the dissension at the Guerbois persisted.

What Renoir thought of all this is a question. He posed because it was politic. He admired Manet's work, though without any intention of following him to the letter. In any event his thought, like that of the hard-pressed Monet (back on the river at Saint-Michel near Bougival for winter and spring) and Pissarro (Monet's near neighbor at Louveciennes), was all for the next year's Salon. They talked about it whenever they met, which was as often as Monet and Pissarro could raise the fare into Paris. The well-known picture by Bazille shows them together: Monet and Manet studying the almost completed canvas on its easel in one corner of the studio, with the figure of Bazille (brushed in by Manet) leaning over the easel, waiting for their judgment, Maître playing the piano in the opposite corner, and Renoir chatting to Sisley from the staircase at the far end.[13]

Bazille was just as worked up as his friends about the 1870 Salon and for the same reasons, because he believed in the canvases he was submitting and because he needed money from sales or commissions, either or both of which could follow a

Salon showing. He had expensive tastes, he was gregarious, and his allowance from Montpellier was limited. Just before the Salon opened, affairs in his studio reached a crisis, crystallized in a note scribbled by Renoir on the back of an unpaid bill which had been brought in person by an irate creditor when Bazille was out: "My dear chap, he says he'll sell you up if you don't pay up." [14]

A few days later the ménage broke up unwillingly. Bazille moved into new and smaller quarters across the river, well away from Batignolles creditors, and the day after the Salon opened, wrote home cheerfully, "I'm delighted with my studio in rue des Beaux-Arts even though it's on the sixth floor. Renoir can't stay with me any more so I shall be on my own, but a friend lives in the same house and I'm only a step from Maître in rue de Seine." [15] He was soon only a step from Renoir too; Auguste missed his cultured insouciance, thought he would not mind a spell on the Left Bank, and, having a few francs in his pocket, at once translated the wish into action; he rented an attic studio in rue Visconti not one hundred yards away. So Bazille had Renoir, Maître, and Fantin-Latour (the friend in the same house) nicely gathered around him, and in his attractive way was soon declaring himself much better off and the Batignolles studio a waste of space and money.

Bazille's cheerfulness in the move no doubt owed much to a Salon acceptance of a nude study *La Toilette*, one of his two offerings. Renoir fared still better with two acceptances, both Lise pictures, *La Baigneuse* and *Femme d'Alger*. Monet was once again rejected, this time after an unprecedented scene in the jury room, Daubigny and Corot both walking out in disgust at the jury's bias against this painter. [16]

So Renoir was in, Monet out, though in terms of hard cash the result was the same for both. Renoir sold nothing, Monet sold nothing. Both were facing yet another year of struggle and hardship when their preoccupations were given a new and even worse complexion: France declared war on Prussia.

CHAPTER VIII

WAR, COMMUNE, AND AFTER

1870-1873

W AR BROUGHT OUT a new and unexpected side of Renoir.
The idea of him as a heroic figure is not easily acceptable—
no straining of the imagination is necessary to hear his laughter—yet the bare facts are impressive.

A short time after the declaration of war in the middle of
July, 1870, Paris was almost bare of painters. They had gone
into the country, they had gone out of the country. Cézanne
retired to the south and took peculiar pains to avoid being
called up for military service. Monet, Sisley, and Pissarro
crossed the Channel to London. They were but three of a
multitude, most of whom sought sanctuary in Belgium and
Switzerland.

Cézanne, Monet, Sisley, and Pissarro believed and said openly
that war was an evil and a threat to art, theirs and everybody's
in France. They refused to allow their work to suffer. They
stoically faced the stigma of cowardice. They thought that the
greater cowardice would have been to stop painting.

Renoir also disliked war. He was to say many years later that
he was almost sorry he had drawn a lucky number on his
twentieth birthday and had been exempted from conscript
service, seven years of it. He explained that he had thereby
missed the opportunities of romance and color in Algeria,
where most recruits were sent,[1] but the explanation must be

99

taken with a grain of salt. It originated in conversations with Monet, for Monet had not drawn a lucky number when his time came far back in 1860; he had been sent to Algeria. He escaped the full seven years only because, after two of them, he went down with fever and was bought out by his father on condition that he study painting at the Beaux-Arts.[2] He soon forgot the fever as he had soon forgotten the promise to his father and could remember only the colors, the light, and the unusual motifs awaiting the painter in Algeria. Renoir, already a devotee of the Algerian work of Delacroix (the pioneer of painting there), listened to Monet and promised himself a painting holiday there as soon as he made enough money. Eventually he did earn the fare and enjoyed painting there so well that he forgot, as Monet had forgotten, how much a holiday differed from the spare-time hobby of a soldier.

But this unrealistic remark did not alter the fact that Renoir disliked war as much as his friends who had left Paris so suddenly, though he would no doubt have described it as stupid rather than evil. And he went further than they; he admitted that he could not endure the physical accompaniment of war, the sound of gunfire.[3] Like them he loved painting, though without their sense of dedication, and wanted nothing better than to be left free to get on with it.

He did not go so far as Degas, who "has joined the artillery. According to him he hasn't yet heard a cannon fire. He is anxious to hear the sound so that he can tell whether he can endure it." [4] But he made no attempt to leave Paris, and when offered a comfortable staff job by Bibesco he refused it; he preferred, he said, to enlist normally and see where he was sent.

It could be that his attitude owed something to the glib jingoism of the crowds, whose street chants "à Berlin!" of the early days turned to catcalls after the Empress Eugénie as soon as they realized, a week or so later, that the supposed French walk-over was likely to end in the siege of Paris. Renoir hated extremism of any kind; disgust of the turncoat rabble may well have driven him into active patriotism at the expense of his painting.

Down in the south Bazille was working hard in his parents' country house. "I shall shine this year," he assured Maître, still in Paris, adding typically, "by the number of my completed canvases, at any rate." He begged for news of his friends: "Renoir should be very nearly a father by this time—has he delivered himself of a child yet? I don't ask you to tell me about Sisley, I know very well what he's doing." [5]

The day after he wrote this friendly dig at Sisley's absorption in landscape the French armies suffered two resounding and, as it afterward appeared, decisive defeats. The moment he heard of them, one week later, Bazille threw up his cherished painting and his security (his father had bought a substitute recruit for him) and, refusing to listen to the protests of family and friends, joined the Zouaves, famed for being thrust into the forefront of every battle. Less than four months later he was dead.

Renoir's war record was very different. He must have smiled at the quirks of the fate he relied on. The supposedly sheltered staff job in Paris would have been dangerous and extremely uncomfortable when the long siege of the city began. His luck held; he was directed to the safest part of the country, Bordeaux, where not a shot was fired during the entire campaign. A more gratifying vindication of the happy-go-lucky attitude, which in this case was also courageous, would be hard to find.

He must have smiled even more broadly when, arrived in Bordeaux, he found himself enrolled in the Tenth Light Cavalry Regiment. He had never ridden a horse in his life, but this is not the kind of detail that would worry him. There is no record that he ever sat a horse after leaving the army, yet he seems to have taken to riding straight away.[6] This and his knack of getting on with people of every kind except poseurs made him a general favorite. He was soon at work on portraits of his captain and his wife, both of whom were charmed with him, and of their daughter, whom he began to teach modern painting, a gesture that would have amused his friends.[7] When he was demobilized after the armistice early in 1871 he left behind three good friends in the Darras family, and when they too returned to Paris he was given a further commission, *Cavaliers au Bois de Boulogne,* a study of Mme. Darras riding by the lake.

In March, 1871, he was back in Paris where he fell slap into trouble. As a man who did not like the sound of gunfire he must have wondered why he had ever left the calm of Bordeaux. Officially there was peace, but scarcely had the French and Prussians stopped fighting than the Commune took over Paris, the Prime Minister, Adolphe Thiers, and his army retired to Versailles, and the two sides began to fight it out. Paris was once again plunged into bloodshed and a renewal of the gunfire and the shortages which had forced Manet a few months earlier to eat his servant's cat.[8] Parisians were in treble danger, of being hit by one of the shells fired into the city by the Versaillais or by one of the shells fired rather inefficiently by the Communards from their great battery on the hill of Montmartre, or of being arrested and shot as a spy. No one trusted his fellow, and the Communards were conducting a witch hunt of supposed Thiers supporters. Arrested men were lucky if they received the formality of a trial. Add to this the fact that the Communards were busily setting fire to all the buildings (the Tuileries Palace, for instance) which reminded them of the regime they detested, and that Paris was in consequence often covered by a pall of black smoke, and it will be seen that Renoir could not have returned at a more hectic moment.

His feelings were mixed. In theory he sympathized with the Communard aim of equality of opportunity and reward. In practice he found them a cross between a joke and a menace; the sight of the leaders in the Hôtel de Ville, most of them the worse for drink and madly overuniformed but all desperately earnest, made him smile, they were such children; the sight of them cheerfully burning some of the best buildings in Paris because of their political associations was quite another matter; the mounting toll of their shot victims was altogether horrible. Courbet, elevated to the new post of Guardian of Fine Arts and announcing that he would make a clean sweep of the Beaux-Arts and encourage the talented everywhere, was admirable if headstrong; Courbet's insisting that the Vendôme Column be blown up as bad art and a reminder of bad politics reduced Renoir to humorous despair. No one seemed to be thinking of the people of Paris at that moment, desperately short of food and threatened with pestilence because no attention was being paid to the sanitary condition of the city.

But what probably affected Renoir most was the almost complete solitude. None of his close friends had returned. Duret, who had not moved, told Pissarro, still in London, that there was "dread and dismay everywhere and as for painters you wouldn't think Paris had known such people." [9]

But Renoir stuck to it. He was obstinate in his quiet way; he had come back to Paris in the expectation of painting all day and every day after months of army life and intended to do it, Commune or no Commune, smoke, shells, firing squads, threat of disease, solitude notwithstanding. The only gesture he made was to move out of the direct line of fire; he took a small studio on the corner of rue du Dragon just off Boulevard Saint-Germain.

Perched there away from the line of fire but still uncomfortably close to noise and danger he began to work solidly for the first time in several months. His brother Edmond comments often on his extraordinary power of concentration, and this period in a Paris convulsed by civil war seems to prove that when painting or making sketches for a painting he neither saw nor heard nor thought of anything but the canvas or sketchbook in front of him. The amount of work he could do in his studio was limited, and he spent much of the day ranging Paris and the country around it in search of motifs. He painted in the streets, in the Tuileries gardens, on the Terrasse des Feuillants, and with even greater daring crossed more or less lightheartedly the no-man's-land between Commune and Versailles territory to reach the river country he loved. He spent weekends with his parents at Ville d'Avray (held by Thiers' troops) and painted in the nearby river villages—Bougival, La Celle-Saint-Cloud, Louveciennes.

It is difficult not to see this as an outstanding example of devotion to family and to art, yet nothing is clearer than that if such a proposition had been put to Renoir he would have laughed at it. To himself, he was merely, as always, doing what he did because he wanted to. He knew that if caught without a pass by the patrols of either side his life was likely to be a short one, but he intended it to be a merry one.

2

As it happened his one close flirtation with death did not come from bullets, shells, or a border patrol. This story has been told many times and in many ways. Three versions are compared here; they indicate that Renoir was no more exact in his reminiscences than most of us.

First, the story as he told it to Vollard in middle life: During one of his painting excursions near Marlotte before the war he saw a man sitting in the forest, dusty and obviously in trouble. When he had finished painting for the day and was about to go back to Mère Anthony's, the man came up to him, said his name was Raoul Rigault, that he had been editor of *La Marseillaise*, a revolutionary paper which had just been closed down by Louis Napoleon and its staff arrested. The police, said Rigault, were after him too. He asked for help. Renoir took him back to the inn, where he was put up. Later he went off (he had in fact escaped to England), and Renoir heard no more of him.

The story then moves to Paris under the Commune. One day Renoir was making a study on the Terrasse des Feuillants when a Communard officer came up to him and warned him; he said that his men were convinced that the painting was a blind and that Renoir was really a Versaillais spy making plans of fortifications. Renoir took the hint and moved off. Soon afterward he saw in a shop window large engravings of the Communard leaders. In the center he recognized the fugitive of the forest; he was Public Prosecutor for the Commune.

The next day Renoir went to the Hôtel de Ville, asked to see Rigault, and was honored by a rendering of the *Marseillaise*.

When he asked for a free pass to paint where he wished and a safe conduct to cross the Versailles border, Rigault gave them at once. Thereafter he painted at will and not only visited Ville d'Avray safely (as long as he was not caught by the opposing side) but lent his pass to friends who wanted to make the journey.[10]

The story as told to his son in his old age is more dramatic. In the forest near Marlotte, Rigault has become a starving, mud-spattered fugitive who suddenly appears from a clump of bushes and begs sanctuary. He was dying of hunger, he said, and would have to give himself up unless Renoir took pity on him. Renoir went back to the inn and fetched an artist's smock which he gave him as disguise. Rigault afterward stayed several days at Mère Anthony's until Pissarro got in touch with his friends, who arranged for him to escape from France.

The second part of the story, during the Commune, has altered even more radically. According to this account, Renoir was sketching on the banks of the Seine in Paris when a Communard soldier became suspicious and told his comrades, who in turn told passers-by. A hostile crowd gathered round the painter and were for throwing him into the river. The soldiers decided that he must be taken to the nearest headquarters and shot. He was "dragged" off to the Hôtel de Ville of the 6th Arrondissement where a firing squad awaited just such emergencies. He was condemned and on his way to the place of execution, the square before the building, when he saw the man he had rescued years ago passing by in full uniform and with an equally gorgeous staff in attendance.

The doomed painter called out, Rigault heard him, turned, recognized his face, ran up to him, embraced him and delivered him from his escort. The escort made a violent volte-face, presenting arms as Renoir walked away with Rigault. Soon afterward Rigault took Renoir out onto the balcony before the huge crowd waiting to see him shot in the square below, introduced him as Citizen Renoir and called for the *Marseillaise* to be sung in his honor.

The version about the safe conduct has been rounded off

neatly by the addition that Bibesco, then with the Thiers party at Versailles, heard that Renoir was working by the river near Ville d'Avray, came to see him and presented him with a Versaillais safe conduct. So Renoir was nicely placed with a safe conduct from each side. He did not keep them in his pocket, which would have been asking for trouble, but in the hollow of a tree trunk on the border. He took out the one he required at the moment according to whether he was going into Paris or out of it.[11]

Yet another variant appears in the account given to Rivière, his special friend of the eighteen-seventies. In this he went to the Hôtel de Ville to ask for a safe conduct, had to pass through several rooms filled with drunken Commune soldiers, and had great difficulty in reaching Rigault, who was surrounded by officers with so many stripes on their sleeves that they reached from the cuff to the elbow. Rigault gave him the pass but warned him that he would be shot by the Versaillais if caught trying to reach Ville d'Avray. He was caught and was about to be shot by Thiers' soldiers when Bibesco appeared, rescued him, and gave him the Versaillais safe conduct.[12]

Readers can choose what they will from these accounts or amalgamate if they wish. The bare bones are no doubt true and merely prove once again that there is no limit to the workings of Providence and that Renoir's attractive version of courage was suitably rewarded.

3

If there were any friends about, Renoir was sure to find them and find them he did in stricken Paris during the Commune. The only painter he discovered was Norbert Goenutte, an old Gleyre acquaintance, but he was soon meeting two musicians in Maître and Cabaner. He had probably first seen Ernest Cabaner at the Guerbois, and once seen Cabaner was not easily forgotten, an immensely tall, cadaverous, yellow-haired, yellow-bearded man, swathed in a tattered yellow cloak which set off his brick-red face. He had first come to light at the Parnassian gatherings of Nina de Callias in the middle of the sixties and was just the kind of man to appeal to this young hostess, a character who could tell good stories (the fact that he did not know they were good made the joke even better), a true artist even if not a very good one, excessively good-natured and desperately poor. The question of his value as composer remains in abeyance because no substantial work of his is known; at Nina's (and perhaps at the Guerbois, too) he could be pushed occasionally into a rendering, in an unmusical voice, of a song or fragment of the oratorio he was always hoping to finish.

His music was his one vanity—he would admit only Bach as his equal—and as no one could understand what he wrote, his claim could not be challenged. Apart from this forgivable foible he was absurdly modest and uncomplaining; he had to play popular tunes on the piano in a third-rate café six nights a week to earn food, lodging, and cigarettes (he was a chain smoker) but accepted the indignity without a word. He would always put up any man worse off than himself—he was soon to let the young Arthur Rimbaud sleep in his room for a few distressing weeks—and delighted everyone by his perpetual state of dream. He never knew the time, the day, the event of the moment, even when it was bursting around him in the form of enemy shells. His classic error (which appears in a different form in every biography) was to confuse the Versaillais bombardment of Paris with the Prussian bombardment; he had no idea that the Franco-Prussian War was over. One of his best recorded sayings was of the funeral of his father (a man he described as "like the first Napoleon but less beastly") when, as the coffin was laid to rest and all the hats came off, he observed with a certain gratified wonder, "I had no idea I was so well known!" [13]

Renoir loved life's casualties, good-natured ones, and was to be one of the many who gave house room, drink, and cigarettes to this forlorn specimen. Besides, Cabaner provided a stimulating contrast with his other contact of this time, the rather intense Maître. It was from Maître that Renoir heard of Bazille's death, and he felt the stupidity of it. Bazille had been a man after his own heart, gay and not too serious, yet a dedicated painter. This attitude suited Renoir exactly; he too intended to paint but was not going to make a fuss about it. He thought, as many have thought after him, that Bazille had the makings of a fine painter, perhaps even a great one.

These weeks of intimacy with Maître provided one of the first signs of the Renoir to come. With his usual tact Maître helped his friend in difficult times by offering him a commission, a portrait of his wife, and this portrait shows Renoir at the parting of the ways. It is in every way fascinating. Mme. Maître is posed against a wall with a flowered trellis paper. The painter was evidently in two minds how to treat his subject. He began with a literalism which reminds one of the flower piece he had done years earlier after the Dutch masters of still life; his sitter's face, her hands and even the flowers at her right along the window were rendered exactly and with no attempt at a general synthesis. All is naturalistic and carefully painted. Then Renoir is caught by the sweep of her dress and even more by the trellised background. Abruptly he drops realism and rises to poetry; on the dress and the wallpaper background he uses color in what was to become known as the Impressionist manner. Was he reliving those weeks at La Grenouillère with Monet? Whatever the influence, he uses color skillfully. The flowers on the wallpaper become colored blobs indicating distance and throwing up the figure before them; they are graduated, the color burning bright in the space to the left of the sitter, subdued behind and to her right.

A few more weeks and he has apparently abandoned realism altogether. Not long after this portrait he painted *Le Déjeuner*, a man and woman sitting at a table at the end of a meal. Bounding lines had gone, the light was used to bring out the features of the faces and to throw up a loaf, the wineglasses on the table. It was wholly Impressionistic.

More weeks still and he made one of his most significant canvases of the year. The Paris theatres carried on regardless of political differences, of shells and street battles, and Renoir was forever climbing to the gallery. He came to know one of the young stars of the Comédie Française and her mother, Mme. Henriot. Accompanied by the faithful Edmond he made a study of mother and daughter at a riverside picnic at La Celle-Saint-Cloud. He placed Edmond at the side of the picture as a painter making a preliminary sketch, notebook and pencil in hand. In the center reclined the young actress, her mother sitting behind her. The picture is an early Renoir study of happiness in the sunshine, gay with color, black reduced to a minimum, contours left to the light to determine and stress. Once more he had made an Impressionist painting long before the word had been coined, faces subordinated to pose and color which told everything, figures plastic and merging with the grass and trees.

Looking at this and at *Le Déjeuner* one might assume that the Impressionist Renoir had arrived. Not at all. A few months later he had completed and offered to the 1872 Salon his *Cavaliers au Bois de Boulogne*. Here everything is detailed. Captain Darras, who watched his wife pose for the picture, rallied Renoir on his coloring: "Blue horses! Whoever saw such a thing!" And after the Salon had refused it, the captain cried sadly and triumphantly, "I told you so! If only you had listened to me!" [14]

The Salon jury was under no obligation to explain its reasons for rejecting a picture, but for once it did no more than its duty. This excessively literal picture is poorly drawn, very stiff, and in some directions—the pony, for instance—so indifferently done that one would be excused for wondering if the painter had ever carefully examined a horse. He succeeds in the very particular criticized by the captain, his coloring, and in nothing more so than the horse's coat; his use of blue and green is most skillful.

Renoir dated this canvas 1873, which suggests that he tinkered with it after the Salon refusal of the previous year. It remains a backward step. However, there is one pointer to the future in it. The sketch for Mme. Darras was entitled *The Amazon*, and it is evident that this lady fascinated the painter. She is the first of what is now known as the Renoir women—big-breasted, round-faced, usually auburn or fair-haired—and her face, in contrast with the careful treatment of hands and body, is painted with a certain freedom. It is in fact what one thinks of as typical Renoir, perhaps above all in the treatment of the eyes, the enormous pupils widely spaced and appearing to crowd out the whites. Unlike almost every other painter, Renoir often refrains, as here, from bringing the pupils to life by the addition of a tiny spot of white; he leaves them dark, huge, mysterious. It has been suggested that this canvas, which recalls Renoir's Courbet period, was begun much earlier, but as he did not meet Mme. Darras until the late summer or fall of 1870, his first sketch for the picture must have been after that time.

This is not the first or last time that the painter disconcerts tidy-minded critics; he puckishly will not conform to periods, but goes from style to style according to his mood. In this latter part of 1871 and the early months of 1872, he made another canvas which has no rapport whatever with the Courbet of the equestrian picture or the Monet and Pissarro of the picnic or, one could say, with the true Renoir. This canvas, *Parisiennes habillées en Algériennes*, was also offered to the 1872 Salon and rejected. The rejection is surprising only because this picture has a certain tastelessness often found in Salon canvases. Renoir had again gone back to the Delacroix of *Femmes d'Alger*—"the most beautiful picture in the world," [15] he thought—but this time, unlike his own *Femme d'Alger* for which Lise posed and which relied on inspiration rather than imitation, *Parisiennes* leaned altogether too heavily on the master. His models had not taken the trouble to dress themselves with any conviction, they were poorly disposed, the colors were dirty, the tones did not harmonize. Not for the first nor last time this colorist is caught napping, and his sense of design, usually sound, is at fault. Renoir's taste was instinctive and depended on the enthusiasm of the moment. He was not a Delacroix, however much he admired his work, and when he deliberately copied him all his weaknesses were exposed.

The Louvre, Paris

Frédéric Bazille, 1867

National Museum, Stockholm

Mère Anthony's Inn, 1864

Renoir, painted by Bazille in 1867

La Grenouillère, 1869

The Studio, painted by Bazille in 1870

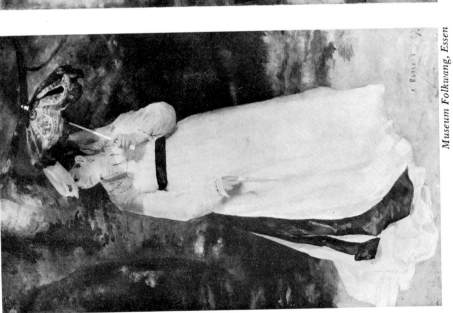

Museum Folkwang, Essen

Wallraf-Richartz Museum, Cologne

Lise with Parasol, 1867

The Sisleys, 1868

The Henriot Family, 1871

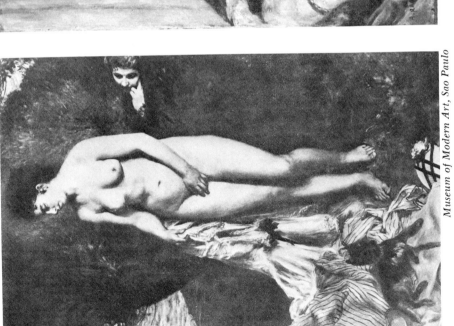

Bather with Dog, 1870

The Box, 1874

Claude Monet, 1875

Portrait of M. Chocquet, 1875

The Cup of Chocolate, 1878

The Metropolitan Museum of Art, Wolfe Fund, 1907

Mme. Charpentier and Her Children, 1878

Ittleson Collection, New York

Portrait of Cézanne, 1880

Le Moulin de la Galette, 1876

Mussel Gatherer at Berneval, 1879

The First Outing, 1880

Gondola on the Grand Canal, 1881

The Bathers, 1887

The Dance at Bougival, 1883

The Luncheon of the Boating Party, 1881

Mme. Tilla Durieux, 1914

The Artist's Family, 1896

Mont Ste. Victoire, 1889

Coco's Writing Lesson, 1906

4

The *Parisiennes* and the *Cavaliers* were painted in a new studio, the last Left Bank studio Renoir was to occupy. He settled, somewhat precariously, in rue Notre Dame des Champs off Boulevard Raspail and only a few steps from the Luxembourg Gardens. This was in the winter of 1871 after a summer by the river which produced the entrancing *La famille Henriot*.

Renoir was a gregarious man, he liked crowds, bustle, animation, and he found Paris very gay. The siege was over, the war was over, the Commune was over, a stable republican government under Thiers was in power, and the whole nation, freed from militarism, rose into prosperity with an astonishing exhibition of unity. The supposedly crippling Prussian indemnity was paid off in record time, government loans were oversubscribed, new roads, railways and factories were built, large stores opened in all the main cities, business flourished, unemployment vanished, and Paris in particular took on an air of almost universal well-being. The streets were crowded with shoppers and promenaders, women were once more highly decorative, cafés were crammed with laughing, chattering people.

Recognized painters, Beaux-Arts men, and regular Salon exhibitors were taking a handsome share of the general prosperity; the tycoon of the day (there were plenty of them) felt instinctively that he must live up to his position by covering the walls of his fine new house with portraits of himself, wife, and children. Renoir and his friends remained unknown and poor; commissions were hard to come by and, when obtained, were poorly paid. But in spite of perpetual privations Renoir responded to the nationwide display of relief. He expressed his love for the busy streets, the colorful dresses, the bright smiling faces, with some cityscapes in the spring of 1872. Two of these, the *Pont Neuf* and the *Quai Malaquais*, stand out as the sunniest examples of what was to become typical of this interpreter of light and movement. No man ever painted happier pictures.

Edmond, at his heels again, has told how his brother made

practical use of him, not merely as a carrier of painting gear but to provide models. Edmond used to speak to passers-by so that the painter could quickly sketch them in as they stood talking, and when he could not delay anyone long enough he would stand by a bridge or in a street and pose as long as he was wanted.[16]

Perhaps the most significant proof of Renoir's preference for creating joy in a picture is shown by comparison with Monet. Monet was back in France and was again painting side by side with his old companion. That spring of 1872 each man painted the Pont Neuf from precisely the same position, on the upper floor of a café on the corner of Quai du Louvre and rue du Pont Neuf. Renoir chose a day of sunshine and parasols; his canvas shines and gleams, water, pavements, road, buildings across the water, dresses, cloud-flecked sky all bright and gay. The general effect is airy. Monet chose a rainy day, a day of umbrellas and slippery roads, of men and women muffled up, of somber skies. His people, like his buildings, are vague splashes of color. He has eliminated detail almost completely. In the background, for example, the buildings lining the waterfront are virtually windowless; they are merely the impression of buildings, and the equestrian statue before them stands out blackly. In the Renoir canvas the windows are used to obtain contrast of color, the dark against the light, and the statue almost merges into them. By comparison with Monet's, his picture, suggestive though it is by the standard of the popular painting of the day, seems highly detailed, spots of color picking out the highlights, heavy use of white.

The canvases illustrate the two men, yet of the two at that moment in 1872 Monet had the better cause for optimism. He had come back from London and Holland determined to paint nature truthfully and to carry others with him. Everyone noticed the change in him. His old master at Le Havre, Boudin, met him at the Guerbois, was very much impressed and wrote to Père Martin when he had gone home again: "He seems to have a strong intention of making a position for himself. He is settling down nicely, has brought some very beautiful studies back from Holland. He is, I believe, destined to play one of the most important roles in our school." [17]

Renoir, of course, noticed the increased confidence. Since the prewar days of La Grenouillère he had respected Monet as the man who would not give in, the man who refused commissions if he did not feel impelled to paint what he was asked to paint, who would not only starve but let his wife and child go hungry rather than compromise. This firmness was incomprehensible to a Renoir who simply enjoyed putting brush to canvas no matter what the canvas represented, but he recognized in his friend the kind of man who advanced the cause of art and was always to remember with gratitude that in the blackest moments of those years Monet had held him to painting.

What he thought of Monet is seen in a portrait made this year. Monet sits at a table reading, pipe in mouth, the strong bearded face calm, powerful, relaxed. It is a splendid portrait (though almost surely executed quickly) because it expresses the man behind the Norman mask, a leader, a prophet, and if necessary a martyr.

5

The reason for Monet's optimism was clear enough and was explained to Renoir. In London he and Pissarro had met Paul Durand-Ruel, also a refugee. The Paris dealer liked their work, bought it, and showed it at a gallery he had opened in London. What was more, he understood the principles behind it and listened receptively when Pissarro talked about the new land-scape painting: no bounding lines in nature—observation showed that color merges into color—and no black shadows, the shadow being a pale reflection of the object that casts it; linear form not necessary because in the act of painting one draws, accuracy of tone revealing the light and shape of the object.

This was revolutionary talk. Durand-Ruel and his father before him had supported the Barbizon painters, but Pissarro and Monet posed an altogether more drastic change. They would obviously be difficult to sell. To his immense credit Durand-Ruel, faced with their work, immediately appreciated it. "I wanted," he said afterward, "to be an enlightened patron." [18] He was certainly that. He told them that he would support them when they all got back to France, and when he was settled in his new Paris gallery in rue Laffitte he not only bought more pictures but asked to be introduced to their friends. When Monet and Renoir met again, Durand-Ruel had already seen Manet's work and had bought everything the painter was willing to sell him. He had met Sisley in London and bought his work, too—a notably good turn since Sisley's father had been ruined by the war and Sisley now depended entirely on his pictures for a livelihood.[19]

Nor was this the end of his favors; he recommended the work of what was still known as the Batignolles group to a number of his advanced clients, the baritone Faure, the Rumanian doctor De Bellio, and the cashmere merchant Hoschedé, owner of a large Paris store, the Gagne-Petit.[20]

So Monet had good news for Renoir and a promise to introduce him to Durand-Ruel, and when Renoir went down to the river for the summer he did so lightheartedly as his canvases clearly show, and none more than his study of a regatta. As it happened, he met another helper before Durand-Ruel; this was the art journalist Théodore Duret. Apparently Degas, before he visited the United States in the fall, introduced Duret to him at the Guerbois, a curious gesture because Degas was no lover of Renoir or his work; he thought the man common and his paintings vulgar: "he plays with colors as a kitten plays with a ball of colored wool." As for these colors: "Lord, what acid tones!" But Degas was kindhearted for all his caustic speech and he made the introduction. Duret liked both Renoir and his work and was to remain one of his few supporters in the dim days ahead.[21]

The dim days were never far from Renoir no matter how much he loved the newfound gaiety of Paris and the crowded river excelling the prewar opulence and good fellowship of La Grenouillère. The Salon rejections had hit him hard. He spent much of that summer with Sisley, who had settled at Louveciennes, Pissarro's old riverside village, and they painted together, talked of the lost Bazille, and discussed their prospects too.

When they touched on these last they must have had hard work to keep cheerful, but Sisley could tell his friend about Durand-Ruel and Renoir could offer to introduce Sisley to Duret when he came to Paris. It was to be a heart-warming unwritten rule among the men called Impressionist that one passed on to the others whatever good fortune came his way, usually an introduction to a dealer or collector. No degree of poverty (and they were almost all unbelievably poor) would hinder him from sharing a patron even though it usually cut his own chance of sales. Renoir was perhaps the most unselfish of all, and this in spite of his strong feeling that imprudent marriages should not be weighed against the man who had had the sense to remain single.

Sisley may have been conceded an exception to this typically antisentimental attitude. Sisley married when he could reasonably expect to keep a wife and family in luxury for the rest of his life. If Renoir still had reservations about the effect of domesticity on work he soon lost them this summer of 1872; the Sisleys were a devoted couple, the two little girls charming, and the family bound up in Sisley's painting. There was no harking back to the days of plenty before the war.

It seems that Renoir had only to see a friend put up his easel before a motif to feel an irresistible temptation to do likewise, and this amiable weakness led on this visit to at least one delightful canvas, a study of Sisley's home. *Louveciennes: Rue de Voisins* is not an Impressionist picture; it is Renoir with his feet on the ground and head in the clouds, a disarming blend of realism and suggestion. The coloring is inspired: the old rose of the crumbling brick end of the cottage, the faint blue shadows of the trees, the turquoise of the retreating cart. He followed this with a portrait-sketch of Sisley. Alone of all the Impressionists he loved to portray his friends, and we have to thank him for making great names so plain to us as real men.

Before he went back to Paris that fall Renoir had several times accompanied Sisley upriver to see another devoted family, the Monets, reunited after the war and settled closer to Paris, at the yachting center of Argenteuil. Renoir, Sisley, Monet, were all vast walkers and the two friends would make the ten-mile cross-river journey to Argenteuil without giving it a thought. They had standing invitations to come over, stay and paint. The unmarried Renoir was free to move when and how he pleased. When the weather was closing in, however, he could think only of the studio in Paris, which would be snug for as long as he could afford to keep the stove lit. When he could not, there were always the cafés, warm and steamy, where for a few sous one could sit more or less indefinitely over a coffee or glass of wine. Nor was this all, for if, like Renoir, one had an appealing personality and often appeared with a sketch, there was more than an outside chance of a free drink or even a meal. The patrons and patronnes of the smaller bistros respected art even when they understood nothing about it and were sometimes prepared to make in its name the greatest sacrifice known to them, the handing out of what was in effect good money.

That winter there must have been many days with the stove unlit. The Lejosne commissions of prewar years had disappeared—with the death of Bazille, Renoir lost this valuable connection—and there was little to take their place, only an occasional niggardly purchase by old Père Martin or some similar small dealer on the fringe of the art world. It was a sort of winter that Renoir knew only too well, of appeals to friends: "I must get hold of forty francs before midday and I've only three." [22] This meant that he had run out of colors or canvases and his color merchant had run out of patience; the bill had to be settled before another account could be opened.

A note to Duret tells a similar story. "I am completely stony-broke, everybody has let me down over the rent. I couldn't feel more fed up. I beg you to do what you can. Whatever you can manage would be a great service to me—I seem to be in a bottomless hole." [23]

Duret no doubt sent him something but there always seemed

to be only one end to this kind of dependency. Later in life Renoir was to look back at it through rose-colored glasses: "I used to love those digs from which one cleared out carrying all one's belongings in a hand cart—and often there wasn't even enough to fill the cart! No trouble about getting rid of anything, there was nothing to sell." But he added, "It was also true at that time that there was nothing I wanted more than to sell something." [24]

One day the studio in Notre Dame des Champs saw him no more; he was forced to decamp, leaving in payment of rent the traditional stacks of canvases. These canvases would have made the fortune of the landlady twenty years later, but this she could not know. Duret faintly suspected it, however. When he heard of the departure he hurried around to the studio and bought the *Lise à l'ombrelle*, which he thought the finest thing Renoir had done.

Meanwhile Renoir, again in traditional manner, had put some miles between himself and his creditors. Naturally thrifty, he also took the precaution, he explained later, of putting a mile or two between himself and the influence of the Latin Quarter style of painting, mannered, inclined to the phony, and typified by Fantin-Latour, which he thought was beginning to show itself in his canvases.[25] He did the move thoroughly; he set up house on the other side of the river, in Montmartre.

CHAPTER IX

—

MONTMARTRE AND FIRST EXHIBITION

—

1873-1875

IT IS SURPRISING that Renoir had not made this move years earlier because Montmartre possessed everything he loved, from dance halls to circuses, from music halls to the café-concert, and its busy streets were filled with the kind of people he liked and respected, the workers of Paris. There one saw pretty girls by the hundred, midinettes, dancers, acrobats, equestrians, and the notorious blue-bloused men from the abattoirs up on the hill who were to prove such a useful attraction to the tourists soon to take over Montmartre.

In 1873 the village was still a village and the life led there was genuine French in its lighter mood. Even then it had night clubs and exclusive restaurants ready to extract a monstrous price from rich people who drove up the hill for a night out, but in general the entertainment for which and by which Montmartre lived was cheap and offered excellent value for money. The legend of the "gay" French originated here, and in the seventies the people were truly lighthearted; the time for manufactured gaiety to attract foreigners had not arrived.[1]

Montmartre was, of course, stuffed with painters, for there was so much to attract them, a cheerful life and wonderfully varied motifs with cheap models by the score. Renoir settled between the village and the center of Paris; 74 rue St. Georges, where he rented a studio, is midway between the great boulevards and the Place Pigalle, the entry to the village and the hub of Montmartre night life, then, as now, crowded with cafés and places of entertainment. Renoir was also a few paces from the birthplace of Gauguin, at that time coining money on the Bourse, and he could walk up to the Guerbois in ten minutes and down to Durand-Ruel's gallery in five.

This last had become important to Renoir and explains how, although so poor that he had to fly from one studio, he could rent another. It was customary for young painters to make the rounds of the poorer studios, holding out in each one for a few weeks in the hope of making a good sale or two and gaining a studio of his own with rent paid more or less regularly. Many of them liked movement for the sake of it, too; it satisfied a spirit of adventure, put fresh motifs within easy range, opened up new cafés and the possibility of new friends and models.

Renoir was like all the rest, but by 1873 he was in his thirty-third year and possibly growing out of the first careless rapture of living from hand to mouth, if indeed he had ever felt it. He managed to stay on in rue St. Georges because he at last met Durand-Ruel. It does not seem that the dealer found his work so original as that of Monet, Pissarro, and Manet. Renoir, unlike his friends, was not working to a firm principle; a view of any half dozen of his canvases could confuse a dealer, since at a quick glance they might have been painted by two or three different men.

But Durand-Ruel liked Renoir personally and could see enough in his work to be able to imagine profits in later years. He bought a picture or two. He did not pay much, from fifty to one hundred francs, yet as a man with simple tastes Renoir could just get by on five francs a week, and as Renoir had a second home at Ville d'Avray, the dealer probably saw himself as generous; after all, he had no guarantee of finding a buyer. Renoir no doubt felt well off for the moment; a sale was a sale and he was not one to worry much about the day after tomorrow. "All his life," says Rivière, "he hated 'business.' He wanted to sell just enough to pay for a fresh model. When he became famous he used to recall the fate of the work of Watteau,

Fragonard, and Boucher in the first half of the nineteenth century, how it went out of favor and did not sell. 'If the same thing happens to my work I have now put enough by to allow me to go on painting without having to rely on sales to dealers.' " [2] He did not complain of Durand-Ruel's prices—he was too glad to have the money—but he did not forget them.

His new studio was to become notable for the work he did in it and the men he entertained there; for the first time he was to form a social group of his own in distinction to his Gleyre friendships based on a common love of painting. The studio, says one of the Montmartre friends, "was rectangular with one of the long sides entirely glassed in. It faced west and during summer the sunlight filled the room with light in spite of the thick canvas curtains intended to soften it. The walls were papered pale grey and some unframed canvases were pinned to them. Propped against the walls were heaps of canvases, painted and unpainted, of which one only saw the backs. The only pieces of furniture were two easels, some cane-bottomed chairs of the most ordinary kind, two ancient armchairs, tub style, covered with a very faded flowered cretonne, a tired-looking couch re-covered with a neutral-colored material and a white wood table on which lay, all mixed up, tubes of colors, brushes, bottles of oil and turps and some cloths spotted with paint." [3] During all the years Renoir was to use this studio the only addition he made to his slender stock of furniture was a dark wood table with a red plush top. He was delightfully practical. He bought for a room only what helped him to work without fuss or loss of time, having all his materials ready to hand. For the rest, he expected friends to put themselves where they could find room; most of them were used to sitting and sleeping on the floor.

His working day was as sensible. It is a little difficult to imagine a man working office hours and doing just what he pleased; yet the apparent contradictions were united in Renoir and effortlessly too. He concentrated on one canvas the moment his mind was made up; no one could have been more businesslike. "He began work at eight in the morning, stopping only to smoke a cigarette or to let his model rest. About midday he went out to go across the street to lunch at Camille's small dairy where there was room only for six people. Back again, he worked till five. Although he always kept open house for his friends it was generally understood that they would not come until the end of the day." [4]

At the beginning his work merely added to the piles against the studio wall. He sold nothing and his two Salon entries for 1873 were rejected. He kept cheerful; he had admirers in Durand-Ruel and Duret, he was gathering a band of friends, he loved the nights at the circus, theatre, or dancing hall, all very cheap, and the Montmartre girls, cheerful and decorative. So he took the new Salon rebuff philosophically and in summer went cheerfully to the river, to his parents at Ville d'Avray and to Monet at Argenteuil.

2

It seems that history was always to be made when Monet and Renoir came together, and this summer of 1873 was no exception. Since that prewar summer and fall at La Grenouillère, Monet had gone far. He had learned much from Pissarro at Louveciennes just before the war; he had experimented in London, in Holland, and again in the Paris streets in very different lights. He now, at Argenteuil, had reached the point where he could feel that his experiments were succeeding sufficiently even to please himself.

It was then that Renoir descended on him as in the old days, but happily without the need to bring food in his pockets to keep them alive. The Monets were not flourishing but at least they were not starving and had not the strain of unpaid rent and tradesmen's bills. They were just about paying their way. The two men took up their old relationship and began to paint together again.

To a man like Monet, intolerant and inclined to impatience, Renoir was a boon. Monet did not suffer fools gladly nor did he take kindly to argument. Renoir got on with the job and said nothing. If Monet had wished to split hairs, his companion painted with an almost indecent speed in strong contrast with his own patient buildup of a canvas. But he was so good-humored about it all that Monet, who perhaps felt his own solemnity at times, gladly if imperceptibly relaxed.

As for Renoir, he was fond of the child, he admired Monet and Camille, he loved the feeling of a family standing together. And he by no means objected to having his mind made up for him. When Monet set his easel in front of the duck pond behind the cottage and began to paint it, Renoir took it as a happy challenge to do likewise. Why not paint a duck pond? It was a refreshing change from the kind of subject one saw in the Salon. Moreover Monet's principle of painting in the open air and finishing the job under approximately the same light in which it was begun appealed enormously to Renoir, who preferred to finish quickly; he took this too as a challenge, to work at top speed.

He saw at once that Monet's technique had developed, and copied this too. At Louveciennes in that last winter before the war Pissarro and Monet had gone far to establish the scientific palette: the division of tones, the juxtaposition of complementaries, primary colors only, pure, never mixed. Monet was now in his own way applying what he had learned. The small brush-strokes of La Grenouillère had become smaller, mere dabs and commas of color, all heavy brushstrokes had gone, all solid masses of color.

As Renoir knew, no one was less of a theorist than his friend. Monet could repeat after Pissarro that color was form; the only point of interest was what he intended to do with the dictum and all the rest he had taken over. What Monet wanted was to reproduce his sensations before the motif. These sensations came through the eye and, in his case, an eye so penetrating that it saw beyond what the normal lazy eye sees as solid forms and the obvious effects of sunlight and shadow. What Monet saw when he looked at a landscape was the air that surrounded the forms and created their color and life. He intended to paint this air; all his experiments had been with this one aim because he believed that only then would his re-creation of nature reach absolute truth.

With Renoir by his side in this summer and fall of 1873, Monet used this delicate, evanescent technique of the tiniest of brushstrokes of pure color, juxtaposing the colors, to re-create on canvas the effect of the vibrations of light, and so reproduced for the first time a scene precisely as it was at that particular time on a particular day. All great painters have won their greatest triumphs as a result of years of observation. They have discovered by sheer application what the ordinary person never thinks of and the ordinary painter never sees. Monet had used those wonderful eyes of his ever since he painted side by side with Boudin fifteen years earlier. At Argenteuil the reward of those years was won; he painted the first great Impressionist pictures.

Renoir, who had observed in his way, once more followed this impressive friend. Side by side with him he painted *La Canardière, Prairie,* and the exquisite *Pavots sauvages* with Camille and her little son walking in the poppy field near the cottage. He followed Monet's technique exactly, and the canvases of both men are wholly delightful, radiant with the new-found light bathing all. When Monet turned to a study of his garden, Renoir promptly painted him at work; he was glad of the excuse, as his preferred subject was a human being; nature as such did not fill him with the passion of Monet, Sisley, and Pissarro.

The question has often been asked, possibly because of this preference of his, whether Renoir was a true Impressionist painter. Technically he undoubtedly was in these years, and such was his skill that he rivaled his friends in portraying their chosen motifs. An Impressionist by conviction, however, he was not. He felt nothing of their sense of dedication to a certain kind of painting and a particular technique. In time he was to make this clear, but the signs were ever present. They existed for all to see in the way he seesawed between style and subject. He would cheerfully paint with and after Monet, then turn to a different subject and manner; Courbet and Delacroix, for example, were still with him as influences. Many years later he was still saying that he had not found himself and that all was experiment, a confession that only makes his successes in every genre the more remarkable.

His unspoken difference from the other Gleyre friends was shown in these years in another way; he alone persisted in offering works to the Salon after the war. They abstained because they disliked the paintings shown there and resented the Salon jury's treatment of them before the war. Renoir, practical as ever, continued like Cézanne and Manet to submit canvases. His answer to reproaches was simple: where else could he show his work, if he could not show it how could he sell it, and if he could not sell it how could he continue to paint? [5]

This question rose to boiling point at the Guerbois in the winter of 1873–1874. Neither Monet nor Pissarro had forgotten the abortive plans for an exhibition of "twelve young painters" in 1867 and thought the time ripe for another attempt. They had several reasons for this. One negative reason was Manet's success at the preceding Salon with *Le bon bock* (a portrait of Bellot sitting before a pot of beer), a skillful pastiche of Frans Hals whose work Manet had been studying. They took the success as yet another sign that the Salon was no place for adventurous painters with a conscience.

Positively, they had some reason to think that the public might take an interest in their work. Durand-Ruel had just prepared the ground with a sumptuous catalogue of his stock in three large volumes. It was edited by a Guerbois habitué, Sylvestre, who argued in his introduction that the work of the new landscape painters was not so much a revolution as a natural development from Delacroix, Courbet, Millet, and Corot. After this attempt to make the new men respectable, he spoke in general of their work with some perception—"It is above all harmonious . . . a very delicate and very exact observation of relationships of tone"—and praised the common feature of their pictures as likely to appeal to people in those days: "They are flooded with a golden light and everything in them proclaims gaiety, clarity, the very spirit of Spring." [6] He discussed them individually in subdued but complimentary terms.

In the early months of 1874 Sylvestre's prediction that their work would soon become acceptable seemed to be coming true. Hoschedé auctioned several canvases by Monet, Pissarro, Sisley, and Degas and obtained prices which to three of the four painters must have seemed too good to be believed; they ranged from five hundred to one thousand francs, about five to ten times more than they had ever been paid before.

The encouragement was enough; in vain Manet urged them not to "leave him in the lurch" [7] at the Salon, in vain Duret told Pissarro that this was the psychological moment to go back to the Salon with its ready-made audience of some forty thousand visitors. The landscape painters had no faith in the Salon jury's accepting their work, and even if it should, they resented the thought of being hung side by side with painters they despised.

Renoir's function in these discussions was, true to his principles, to avoid anything that smacked of extremism; he successfully opposed Pissarro's attempt to impose rules, regulations, and fines on all members [8] and supported Degas' suggestion to exhibit under a noncontroversial title, though not for Degas' reason: to keep in with the respectable collectors. Renoir wanted simply to avoid the inevitable charge that they thought of themselves as "a new school." [9] He had never cared for self-sufficient and self-satisfied groups; he did not want to work under a label and did not consider himself as preeminently a landscape painter and still less a painter who followed a formula. It is significant that he had not been included in the Durand-Ruel catalogue, possibly because the dealer had not bought his work early enough but more because he was not taken so seriously as Monet, Pissarro, and Sisley. Renoir would have thought Manet's *Le bon bock* a normal piece of work, and indeed it did not differ from his own attempts to follow Delacroix except that it was more skillfully done.[10] He agreed with Manet and Cézanne, and with Duret's advice, that they should continue to submit to the Salon jury, and made his position clear by the all-embracing slogan "show it wherever you can," [11] advice at once businesslike and sensible.

However, he had the militant Pissarro to contend with. Pissarro early made clear that their exhibition must be in direct opposition to the Salon, even timed to anticipate it, and that no exhibitor should be allowed to try for the Salon.[12] This was a hard rule for the noncompetitive Renoir to accept. He detested limitation or exclusiveness in art; as he was ready and happy to paint anything and in any style within reason, so he was ready to sell a picture wherever he could find a buyer. What did it matter to him whether the francs came from the pocket of a visitor to the Salon or to their own exhibition? Yet he could not oppose Pissarro in everything; the revolutionaries for whom Pissarro chiefly spoke were his friends, they were serious men, they might even be right when they predicted that a separate small exhibition would make their name as they could never hope to do amidst the swarm of Salon exhibitors. The voluble and convincing Pissarro, being naturally optimistic, failed to see the reverse of this argument, that in a small exhibition a man is more exposed to criticism. He honestly believed that their work had only to be well hung to be at once hailed as the painting of the day. One wonders whether the clear-minded Renoir wholly accepted this naïve conclusion. But his philosophy was to go where the current took him. If it took him to a separate exhibition, he hoped for the best.

Any doubts he may have had vanished a few weeks after the Hoschedé auction when Durand-Ruel virtually went out of business. The postwar boom was followed abruptly by a slump, and the dealer found himself with a large and unsalable stock of pictures, not so much the Impressionist pictures he had recently bought as, ironically enough, the moderately respectable Barbizon painters. His enthusiasm sometimes swamped his judgment. He had tried to corner the Barbizon market only to find that there was no market. The rich collectors did not stop buying pictures during the slump, but they confined their buying to easily resalable ones, the Gérômes, Bonnats, Cormons, Coutures.[13]

So the dealer had to tell his new friends that in spite of his faith in their work he could buy no more of it; he could only hope that the boom would return. He did not tell them what was also true, that his championship of them, even the mere existence of their pictures in his gallery, had done him great harm with conservative customers and that this played its part in his sudden financial embarrassment.

The news convinced everyone but Manet and his followers that a separate exhibition was now essential. Degas surprised the landscape painters by offering to come in, surprised and embarrassed them too. Monet and Pissarro were artists, not businessmen; they had not considered the cost of mounting the simplest of exhibitions. Even when the Guerbois habitué Nadar offered them his studios rent-free, they found that they were still unable to afford the many outside expenses. Degas' offer saved the plan.

It also changed it radically. The idea had been to mount an exhibition that would show Parisians the new landscape painting, work done in *plein air,* and demonstrate the scientific palette in action. Degas' offer was conditional on his bringing in a number of friends. Neither he nor they were interested in the scientific palette or in landscape; the most that could be said of some of them, Degas especially, from the point of view of the idealistic Pissarro, Monet, and Sisley, was that they were making some attempt to portray scenes of contemporary life, the ballet, the cafés, the circus.

Nonetheless Pissarro and Monet were in a fix. They had not the money to exhibit alone, and if they agreed to exhibit with Degas and his friends the exhibition would cease to be what they had always dreamed of. Indeed it could be seen as the reverse, since some of these friends were unashamed Beaux-Arts men. Degas was trying to make sure that the effect of the Guerbois rebels' work would be counterbalanced in the exhibition rooms by his friends' soothing classicism, and his ruse was understood by all.[14] Renoir has not left his views on this internal crisis, which was not without its humorous side, but he would surely have sympathized with Degas.

Monet and Pissarro had to bow to the inevitable, and on

April 15, 1874, a month before the Salon, the exhibition of the
Société anonyme des peintres, sculpteurs, graveurs, etc., opened
in the photographic studios Nadar had just vacated on the
corner of Boulevard des Capucines and rue Daunon. The
studios were well placed though not well lighted and were
sufficiently central to draw the crowds. There were thirty
exhibitors, most of them brought in by Degas. Eight could by
stretching a point be described as Impressionist—Pissarro, his
friend Guillaumin, Monet, Sisley, Renoir, Boudin, Cézanne,
and Berthe Morisot.

3

Renoir showed seven canvases. One of these, *La Loge*, was a
masterpiece by any standard, the finest picture he had painted.
Another, *Danseuse*, was a picture Degas would not have been
ashamed to own, and one can scarcely say more.

Renoir was to say later that reports of the scenes at this first
exhibition were very much exaggerated.[15] There were plenty of
visitors and most of them had a good laugh before certain
canvases, those of Monet and Cézanne especially. This laughter
was ominous and Renoir saw it; he and his friends, he realized,
had failed in their first and most important aim, to be accepted
as serious painters with a fresh approach. The inclusion of the
many "respectable" friends of Degas proved as useless to Renoir
as to the true rebels; it soon became clear that most visitors
came to scoff rather than to look at pictures dispassionately;
they ignored the work of Degas' friends and singled out the
landscape painters in order to make fun of them.

Many influential critics of the day did not even trouble to
come to the exhibition, a cruel cut indeed, and those who did
(the few morally courageous Guerbois critics excepted) made
no effort to take the painters seriously. He and his friends were
regarded, says Renoir, as a bunch of young cranks (Pissarro was
forty-three, Monet thirty-three, Renoir thirty-three, Sisley thirty-
four) who wished to attract attention by being silly.[16] A man

who was to become one of their greatest supporters, Victor Chocquet, explained afterward that he had intended to go to Nadar's—he was an inveterate exhibition visitor—but was dissuaded by friends who told him it was not worth even the one franc entrance fee.[17] By "not worth," these friends meant it was a stunt, not even an attempt at serious art.

The hostile critics who did attend first accepted then led the public in the usual reaction of the stupid, to laugh at something they do not understand. The critics permitted themselves some distinctly tasteless jokes and chanced to give the rebels the name by which they were to become famous, a name thrown out as a sneer. The general idea behind these criticisms, which do not deserve to be perpetuated, was that the revolutionary painters were men who, not knowing how to paint, could get no further than an unfinished "impression" which they were trying to beguile Parisian art lovers into accepting as a completed work.

Renoir escaped direct allusion, in its way an even greater slight than the abuse and coarse witticisms directed especially against Cézanne and Monet. He understood this well enough and spoke of it whimsically, but it is true that the pictures he submitted were less obviously advanced than those of his two friends and so were not considered worthy even of attack.

He had two favorable notices, both by men he had met at the Guerbois, but, the men preferring prudence to principle, both unsigned. Catulle Mendès in *Le Rappel* praised his three portraits quite fulsomely and Philippe Burty gave him a good write-up in *La République Française*: "M. Renoir has a great future. *La jeune danseuse* is strikingly harmonious. His *Parisienne* is rather less good, his *Avant-Scène (La Loge)* creates a complete illusion, particularly through the handling of the light. The impassive, made-up figure of the woman, her white gloved hands, the one holding opera glasses, the other buried in a muslin handkerchief, the head and shoulders of the man who leans back, are pieces of painting as worthy of eulogy as of attention."

This no doubt made pleasant hearing, though written by a well-wisher who had not the courage to put his name to it, but

Renoir was concerned with hard facts, and these were that neither he nor any other member of the Impressionists sold a single picture during the month of showing. Worse, not even the most optimistic could persuade himself that the exhibition had made a breach in public devotion to the glossy perfection of technique, with every "i" dotted and every "t" crossed, of a favorite like Gérôme, who that same month of May was awarded the medal of honor by the Salon jury. The exhibition merely convinced Parisians that the Impressionists were exhibitionists in a very different sense.

There had, in fact, been the occasional perceptive visitor. The most notable convert was Count Armand Doria, who said after studying the Cézanne canvases that were causing such amusement, "Certainly we know nothing. There are first class things here. I must have something by this painter." [18] Although he did eventually form a small Impressionist collection, he moved cautiously; as far as the painters knew, when the exhibition closed they had sold nothing.

There was general despair in the landscape camp but no surrender. At Pontoise, Pissarro, with a large family to support and a wife who had no faith in his work, admitted to "frightful sufferings" but declared that if he had his time over again he would do the same.[19] Sisley kept afloat only with Duret's support and a loan from England.[20] Monet again had to leave his cottage hurriedly, submerged by debts, and was heading for starvation when rescued by a sailing friend he had met at Argenteuil, the marine engineer Gustave Caillebotte.

Renoir was more fortunate; soon after the exhibition closed he was offered 425 francs for La Loge by Père Martin. He accepted at once; such a price from a niggling dealer was a rare compliment. Practically, it meant a breathing space for a man who lived simply and whose many enjoyments were mercifully low-priced. He was always ready to carry out the odd commission that came his way, and eased his position further by painting Madame Hartmann au piano—wife of the music publisher introduced by Clapisson—and incidentally followed Degas and anticipated Toulouse-Lautrec and Van Gogh in depicting a woman at the piano.

By summer Renoir was back by the river in high spirits, and, as usual, he carried these spirits over to the Monet household now settled in a cottage belonging to the Aubry-Vitets, friends of Manet.[21] Berthe Morisot had become engaged to Manet's brother Eugène and used her position as prospective sister-in-law of the painter to urge him to help the strongest of the *plein air* men who had also been hardest hit by the failure of the exhibition. She was determined that Manet should take a closer view of Monet and his work. She succeeded. Outside his spurts of temperament and a tendency to snobbism, Manet was a just man and a generous one. He did take a closer look and, as a result, recommended the homeless Monet to his friends. Then, having assured him of a roof over his head for a few months, Manet came down to see what he was doing.[22]

When he arrived, he found Renoir painting side by side with Monet and Caillebotte. Although Caillebotte had first been attracted to Monet through a mutual devotion to sailing,[23] his devotion quickly extended to Monet and his work. Caillebotte, an amateur painter, at once began to change to the Impressionist style and palette and, in addition to helping by buying one or two canvases from Monet (tactfully, always those most unlikely to sell), took up the question of further exhibitions. He was immensely enthusiastic and refused to consider Impressionism as anything but the inevitable painting of the future. He was delighted with Renoir, such a piquant contrast with Monet, and the three of them quickly became inseparable: if not sailing on the river they were painting identical scenes of or about it.[24]

Manet was not prepared for Renoir as a daily companion and found himself faced with a problem. Whatever he might think of Renoir's commonness, he could not resist his good temper and fun in a boat, but as a painter he continued to rate him impossible. And he had to endure the sight of many Renoir paintings. Anything would set Renoir off—Camille reading under a tree in the garden, Monet painting a family group, a regatta—and the moment he felt the wish to paint he painted. The speed with which he worked struck Manet, as it had struck Monet, as unseemly, and the way he slapped paint on the canvas offended him. His feelings rose to a climax when Renoir decided to follow Monet's lead with a family group, setting up his easel side by side with his friend's. Manet stood it for a time, then walked over to Monet and whispered, "For heaven's sake try to persuade that boy to give up trying to paint. He has absolutely no talent for it." [25]

It can confidently be assumed that Monet did nothing of the kind, and the "boy" continued to paint, blissfully unconscious of the great man's anguish. He must surely have been amused to watch Manet's surrender to Impressionism when, using pure colors and small brushstrokes, he made a study of Camille and little Jean standing by the river bank watching the yachts, the celebrated *La Seine à Argenteuil*, as well as the equally Impressionist *En bateau*. Manet admired Monet's strong technique; he admired his unimpaired sweetness of disposition after years of unjust abuse (Manet had also concealed bitterness); did he not also feel a certain kinship with this man who painted just as he wished regardless of groups or theories? Manet went straight from Argenteuil and Impressionism to quite another style, then back again to Impressionism in Venice. Renoir went back to Paris that fall to make his nude study *Anna*, which was without a trace of the Impressionist technique; it had bounding lines, it made use of black in liberal quantities.

In December his father died at Ville d'Avray at the age of seventy-five. Mme. Renoir was not left alone; she had her daughter and Leray with her and frequent visits from the flourishing sons. The unflourishing son could go back to his Montmartre studio carrying with him her affection and faith.

4

By this time he had formed his own set, and a lively one it seems to have been. The man who has written about it at length was a friend salvaged from the apparent wreck of the exhibition. Not everyone went to the Nadar studios to laugh and jeer. The young Georges Rivière, journalist, poet, and budding critic of art, was immediately struck by the possibilities of Impressionism. Like all advanced critics, Rivière believed wholeheartedly in the theory that art should take as its subjects the people and things of the day and that beauty resided just as much in astringent studies of modern life as in romantic studies of the past. Renoir and Degas were the obvious examples of painters after Rivière's mind—*La Loge* (for which Edmond posed) was the eighteen-seventies to the minute.

In those days the Paris art world was small, and it was no difficult matter for the two men to get acquainted; they were almost certain to have friends in common. As it turned out, the Franc-Lamy of Gleyre's and Mère Anthony's had become an intimate of Rivière's since the war, and this friendship began to blossom into a group based on Renoir and his studio.

Unlike the Gleyre group, the men at Renoir's had diverse interests, and the fact that their host managed to keep them happy and to control the inevitable friction puts him in a new light, as a leader. Rivière, a bright young man, can be seen lifelike in the portrait Renoir was to make of him the following year, 1876. He had a shock of brown hair, red cheeks, bright eyes and, rare in such circles in those days, no beard. Rivière's painter friend Frédéric Cordey, a gaunt young man, bearded, wearing pince-nez and with a long and razor-sharp nose, soon turned into Renoir's shadow. The Home Office clerk Lestringuez was a typical product of the time; blond-bearded, impeccably turned out, he would arrive at the studio most afternoons soon after five and settle down to talk about his latest experiments in occultism for as long as Renoir managed to keep a straight face. Diverted from this passion he would discuss books or the theatre knowledgeably if he could not drag his host off to the dance or circus, for he and Cordey were keen on the dance halls.

Sometimes he brought a fellow Home Office clerk with him, the vivacious Emmanuel Chabrier; then the conversation swiveled between painting and music.[26] When Cabaner walked in, stooping heavily, on his one free night from the café piano-playing, he would talk of the new musical language he hoped to invent, of inaccessible harmonies he dreamed of, rather after the manner of his successor Alexander Scriabin. If the conversation was deflected briskly by Chabrier or another to painting, Cabaner would repeat happily enough how he came to own a Cézanne. Everyone had seen this canvas. It was the sole decoration in Cabaner's latest hovel, a huge bare room in a court between rue Fontaine and Place Pigalle, furnished with a four-poster, a piano, and a harmonium. Cézanne had come across Renoir one day, and when asked by Renoir what had happened to a canvas he had been carrying in the street a few days earlier, a canvas he said he must sell because he had not a sou left, he cried, "I'm so pleased! My picture has had a great success, it's been taken by someone who really cares for it." Renoir thought, naturally enough, that Cézanne had at last made a sale and congratulated him. A few days later Renoir met Cabaner who also announced wonderful news. "I have a Cézanne!" Renoir, knowing that he could not buy himself enough food, let alone a picture, asked what had happened. "I ran into Cézanne carting the picture along. I looked at it, went into ecstasies over it. He said at once, 'Please take it, then!' " [27]

If no one would listen to his dreams about music or his Cézanne story, Cabaner could sit through an entire evening without saying a word, endlessly smoking Renoir's cigarettes and marveling at Paul Lhotte, a young painter who believed in action and boasted of the number of duels he had fought. But Lhotte could talk well, was good-natured under the martial exterior, and found a foil in the occasional visitor, Marcellin Desboutin, painter and writer of verse tragedies. Desboutin could outswagger Lhotte and had some twenty years' more experience of life. He was always swathed in a discolored cloak, a pipe permanently stuck in the side of a half-paralyzed mouth. He was in his fifties, gray-haired, and bearded and would talk of his days in Florence as a rich man, days so far removed from these poverty-stricken Paris appearances that when Manet first saw him at the Guerbois he mistook him for a strolling player and was on the point of giving him a few sous. A watercolor portrait by Manet gives an excellent impression of this Rabelaisian character.[28]

Add Goenutte, Maître, and the occasional visit of Pissarro or Monet when in Paris, and the Renoir circle is complete. It consisted largely of oddities, since Renoir, himself anything but odd, typically preferred his opposites, and, more important, of men who loved life and believed in using it to the full. Renoir usually sat as Bazille had painted him, feet up on chair, knees between arms, a cigarette between his lips, listening and occasionally throwing in the decisive word. He disliked discussions of his work—his canvases were turned face to wall—and was not much more anxious to join in the worship of Wagner and Berlioz then at its height. He did not go to the Pasdeloup concerts, the shrine of Wagner. When he grew tired of superlatives he would merely say in his dry way that the moderns might be all very well but personally he preferred the musicians of the time and manner of a man like Watteau—Bach, Handel, Couperin, Albinoni.[29]

In literature he played a similar role, deprecating his friends' admiration for the *Ruy Blas* and *Hernani* of Hugo and allowing himself a few scathing remarks about Zola, who had become the favorite novelist of the naturalistic school. He said of one of Zola's much praised purple-passage descriptions of a storm, "Yes, it may be all you say but Alexandre Dumas père would just have written 'it rained' and that would have been good enough for his readers." He recommended Verlaine as a great poet who knew exactly how to use words without preciosity.[30]

Renoir, it will be seen, provided this collection of rather wild enthusiasts with a steadying point; they relied heavily on his common sense even when they contested it. But this alone would not have won him the affection of men so varied in age and experience. Renoir possessed a rare gift, he could be sensible without a trace of priggishness; and when (as he much preferred) the discussions were abandoned for a dance at the

Moulin de la Galette or a night at the Cirque Fernando, he was often enough the life and soul of the party.

Occasionally he sold a picture to or by way of one of these friends. Chabrier, for instance, bought the nude painted that winter—possibly after the "crouching Venus" in the Louvre. He circled the canvas half-fascinated, half-horrified (it was "outrageously nude," he said), offered three hundred francs for it, and was delighted when Renoir agreed. "I shall never part with it," he declared, "not if I'm offered ten thousand francs!" This flight of fancy (Chabrier was renowned for his exaggerations) aroused incredulous laughter, from Renoir as much as anyone; who could dream that *La Loge*, which Père Martin had bought for 425 francs, was to fetch one million just after the first World War when the painter was still alive? [31]

Renoir's models sometimes joined the men if they had been posing that afternoon. One girl in particular, the model for *La Loge*, often stayed on, reading novels on the sofa when not wanted to pose and, when the men arrived, moving into a corner with her book. She was very quiet with bright hair, long eyelashes under markedly arched eyebrows, and her pure antique profile fascinated all the painters. Her relationship with Renoir typified the impression he made in Montmartre in his first year there. Nini (nicknamed "Cat's-Paw" because of the two loops into which she fastened her hair) was the daughter of a theatre program seller and an assistant in a shooting gallery. Her mother, the program seller, called at Renoir's studio one day and appealed to his gallantry: "Just imagine, M. Renoir, the dangers she's exposed to—a pretty girl like that is difficult to protect. She needs a serious protector, someone steady who'll make sure of a good future for her."

It may be that at this point she caught sight of Renoir's expression for she hurried on, "I don't think of a Lord or a Russian prince, I just want her to have a good home and someone who'll understand her." As she still did not provoke the necessary suggestion and may well have thought Renoir too modest—it was the invariable impression he gave—she explained, "A man like you, M. Renoir." [32]

Renoir did not take the hint. He did not become an official protector of any of the girls he painted, danced with, escorted to the theatre, and slept with. Nini was eventually to marry a third-rate actor, but the interesting point of her mother's démarche was that Montmartre mothers were attracted to Renoir, entrusted their daughters to him, and hoped against hope that he would "protect" or, a very faint hope, marry them. It was a measure of his charm, the charm of the serious-looking man with little to say and a humorous look in his eye, that at a time when mothers had good cause to worry about their daughters they instinctively relied on him and confided in him. That he might sleep with them was understood; they would probably have felt rather insulted if he did not. What they knew was that he would never desert or ruin them and that if they struck bad times he would try to help them. As he often did. He was much better than the "protector" all these mothers were yearning for; he really thought of their welfare, advised them, sorted out quarrels, handed over loans, and was to carry loyalty to the point, a few years later, of paying for a good funeral for one of his models, Margot, who posed for his first successful picture and died young.[33]

So Renoir enjoyed his Montmartre life, talking, listening, dancing, theatre-going, flirting and, above all, working in a place where the most attractive models were all about him, cheap and willing. But he could not live on nothing and next to nothing sold. More important to such a kindhearted man, Monet and Pissarro and Sisley were at their wits' end to keep going, Monet especially.[34] And it was Renoir, always the practical one, who suggested early in the new year of 1875 that, as no money was available for another exhibition, they might try a public auction.

CHAPTER X

─────

GETTING A FOOTHOLD

─────

1875-1877

RENOIR SUGGESTED AN AUCTION for two reasons: to get back what the catastrophic exhibition (all expense and no sales) had cost them and, more ambitiously, to collect funds to defray the expenses of a second exhibition.

It is improbable that he really wanted another exhibition unless the ban on submission to the Salon were lifted, and Pissarro and Monet remained adamant.[1] Yet Durand-Ruel said of the first exhibition, "The pictures of Monet, Sisley, Pissarro, Renoir, and Degas had so far simply excited curiosity; most visitors regarded them with indifference but without any special hostility." [2] This view, which Renoir shared,[3] strengthened the argument of Pissarro and Monet that only by keeping at the public year by year would they be taken seriously. Durand-Ruel's occasional sales also seemed to point the way; his "advanced" clients, such as Faure, Duret, De Bellio, and Hoschedé, could be relied on to defend the men whose pictures they owned and even to go from defense to attack. De Bellio, for instance, was a voluble and pugnacious man, forever declaring publicly that Impressionism was a logical and inevitable development of painting. Renoir could not contest the apparent good sense of all this and as usual went the way of men more determined than he.

First came the immediate need to raise enough money to pay

for the expenses of an exhibition—Renoir's auction plan—and he and his friends must have felt jubilant when Berthe Morisot, hearing that there was talk of holding an auction, offered to join Monet, Sisley, and himself in sending canvases to the sale room. She had come to know her fellow exhibitors well—she was on the exhibition committee—admired their work and spirit [4] and was specially taken with Renoir. His no-nonsense manner and air of withdrawal from the world obviously intrigued a young woman brought up in the stuffy and materialistic circles of the upper class civil servant. She was kind, she had just married into a painter's family,[5] and was herself a painter. She was excessively diffident about her gift but her work showed charm and considerable talent, as Renoir appreciated.[6] Her offer to come in pleased everyone; the addition of a painter who had no need of money, was well born, and was Manet's sister-in-law seemed to give the proceedings a much more respectable flavor.

In the event, her entry made not the slightest difference; the auction at the Hôtel Drouot was a calamitous failure. It was more than a failure, it became a Paris scandal delightedly written up by journalists who had condemned the previous year's exhibition. It gave further and final proof, they wrote, that the Impressionist painters had no business to thrust themselves on the public attention.

The auction was preceded by the customary showing of the works to be offered, and it was then that trouble began. The room was invaded by a crowd of Beaux-Arts students [7] who made serious inspection impossible; groups of them circled the room shouting ribald comments in front of each canvas.[8]

The next day, March 24, 1875, they were back in force when the celebrated auctioneer Charles Pillet opened the sale. This time they went further and tried to drown the bids by jeers and catcalls. When one or two intrepid men refused to be browbeaten and shouted their bids, the students began to jostle and push them.

Durand-Ruel, asked by the painters to buy back pictures which did not reach the low reserve prices, was in the auction room from beginning to end. He was appalled by the scenes and particularly because the students had been joined by older diehards who behaved just as badly. "This sale," he said later, "which comprised twenty superb pictures by Monet, twelve by Mlle. Morisot, nineteen by Renoir and twenty-one by Sisley, provoked unforgettable scenes. On the day of the preview and on the day of the sale Pillet was forced to call in the police to stop altercations from degenerating into regular fights. Most of the people there, annoyed with the few defenders of the unhappy artists, wanted to stop the sale; they howled down every bid." [9]

The critics had much to answer for, and Albert Wolff most of all. This influential vulgarian, critic of *Le Figaro,* had not troubled to visit the exhibition at Nadar's, and probably would not have troubled to look in at the auction preshowing if Manet had not asked him to. Manet, in spite of his commitment to the Salon, good-naturedly wanted to help Monet and Berthe Morisot, the one because he liked him, the other because she was his sister-in-law. He begged Wolff to give the pictures a mention. "You may not like this kind of painting yet," he wrote, "but you will one day." [10]

The kindly effort recoiled on his friends. Wolff obliged, but in his own way; he wrote a piece calculated to inflame the unruly crowd of students. Manet's "one day" might conceivably come, he agreed, but to judge by what he saw at the Hôtel Drouot, "the impression left on me by the Impressionists is of a cat walking on the keyboard of a piano or a monkey playing with a box of paints." [11]

The other critics, like the bulk of the people in the auction room, took their cue from him. *Le Charivari* provided the most restrained example: "Perhaps you remember an exhibition held at the old studios of Nadar in Boulevard des Capucines? Certain painters who wanted to break with tradition set up their own temple in opposition to the Salon. Their efforts were not successful. But notwithstanding, four of these people (one a lady) have had the temerity to arrange an auction at the Hôtel Drouot. The new group to which these four belong is called

Impressionist but it has made no impression on the public. This kind of painting, veering from the vague to the savage, seems to us chiefly to display ignorance and to deny the true and the beautiful. It is only too easy to attract attention by turning out work more rubbishy than anyone has ever dared exhibit before." [12]

Against this kind of vituperation, followed by full and exaggerated reports of the auction room hooliganism, the few faint voices raised in the painters' favor carried little weight. One critic, who had not the courage to sign his article, wrote perceptively of the paintings as "small fragments mirroring universal life" and claimed that "the swift and colorful, subtle and charming things reflected in the mirror deserve our attention and applause." [13] In his catalogue preface, Burty declared, "These works earn more than our scrutiny, they earn our sympathy—for their efforts to awaken the memory of fresh and lively sensations in front of nature, for their technical novelties (products of careful research) which reproduce landscape effects without the artifices of a strong foreground or vulgar attractions, for their preference for clear, bright tones and the suppression of detail to the benefit of the whole." [14] He suggested, to encourage bidders, that canvases could be picked up at prices which would soon return a handsome profit.[15]

Only a few brave and principled men listened to him. Most prospective buyers were scared out of the room, or from bidding, by the threat of rough handling by the crowd; those with a little more courage were convinced by the abusive critics that they would be throwing their money away by patronizing painters whose work, however attractive they found it, was considered rubbish by men who ought to know. The result was a mere handful of bids; the few paintings that did exceed the reserve prices fell to the first or second bid.

Durand-Ruel, watching impotently (he could not afford to enter the market), summed up: "What bids there were cannot be called notable. The 72 canvases produced only a total of 11,496 francs." [16] And this paltry figure, an average of 165 francs per picture, came largely out of the painters' own pockets by way of the canvases bought back by Durand-Ruel. Ironically, Berthe Morisot, who did not need the money, got the best of the poor prices, an average of 250 francs, Monet followed her with just over 200, Sisley just under 200, and Renoir last of all with an average of 150.

Yet Burty and Manet were true prophets, as Durand-Ruel pointed out years later. "This was a marvellous collection of works of which the least fine would be treasured today. To give one an idea, among the Monet canvases was *Le Printemps*. It fetched 205 francs at the sale yet was bought not many years later by M. Von Tschudi for the Berlin Museum for forty thousand francs. As for Renoir, his *La Source* which I bought back for him at 110 francs was sold by me some years afterwards to the Prince de Wagram for seventy thousand francs. And *La Toilette* which Duret secured for 140 francs at the auction I bought from him for 4,200 francs in 1894, resold later to America for one hundred thousand and could today easily get two or even three hundred thousand for." [17]

The dealer was writing in 1911 (he died in 1922, aged ninety), and the later prices he speaks of would have been inconceivable to the painters of 1875. Yet the actuality was almost as inconceivable; the few bids and the absurd prices were cruelly beneath the most moderate hopes. A second exhibition was, of course, out of the question that year; all three men were asking themselves one question only, how they were to live through the succeeding months. It was one of their blackest moments.

Renoir's feelings as the instigator of this apparent fiasco can be imagined. Yet out of the scandal good was to come, and the better part of it through Renoir, so that he was able to say in the end that his judgment had not been wrong. The least acceptable good came through the negative adage: rather a bad press than no press at all. The Impressionists were thrust back into the headlines by the renewal of newspaper abuse. Unbearable though it was at the time, this publicity was to have a long-range effect. Parisians were not allowed to forget the name Impressionist, and the public being what it is, the value of the hostile journalists' articles can scarcely be overestimated. With no more than elementary justice, the very exaggerations of the critics fastened the painters' names in public memory.

Positively, one great good arrived immediately, as Renoir was to explain. "This disastrous sale had a happy ending for me. I made the acquaintance of M. Chocquet. He was a civil servant with very little money who had nevertheless managed to form a most remarkable collection." He added ruefully, "It is true that in those days, and later on too, for that matter, it wasn't necessary for a collector to be rich; all he needed was a little taste." [18]

Victor Chocquet is known to millions today from the portraits by Renoir and Cézanne. These present him lifelike, golden-haired, bearded, and kindly. What they do not show is the moral courage behind the handsome exterior and gentle manner. Before the auction, Chocquet had already shown his mettle. It was the rule that all clerks in the customs and excise department in which he worked should file into their director's office every first of January to be told that they had been granted a salary raise of fifty francs per month. They were expected to wear their Sunday best for the occasion and to appear obsequiously grateful to this man whom they never saw on any other day in the year.

On this particular January first, Chocquet walked into the director's office in a coat out at the elbows and trousers with frayed turnups and shiny from years of sitting on his stool.

His chief stared and frowned. "What is the meaning of this get-up, Monsieur Chocquet?"

Chocquet replied politely, "Monsieur, it is the get-up suitable for a man who is given a raise of fifty francs." [19]

Later, after he had met Renoir and had begun to collect Impressionist paintings, Chocquet was visited in his rue de Rivoli apartment by Alexander Dumas fils. Dumas asked if he might see the collection. Chocquet took him round, stopping from time to time to praise his Renoir, Cézanne, and Monet canvases.

Dumas did not listen; he was there for one purpose only, to see and if possible buy Chocquet's Tassants. At last he lost patience and said, "Your Tassants are very fine, Monsieur Chocquet."

Chocquet agreed: "Yes, true enough, I like them pretty well. Of course they aren't Renoirs or Delacroix but they're pleasant trifles."

The incredulous Dumas, thinking himself on to a good thing, snapped in with "That's splendid, Monsieur Chocquet. Then you'll let me have them? I'll give you thirty thousand francs for the lot."

Chocquet, who had never seen such money in his life, struck an attitude. "What! You ask to see my pictures simply to make an offer for them! You wish to insult me, I think. I'm not a shop, monsieur. I will wish you goodbye." And Dumas was shown the door.[20]

Such was the man who, Renoir explained, "looked into the Hôtel Drouot by chance when our canvases were being shown. He chose to see some resemblance between my canvases and the work of Delacroix, his god. On the evening of the sale he wrote to me, paying me all kinds of compliments on my pictures and begging me to make a portrait of Mme. Chocquet. I accepted at once."[21]

Renoir qualified his last sentence with a remark, made slightly on the defensive, about commissioned work. "I didn't often refuse portrait commissions. When the sitter was a bit dotty I took the job as a kind of penitential act—it's good for the painter to do something boring from time to time."[22] He allowed for exceptions. "It is true that when asked to paint the portrait of Mme. L. I replied that I didn't know how to paint wild beasts, but that wasn't at all the case with Mme. Chocquet."[23]

Chocquet made only one stipulation, that Renoir should paint his wife with a Delacroix picture on the wall behind her, and he rendered the stipulation innocuous in typical fashion by adding, "I want to see you together, you and Delacroix."[24]

He and the painter took to each other at once; he admired Renoir's spirit as well as his talent, Renoir admired his new friend's good taste and strong principles. He quickly had entrée to the Chocquet apartment and made characteristic use of this unexpected stroke of good luck. He painted portraits of husband and wife and sold Chocquet five of his pictures. When Chocquet died twenty-four years later and his collection was sold, it included eleven Renoirs.

The collection also included a Pissarro, a Sisley, eleven Monets, and thirty-one Cézannes, and this was wholly due to Renoir. The meeting with Chocquet had got him out of immediate trouble after the failure of the auction, but that was not enough for him; it was one of the happiest features of the Impressionist painters that they shared good fortune as well as bad, and Renoir, most generous of men, immediately followed this unwritten law.

How he did so requires the introduction of another character, the Breton Julien (known as Père) Tanguy, the man immortalized by Van Gogh.[25] Before the war he had been a traveling salesman in painter's materials. His round covered the Paris suburbs. He met Pissarro and Monet and, realizing that they were true artists, unpretentious men, and very poor, often let them have colors and canvases free. The gesture expressed the man; he loved painting when the painter was sincere.

Like Pissarro he was an extreme radical. Unlike Pissarro he put his principles into practice, joined the Commune forces, was caught by the Versaillais and would have been shot but for the intervention of Degas, apparently through the medium of the ever-useful Bibesco. When freed under a general amnesty a year or so later, he set up a small paint and color shop in rue Clauzel on the way up to Montmartre. The business did not flourish because Tanguy was too kindhearted. He would give free colors and meals to hard-pressed young painters, allow them to use his shop as a debating center, and take their pictures (virtually unsalable) when he thought well of them. He thus had by 1875 a collection of advanced pictures, all theoretically for sale but mostly a dead weight on him.

Pissarro had kept in touch with him, and after the return to Paris (Tanguy had been deported along with many Communard sympathizers) he introduced his friends to the shop. One of these friends was Cézanne, who brought a canvas with him. This was a year before the Drouot auction, a year afterward claimed by Tanguy as the most notable in his life. He was instantly enraptured by Cézanne's work, begged for more, and by the time the auction was held had become the only man in Paris who could claim to have a Cézanne collection.

Renoir knew Tanguy well and liked him but does not seem to have visited the shop often. This is easy to understand; Tanguy's was usually full of young painters earnestly discussing painting, and Renoir preferred painting to discussing it. But when the remembrance of Tanguy and his collection was practical he remembered it. As then. "The moment I met Chocquet," he said later, "I thought of selling him a Cézanne!" [26]

In other words, Renoir was acute as well as generous. He had no sooner met and listened to Chocquet and seen his collection than he realized that the man whose work this Delacroix enthusiast would really take to was Cézanne. So: "I took him to Père Tanguy where he bought a small nude study by Cézanne. He was ravished by it and while we walked back to his home he kept exclaiming, 'How good this will look between a Delacroix and a Courbet!' [27]

"But just when we had reached the house and he was about to ring the bell, he stopped. 'But what on earth will Marie say? Listen, Renoir, do me a service, tell my wife that the Cézanne is yours, forget to take it away when you leave, then Marie will have time to get used to it before I admit that it is mine.' [28]

"This little ruse was completely successful and Madame Chocquet, to please her husband, quickly made herself accept Cézanne's style." [29]

Cézanne carried on the pleasant Impressionist habit of co-operation; he took Chocquet down to lunch with Monet at Argenteuil. There Chocquet repeated his childlike and irresistible burst of enthusiasm, bemoaning the fact that he had listened to friends who had warned him off the exhibition at Nadar's. "When I think that I might have known your work a year earlier!" he cried to Monet. "What wretched luck, to have been robbed of such pleasure. Imagine how I feel, having lost a whole year of you!" [30]

To Monet, rapidly approaching his prewar state of abject poverty, these words must have sounded sweet. All knew that whatever they had to face in the future, they had found another supporter, even though with a limited income, to be added to the short but splendid list of forward-looking men—Durand-Ruel, Duret, Faure, Hoschedé, De Bellio, Comte Doria, Dr. Gachet, Tanguy, Henri Rouart, friend of Degas, and the Arosa brothers.

2

The list was shortly to be enlarged by another name. The surprises of the auction aftereffects were not yet over, and again Renoir was the lucky one. Of the few pictures genuinely sold, his *Pêcheur à la ligne* was bought by Georges Charpentier. It seems probable that Charpentier had been reminded of Renoir by the musician Léon Clapisson, who had already commissioned a portrait from the painter. Charpentier was one of the coming men in publishing by this time—he published the popular Daudet and specialized in Zola and the modernists—and had no doubt forgotten the meeting at La Grenouillère, but if so, he soon made up for the lapse of memory. Renoir came back to him as a man, and the painting Charpentier bought at the auction and took home was to advance the artist notably as a painter—by reputation, at any rate.

Charpentier had an ambitious wife determined to establish a salon of all the cultures (including politics) which would outshine the efforts of every other Parisian hostess. When Renoir met her she had gone far toward her goal. An advanced and wealthy publisher is in a good position to surround his wife with interesting people, and by 1875 Mme. Charpentier's luxurious apartment over the publishing business at the corner of Quai de Louvre and Place Saint-Germain l'Auxerrois was satisfactorily filled in her reception days. There one could find Gambetta, Daudet, Zola, Flaubert, the Goncourt brothers, Maupassant, Turgenev, Huysmans, De Banville, Bergerat.[31]

But there was a lack, and one of which Mme. Charpentier

was very conscious. She was weak in painters. Manet was to be seen from time to time at the Charpentier soirées, and as the most famous rebel painter of the day his presence was gratifying. But Manet held his own receptions; he was well-to-do, independent, established. The society hostess with a leaning toward the arts wants to make her own discoveries, to spot genius before anyone else, to bring it on, to share the glory.

When Mme. Clapisson told her that Renoir was a charming young man and good painter though unknown and poor, and Charpentier, recalling the La Grenouillère meeting, confirmed the report, it appears that Mme. Charpentier scented the possibility of a find. If she sounded Manet she must have been told that Renoir had charm but not much of a gift. This would merely put her on her guard. She was cautious, she was also masterful. She would be unlikely to accept any verdict but her own as final. Her husband was willing to experiment. He was sympathetic to modern art; he not only published Zola but was friendly with him and agreed with his view that painters must take subjects from the present day and treat them as realistically as he did in his novels. He was not at all averse to a reputation as the champion of painters as well as writers.

So it came about that Charpentier picked up very cheaply (he paid 140 francs) Renoir's *Pêcheur à la ligne* at the Drouot auction, took it home, and showed it to his wife. She liked it. She liked Renoir even more when he was invited to call about a possible commission. She decided to test him out; she asked him if he would make a portrait of her mother-in-law.[32]

3

This was the beginning of a string of commissions for Renoir from the Charpentiers and their friends, but in the fall of 1875 all he knew and all he cared about was that he had picked up a good friend in Chocquet and several commissions from the apparently calamitous auction and would not have to worry about money for a space. He was at that moment much more concerned with the commission from Léon Clapisson. He had known this family some time—he met them in 1872 through Maître—found Mme. Clapisson "charming," [33] and must have been astounded by his good luck when her husband offered him twelve hundred francs for a portrait of her and her two daughters.

He made *Mère et enfants en promenade* and before he had finished it had decided what he would do with the money; he would take rooms in the heart of Montmartre, that still charming village surrounded with trees on its hill overlooking Paris. He and Rivière began looking about. Before he had decided on the rooms, he had become involved in a second Impressionist exhibition. In the summer weeks with Sisley and Monet both men had talked much of another exhibition, Monet especially, and a powerful helper declared himself in Caillebotte. The engineer was determined to compel the public of Paris to acknowledge the new painting. He had money as well as faith. He admired Monet and Pissarro to the point of idolatry and would not hear of accepting the result of the first exhibition as final.

Caillebotte's youthful enthusiasm heartened them all. The problem, as always, was money, but with a Caillebotte eager to help out they thought an exhibition might just be managed if a cheap gallery could be found and if Degas and Berthe Morisot, both monied and socially reassuring, would join them again. Sisley was very anxious for the exhibition; he had just painted his finest canvas to date, *L'Inondation à Port-Marly*, was beginning to feel his strength, and for the first time conquered his reticence sufficiently to take a strong line.

Renoir was deputed to approach Berthe Morisot and Degas and did so with success. She was enthusiastic, Degas accepted with a proviso that the word Impressionist must not be used.[34] By the time both were rounded up, Durand-Ruel had told Pissarro that they could use his gallery in rue Le Peletier rent-free for the month of the exhibition. He felt guilty at being obliged to drop them so soon after taking them up, and here was a simple and effective way of making slight amends.[35]

There was a considerable change in the exhibitors, in both

number and quality. No fewer than seventeen of the original
thirty fell out. Three of these—Cézanne, Boudin, and Guillaumin—could be considered Impressionist painters, but the
remaining fourteen were all friends of Degas, a group of moder-
ates led by Braquemond, who had been shocked by public and,
still more, critical reaction to the first showing and who were
terrified of being associated twice with the wild men of painting.

Their withdrawal left Impressionist painters very much in
the ascendant. Monet showed eighteen pictures, Berthe Morisot
seventeen, Pissarro thirteen, Sisley eight, and Renoir fifteen. Of
the seven painters newly represented by their works, four—Caillebotte, the deceased Bazille, Desboutin brought in by Renoir,
and Legros introduced by Pissarro—were sympathizers. Two of
the remaining three, Millet and Tillot, were represented by
landscapes. In short, sixteen of the twenty exhibitors in this
second exhibition were wholly or primarily landscape painters,
and the bulk of the pictures shown were not merely landscapes
but *plein air* studies.

The exhibition had moved close to the original aim of Monet
and Pissarro, to demonstrate nothing but the new painting to
Paris art lovers. Degas, it is true, had the largest showing with
twenty-four pictures but, his conventional friends having deserted en masse, remained heavily outnumbered. He evidently
worried a great deal about this and felt he had been left to the
mercy of a band of reckless innovators. That was why he fought
tooth and nail to keep the word Impressionist out of the title.
The show was called simply Exposition de Peinture.

To the present-day lover of pictures the qualms of Degas
must seem curious. Certainly he did not care for landscape and
thought Pissarro's scientific palette an abomination.[36] But his
own exhibits included superb but highly unconventional ballet
studies as well as four pictures of ironing women who were not
then regarded as permissible subjects for the serious painter. He
was, in fact, as revolutionary as the men he feared to be shown
with, not only in subject but in treatment, but this he did not
seem to understand; he thought of himself as painting in the
traditional manner, particularly in the emphasis on drawing.

It may have been to mollify a nervous Degas that Renoir did not include a single landscape in his fifteen entries. Six of these were lent by Chocquet, showing how quickly this new friend had supported him practically, and ten in all were commissioned portraits. Apart from Chocquet he had found three new patrons; one of them, Jean Dollfuss, a rich businessman from Mulhouse, was to become known for his small but choice Impressionist collection. Renoir had begun in time-honored fashion by making a portrait of Mme. Dollfuss, then sold her husband two more portrait studies. But the best and most unconventional of his offerings was not a commissioned work. *Liseuse* is a daring study in light and color.

This canvas was singled out by no less a man than Wolff when the critics got to work. "How can one prove to M. Renoir," he asked in a long and vicious article, "that a woman's body is not a mass of decomposing flesh made up of green and purple spots?" [37]

The entry of Wolff into the lists after ignoring the first exhibition was a compliment of a kind, and the reaction of the Impressionist painters to his abuse was astonishingly calm. Berthe Morisot expressed it for all when she said, "We are being discussed and this makes us so proud that we all feel happy." [38]

Not all the discussion was unfavorable—a few kind words were said in *La Presse*, for example, of Renoir's portraits of Chocquet, Bazille, and Monet, and his solitary nude was hailed as "superbly colored" [39]—but in general the harsh judgment of the first exhibition was repeated. "The Impressionists," said *La France*, "deliberately flout all rules, common sense and truth. They paint trees red or yellow, houses blue, water carmine or bright red. Their figures look like the occupants of the morgue." [40] *Le Soir* spoke of the painters as madmen using "incoherent colors," [41] *Le Soleil* declared that the canvases "aren't worth the wood they are framed in," [42] and even when an occasional hostile critic made an effort to rise above abuse or cleverness he was very cutting, as this extract from *L'Art* shows: "The so-called discoveries of Impressionism already exist in the work of Jongkind—a true artist—and what good taste the Impressionists possess comes from Delacroix and the Barbizon painters." [43]

Monet made one good sale at two thousand francs, of a canvas he did not like, and his friends sold one or two pictures, but all to supporters. Renoir sold nothing but could scarcely have hoped to, since all but two of his exhibits already belonged to patrons. This did not disturb him; what made him ponder was the evidence that neither exhibition had made more than the odd convert and that the Impressionists still depended on a few men already converted like Chocquet, Faure, and Hoschedé. He himself was not greatly concerned—unlike his friends he had before him a prospect of many commissions if he played his cards right—and he listened with some skepticism to Caillebotte, Monet, and Pissarro talking about striking quickly with a third exhibition the following year.

4

He soon forgot all about exhibitions. He had found the rooms he was looking for, and as soon as the exhibition closed in May, 1876, he moved to rue Cortot in the center of Montmartre. He still kept on his rue Saint-Georges studio as a base for winter; the Montmartre rooms were an extravagance made possible by the munificent Clapisson commission. An extravagance but with an aim or, to be precise, three aims in one: he was surrounded by poor families from which with tact he might extract many models (almost all the girls were flower sellers, milliners, or shopgirls); his rooms looked down on an old garden with trees in which he was allowed to work; most important, he was only a few minutes from Le Moulin de la Galette, the dance hall haunted by Lamy and Gervex, which he had decided to paint on the spot.

The move began a very happy period for Renoir. He had money enough for the day and the day after and that satisfied him. He had at least two commissions in hand: Durand-Ruel wanted him to paint his small daughter Jeanne, and having passed Madame Charpentier's first test, personal and technical, he had been invited to make the portrait of an even smaller girl, Georgette Charpentier. There was already talk of further introductions by the Charpentiers, to the great D'Anvers family and the Bérards. He had met the Daudets at the first of the Charpentier soirées and through them the attractive actress Jeanne Samary. From all these he might reasonably expect commissions.

The immediate future taken care of, he could relax and enjoy himself. He danced at the Moulin de la Galette and Élysée Montmartre, listened to the operettas, watched the dramas and comedies, became an habitué of the Cirque Fernando in the Boulevard Rochechouart where the clown Medrano fascinated him as he was to fascinate Toulouse-Lautrec. He entertained his friends in the studio and in a little restaurant at the corner of rue des Saules and rue Saint-Rustique, which he decorated free of charge, rather after the manner of Mère Anthony's. In the garden behind the restaurant was an arbor which he and his friends appropriated in summer for alfresco meals with their models.[44] There they had the best of both worlds, an illusion of being in the country with the comforting knowledge, to the city man, that they were in fact nothing of the kind. They all became very popular with the patron and his wife for their high spirits and the true disdain of the impecunious artist for quibbling about prices, but Renoir was always the favorite; he was cheerful and steady too, a Frenchman at his best.

On occasional evenings he went down to the Nouvelle Athènes, the larger successor to the Guerbois just along the street. He walked very fast and absent-mindedly, as his habit was, but had even less to say when he reached it than in his own home, where he was usually content to throw in the odd but often decisive word. The company at this new headquarters of Manet had expanded in ratio to his increasing importance in the world of art. Zola had dropped away as his vast reputation as novelist tempted him into more worldly fields, Burty was following the rising star of Gambetta and gave less time to art than politics, but in their place came the Parnassian poets in strength: Catulle Mendès with the profile and coloring of a Greek god; the dusky

Charles Cros, poet, musician, inventor, wit; the haughty Albert
Mérat; the posturing Villiers de Lisle Adam who could hold an
audience spellbound and uncertain whether he was genius or
charlatan; and such bright sparks as the young Jean-Louis
Forain, just winning a name for his ferocious cartoons, and Jean
Richepin, who had recently delighted literary Paris with a book
of daring verses.

All these and more with most of the old companions in argument and drink were found there, including Renoir's studio
friends en masse,[45] but he had no more to say than in Guerbois
days, no doubt because of his ambivalent attitude toward theoretical discussion. He liked to be with men; he was never to love
dialectic or overdue earnestness. So: "He came in with his hurried step, serious look [not to be taken too seriously, however]
and abstracted air, his imagination running ahead of him as
usual. He usually sat in a corner, rarely took part in the conversation and often appeared almost indifferent to what was being
said round him; he would roll a cigarette, light it, then let it
smolder away while he doodled on the marble table top with
the burnt match." [46]

If George Moore is to be trusted (he was one of Manet's latest
disciples), when Renoir did speak it was to express his dislike
of the century in which he lived. He was thinking of the decline
in craftsmanship—he had never forgotten the ominous rumbles
of a mass production world when he lost his workshop job—and
according to the Irishman busily taking notes of these fascinating Frenchmen, he declared that men had lost the art of making
the original and the beautiful, that all the modern man could
do was to copy. Moore is notoriously unreliable but this sounds
like Renoir.[47]

Down in the city Renoir walked into another world, the cultured quiet of the Chocquets, the smart chatter of the Charpentiers and their friends, but took the change in his stride. He had
the Lejosne soirées behind him and his own native wit; he liked
change, liked well-dressed women, liked the feeling of wealth
and luxury as long as he did not have time to stifle in it. As a
result, outwardly at least he appeared as much at home among

the literati of Paris as among the workgirls of the dance hall.[48]

He did all this and much besides, but to generations not then born the important fact was that he worked too, and threw all this varied enjoyment into his work in such a way as to infect everyone who looks at his paintings.

Impressionism can be seen as more than a technique of painting. It is an attitude of mind. In technique Renoir could be faulted not because his was less good than the others but because he never once believed as they did that this was the only way to paint; he was interested in a novelty, no more. But in the larger sense, the attitude of mind, he was as revolutionary as any of them and never more so than in these years in Montmartre.

It could be said, looking at Impressionism in this light, that its aim was to give an impression of France as it then was. The Impressionist painter insisted on precise truth of vision and coupled this with the belief that his subjects were all about him, that he need not stir a step to find them, let alone follow the conventional painters into the past.

This belief that the everyday world of the latter half of the nineteenth century provided artist, writer, or painter with the means of achieving beauty was common to almost all the men who met at the Nouvelle Athènes. Manet and Degas just as much as Monet and Pissarro were converts to modernism, Manet while still a student in Couture's studio, Degas after the many discussions in the Guerbois. Monet, Pissarro, and Sisley exemplified the more obvious side of Impressionism; they took as their subject any land, sea or river scape that happened to catch their attention; its supposedly artistic appeal in the old application of the word—romantic, historical, grand—had no more effect on them than its social significance.

In their way Manet and Degas went further, although the one practiced the Impressionist technique only when he felt like it, the other not at all. Before the war Manet had painted the cross-Channel steamer at Boulogne, and the picture's charm rested in truth to the everyday. Degas was making studies of acrobats, laundry women, prostitutes, and ballet dancers, and far from romanticizing them like the few other painters who had dared to touch such subjects, he presented them with devastating candor. The pictures he painted were remarkable in every sense and not least because they were truthful; this gives them a beauty no romantic painter, devoted to the conventionally beautiful, could match.

At the beginning of 1877, a few months after the second exhibition, Monet suddenly invaded the Manet-Degas territory. He painted the Gare Saint-Lazare and made history by demonstrating that there was poetry in the most blatantly unpoetical manifestation of modern life.

So the Impressionist painters and those allied to them were dealing with the look of present-day France. There was a further obvious development, and Renoir made it almost singlehanded. Manet had insisted on naturalism in his long-past canvases of a Tuileries concert, *Olympia* and *Le déjeuner sur l'herbe,* and was soon to paint the ravishing and precise *Au café* and *Un bar aux Folies-Bergère,* but as a chronicler of the social scene he usually limited himself to, and certainly felt most at home with, the well-to-do minority. He had, moreover, an almost clinical interest in his subjects; he is just as much interested in portraying a glass of beer as the girl who is holding it. He does both marvelously well but the effect can be chilling.

It was left to Renoir to provide a panorama of the everyday Parisian. More than any of his friends he loved to paint people, and better than any he knew the people who gave the city its life and character. He was a city man and loved everything about it but most of all the common men and women. And in these years he was to establish himself as the painter par excellence of the people and, to qualify further, the women of Paris.

His studies of women ranged from the aristocratic patron commissioning a portrait, through stage and circus stars to the working girl model. Often he was to show them in their special milieu, always he was to show them to best advantage, in their moments of relaxation and pleasure. He did more than paint women, he created on canvas what no other man had done so well, their femininity. There are men who have a strong sense of the feminine in women, a sense going far beyond appearance.

Renoir was one of these and conveys this elusive but unmistakable property of the opposite sex.

Essentially he was becoming not merely the chronicler of Parisian types but of their life, the night life especially. He was not interested in their work but fascinated by them at play. He loved happiness as much as he loved women and inclined toward it instinctively. He saw no point in the kind of realism Zola preached and wrote about; he saw that as ugliness and the man who thrust it on the public notice as a sadist. He knew that many of the workgirls he painted were in fact sweated labor, but his portrayal of them happily dancing was not less true and infinitely more pleasant. He concentrated on the pleasant, and his pictures ring true because, for all the often monstrous overwork and underpayment of that time, the young people were truly gay and lighthearted.

He gave us Paris of the eighteen-seventies, and Paris then was in many ways a very happy city. It had not reached the point at which moralists would condemn this happiness as shallow, pagan, antisocial, escapist. In those days everything was simpler, the minds of the public most of all. The French have always been realists. They were realists then. To be realistic, they thought, was to earn one's living then forget about it as quickly as possible; if they were paid little, drinks, food, dances, theatres, circuses cost little too. They were expected to put a happy face forward, and as it was in their own interest to do so, and as it is nicer to smile than to frown and just as easy, they concentrated on the smile.

This was Renoir's philosophy precisely, and given his love of women and attachment to his class, it is not surprising that he became the foremost example of the painter who demonstrated that the common people at play could be beautiful as well as heartening. In these summer months of 1876 he was hard at work creating his first painting in this genre. His aim was to make a study of Le Moulin de la Galette as it was at the height of a summer evening, packed with dancers. He planned to paint the whole canvas in situ, Impressionist fashion, and went even further in naturalism, intending to use only his friends and the habitués of the Moulin as models. He wheeled the large canvas to and from the Moulin and his rue Cortot studio in a handcart each painting day.

He had some difficulty in persuading the dancers to pose; the idea of being painted while dancing seemed very strange to these simple people. Renoir tackled the problem with guile. He visited the homes of the girls, flattered the parents, assured them that there was no question of painting their daughters in the nude (their great fear), bribed small brothers with sweets and toys.[49]

He then had to deal with the girls and conquered their bashfulness neatly. Down in Paris he had many times seen *La Timbale d'Argent,* which was enjoying a long run. The leading lady, Théo, created a sensation by wearing a new hat, the Timbale, which gave the operetta its title. The hat was simply a cone-shaped straw hat with a large red ribbon tied round it, but by wearing it on the back of the head the actress framed her face and hair in the most appealing manner, the ribbon floating brightly away from the hat whenever she danced or tossed her head. The hats were cheap but did not look cheap. Renoir bought some, carried them up to Montmartre and offered them to the unwilling models at the Moulin. All fell for the simple bait, snatched a hat apiece and gladly promised to pose for him.[50]

From that moment his difficulty was to avoid mothers desperate to introduce willing daughters to the rich Monsieur Renoir, a man who could produce a handful of hats and give them away with an air. So easily did rumor get around the village that he could take his pick of practically the entire young female population, not merely for posing at the ball but in his studio too. No stratagem was considered too obvious, such as the mother stationing a daughter slightly gone in pregnancy in the route Renoir took every day to his work, and hissing to her as he came up to them: "Here comes Renoir! Hold your breath!" [51]

As all this indicates, the population of Montmartre and the young men and women who filled the Moulin every week end night remained naïve to a degree. And it was precisely because the dances, like them, represented true old Paris at its best that

Renoir loved the Moulin so much. In 1876 the place and its clientèle were still unspoiled. The Moulin de la Galette stood just off rue Lepic and on one of the highest points of Montmartre. It is still there after a fashion, but in Renoir's day and long before it the two eighteenth-century wooden mills formed just as striking a Paris landmark as the Sacré Coeur today; they could be seen from most parts of the city, and the young Renoir playing in the courtyard of the Louvre or running to and from his china workshop must often have looked up at them.[52]

When the mills ceased to make a profit as such, the owner, Debray, and his son decided to take advantage of their situation. They invited people to climb to the top of one mill for a tiny fee and obtain a matchless view over Paris and the île de France. The other mill, its vanes still allowed to rotate gently, was thrown open as a simple café in which were served wine and the small wine-dipped cakes known as galettes. Hence the name.

Just before Renoir came up to Montmartre the Debrays, finding that the pleasure seekers paid their sous in gratifying numbers and liked to eat and drink out of doors, went a step further; they developed the wide terrace on which the mills stood. They turned it into a pleasure garden with a shooting gallery (in which Nini's father was employed) for the fathers, swings and roundabouts for the children, stalls of sweetmeats and cheap gifts for the women, and plenty of tables and chairs on the terrace for drinks and snacks. To cater to the young men and girls they built a dance hall directly facing the entrance to rue Lepic.

Rivière, who came to know the place as well as the back of his hand, has described it: "The ballroom was built of planks painted a vile green which was mercifully being effaced by time. At the back of this room a balcony was reserved for an orchestra made up of a dozen or so poor devils condemned to blow into their discordant instruments for eight hours every Sunday. A raised gallery surrounded the dancing floor. For the most part it was filled with tables and chairs, leaving a very narrow right of way between tables and the railing marking out the dance floor. The crowd pressing through this gallery always had great difficulty in moving on or getting through. Behind the orchestral balcony was a garden, a court, one might call it, planted with mangy acacias and furnished with tables and benches. The ground, made up of bricks and rubbish pressed down, was hard and smooth enough to dance on in summer when the hall itself was open on every side. The mill standing in the garden where we danced still turned, perhaps to waft away the scent of iris roots favored by a Paris perfumer and the Moulin's clients; the other mill, its vanes still, continued to draw in some sous from the curious wanting to see a panorama of Paris." [53]

Everything about the place was unpretentious. Debray intended it for the use of his Montmartre neighbors, and for all the years Renoir lived and worked up there the dance hall and pleasure garden kept their local character. No attempt was made to dress up for the dance—soldiers came in their uniforms, butchers and bakers in their workday clothes, artisans in their smocks, and even the girls were often too poor to wear anything but the frocks in which they went to their shop or workroom during the day. The music and the dances followed the same pattern; they were simple, old-fashioned, hearty, and often extremely vigorous. They differed violently from the sophisticated dance halls such as the Élysée Montmartre down the hill in the Avenue (now Boulevard) de Clichy and the Boulevard de Rochechouart, long since invaded by Parisians au fait with the latest dance sensation and which relied heavily on exhibition dancers.

When Renoir arrived in Montmartre the Moulin de la Galette dance hall was still a novelty, and he and his friends were among the first "foreign" visitors. He was instantly delighted with its homely character and with the old dances, delighted too to see that the poor were still catered to. He knew that they could enjoy themselves if given the chance. He had seen it again and again during his youthful years of theatre gallery-going and later at La Grenouillère and other popular riverside spots; at the Moulin his theory was proved to the hilt. The dances sometimes became rough when the apaches came on to the floor, or the odd workman or painter had drunk too well, but the Debrays were careful to preserve their reputation and the pleasure of the great bulk of their clients. By and large, men and girls loved every moment of their evening and threw themselves into the dance with an abandon of which Renoir could never see enough. He and his friends enjoyed themselves so thoroughly and so wholeheartedly that they were soon accepted in a place which most Parisians would scarcely have dared try to enter.[54]

In his *Bal au Moulin de la Galette* Renoir wanted to catch this gaiety just as Monet wanted to catch the unique effect of light on a landscape or seascape at a given time. How he did so all the world now knows.

That summer in *La Balançoire* he made another study of the simple happiness characteristic of the village life of Montmartre. He painted this in the garden below his rooms, and his model, Jeanne, was the sister of the Estelle who posed for *Bal au Moulin de la Galette*, sitting on the seat in the foreground. He followed this with *La Tonnelle*, a study of the arbor behind the little restaurant in which he and his friends usually ate lunch.[55]

When the days began to draw in, he worked in the studio between visits to the Charpentiers, Durand-Ruels, Daudets, and Chocquets (for another portrait of Chocquet) and turned out a bewildering array of canvases of every kind and style. It was a queer existence switching between the elegant sophistication of the Charpentier soirées with the friends they introduced him to and the homely days and nights of Montmartre, and his work shows the division of interests.

There has been much speculation in recent years about these incursions into the fashionable life of Paris and the visits (a little later in time) to great country houses such as Wargemont. Some say that Renoir was in danger of being flattered out of his way as a true artist, that his partial desertion of the people and places he really belonged to was wholly bad because it diverted him from the source of his strength as painter. Rivière, on the other hand, who often accompanied his friend to the Charpentier evenings, says that Renoir thoroughly enjoyed them and was the better for the change.[56] Renoir, as ever, said nothing, although it is perhaps possible to detect a certain insincerity in his letters to Madame Charpentier, who gave this winter the first clear signs of a determination to lionize him.[57] She was no doubt fascinated by him and his manner, for it is evident that he had the gift of being all things to all men without surrendering his own individuality.

There is no proof that his visits were wholly opportunist, although he was to make the most of them, and his policy of always doing what he wanted suggests that he would not have endured boredom or the wrong kind of patronage whatever the ultimate reward—not, at any rate, over the long period he was to be intimate with the Charpentier circle. It is not difficult to understand the attraction of wealth and sophistication for the humbly born artist. But as a man's work must remain the test, it is beyond question that the society portraits Renoir was to make for the next few years are in no sense the equal of his Montmartre canvases; they were commissioned work and are inevitably without the spontaneity of his studio and outdoor pictures.

That he was stimulated by the diametric differences of Montmartre life and the life of the society soirées is seen in the amount and variety of this winter's work 1876–1877. In a study he made of a studio evening with Rivière, Lestinguez, Cordey, Cabaner, and Pissarro sitting in the accustomed half-circle, he represented himself wearing the then smart small mustache and fringe of beard (interesting to compare with the etching by Desboutin which shows the worn face and thinning hair). He made one of the most feeling of all his canvases, *La première sortie,* with a small girl in a theatre box for the first time. He expressed his passion for the stage in *Madame Henriot en travesti.* He created a study of a girl combing her hair, a positive riot of color. He painted his *La sortie du Conservatoire* or *Après le concert,* a well-contrived group which is notable for the first appearance in a picture by him of the girl later to become his wife, Aline Victorine Charigot, and of the afterward notorious Suzanne Valadon, then one of Degas' models.

He painted, painted, painted through the winter. It could no doubt be said of everything he made that it had the Renoir touch—the sensitive brushstrokes, the rich textures—but in general these canvases are remarkable as much for disparity in treatment as in subject.

Of the others—and there were many—perhaps none is more impressive than *Bouquet devant la glace*. He explained it in his usual frank way. "I give my brain a rest by painting flowers. There isn't the same tension of mind as when I'm faced with a model. When I paint flowers I sometimes experiment, I play about with values fearlessly without the dread of ruining a canvas. I wouldn't dare try it with a figure for fear of spoiling everything. And what experience I gain for my other pictures! Just as landscape is also useful to the figure painter; in the open air one can apply tones to a canvas that one can't even imagine in the studio with its restricted light." [58] Of this particular canvas it can only be said that even if he was merely experimenting or resting from figure work he managed to create a little gem. The color and treatment of this flower study are striking, and the background mirror provides a splendid opportunity to distinguish between color directly seen and reflected color, a device possibly suggested to him by the Impressionist treatment of shadows. In this canvas the old red plush table makes its appearance. It was to become famous in later years when collectors looked eagerly for signs of this prop in a Renoir picture.

By the early spring of 1877 he had stacked against his studio walls by far the largest and best group of canvases he had painted. And it was at this moment that the question of a third exhibition came to a head.

CHAPTER XI

ON HIS OWN

1877-1879

THIS THIRD EXHIBITION bore the name Impressionist for the first time in spite of the protests of Degas [1]—vain protests this year because he no longer held the balance of power. He had lost most of his considerable fortune—whether in the general slump that had hit Durand-Ruel or in helping relatives in America suffering from the fall in prices of cotton is not clear—and was almost as anxious as the true Impressionists to sell his pictures. [2] Of the eight exhibitions to be held it was with one exception the most truly representative—all the Impressionist painters except Berthe Morisot were there, including Cézanne and Guillaumin—and the richest in number and quality of work. So many masterpieces were never to be seen again in one gallery in the lifetime of the painters. Every one of the eighteen exhibitors, except possibly Degas, had some claim to the name Impressionist. Caillebotte was there, of course—it was he who had finally made the exhibition possible by renting a large first floor apartment a few doors from Durand-Ruel's gallery [3]—and Lamy and Cordey had been introduced by Renoir. But the tone of the exhibition was set by the three best landscape painters, who showed sixty-nine canvases between them. Cézanne showed sixteen, Guillaumin twelve, and Degas twenty-five.

Renoir's twenty-one canvases included some of the finest pictures he was to paint. His list was headed by *Bal au Moulin de*

la Galette and *La Balançoire,* the latter already bought by
Caillebotte.[4] He included seven portraits, five of them society
commissions. All but one of the commissioned portraits, of
Mme. Charpentier, of her daughter Georgette, of Mme. Daudet,
and of the Deputy for the Seine, M. Spuller, were richly colored,
technically efficient. Rivière did his best for them when he said,
"One always finds the same search for the right tones to express
life and link the figure with its surroundings." [5]

That Renoir worked hard at them is obvious, that they would
stand out well against the kind of competition he was facing
from the Bonnats of the portraitists' world is equally plain.
What they lack is seen in the fifth commissioned work and even
more in the two he painted to please himself.

The fifth commissioned canvas was of the actress Jeanne
Samary. Renoir had seen her on the stage many times and was
delighted when the Daudets introduced him to her. She was a
girl after his heart—"a ray of sunshine," [6] he called her—and
lived with her parents in rue Frochet a few hundred yards from
his studio. She had a particularly cheerful laugh; she was completely unspoiled and always being surprised by what sophisticated people would find obvious. "What a charming girl!" he
cried after he had begun the first portrait—he painted two, one
full length the other head and shoulders—"And what a complexion! She positively gleams all round herself!" [7] His work
conveys the pink and white skin, shining tawny hair and rose
dress admirably, and the coloring emphasizes the amiable
character of his sitter. He succeeds too in the vividness of the
blue eyes, which stared at one so straight and clear that Dumas
fils once cried, "Jeanne, you have such eyes I almost feel
tempted to put them out!" [8] How good his likeness was can
perhaps be gauged by Mme. Charpentier's comment when she
saw it. Mme. Charpentier was short, plump, and facially un-
remarkable. She stared critically. "Yes," she said, "she's quite
pretty. But what dreadful salt-cellars!" [9]

Sunny though the Samary portraits are, they seem conventional when put side by side with Renoir's other portrait exhibits, of Sisley and of a small girl, both painted because he

felt like it. The girl is interesting, she has the enormous Renoir eyes, but the Sisley is more than a study in color and design. Much had happened, almost all of it unpleasant, since Renoir had made his now famous studies of Sisley and his wife. The change from affluence to almost total poverty within a few months leaves it mark on any sensitive man, and this second well-known Sisley portrait is touchingly true. It is more, it is prophetic; in Sisley's face one sees the future only too clearly.

To the portraits and the Montmartre scenes Renoir added three landscapes, of which two, an autumnal study on the Seine at Champrosay, in which he cleverly contrives the effect of wind, and a May morning study of the Place Saint-Georges with its flowering chestnut trees, are so enchanting as to make one regret his lack of interest in this genre. There were three studies of men and women, Parisian to the last inch, two garden scenes, and two exquisitely painted flower pieces, of dahlias and of wild flowers. His handling of color and the luminosity of his canvases demonstrate how quickly he had learned his trade. The word is used advisedly because that was how he thought of it; he still believed he was struggling to find himself.

Whether this honest opinion saved him from yet another disappointment is another matter. He took two steps to try to propagate the Impressionist point of view. The first was to arrange with Rivière to put out a weekly newssheet, *L'Impressionniste*, during the four weeks of the exhibition. In this Rivière explained Impressionism simply and tried to show the public what each man was trying to do and what his special merits were. It is noticeable that the analysis of Renoir's exhibits is less convincing than those of the other painters and that the piece on Cézanne is stronger than any other. This supports the belief that Renoir inspired most of these comments. He admired Cézanne's work particularly, no doubt because it was so far removed from his own. He would prime Rivière to write perceptively about the one friend he believed to possess genius but would leave him to write what generalizations he pleased about himself. He also got a weight off his chest by writing two anonymous letters to Rivière for publication on the new architecture in Paris; he disliked the work of Louis Napoleon and his henchman Baron Haussman in clearing away the good old and replacing it with poor new; he now said so pungently.

This effort to popularize Impressionism or at least persuade visitors to suspend judgment until they had looked hard and often at the pictures had no obvious success. The articles in the little journal were no doubt too uniformly eulogistic to carry conviction. Rivière would have done well to criticize more often. Nor did Renoir's other definite effort meet with much response. This was uncharacteristic of him; he went to the office of the *République Française*, now run by Gambetta, intending to ask the great man to arrange for a favorable notice. Renoir never asked favors for himself; that he risked a snub shows what he feared for his less fortunate companions.

He not only risked a snub but got one. Gambetta was not there and his editor, Challenel-Lacour, refused the request for quite the wrong reason: "You ask me to speak of the Impressionists in our paper! Impossible. It would be a scandal. Have you forgotten what revolutionaries you are?"

The repulsed Renoir met Gambetta coming into the building as he was going out. He repeated the conversation. Gambetta reacted as he had hoped. "*You* are revolutionaries! Then what are *we* supposed to be?"

Renoir got his puff; Burty wrote it. It caused him little but embarrassment; Burty devoted most of his space and his praise to Renoir and his work. This was the first and last time Renoir tried to influence the press.[10]

There was more cause for embarrassment when it became clear that most of the journals which tried to report the exhibition with a certain objectivity treated him with an indulgence and at a length not granted to his friends. One critic spoke of the "superb color" [11] of his *Baigneuse*; another said, "as a portraitist he is in a class apart"; [12] another that "one would have to go back to Fragonard to find the kind of evocation of special atmosphere M. Renoir has put into the portrait of Mlle. Samary" [13] (that must have pleased him tremendously); and yet another, though dismissing the Samary picture as "less than nothing—simply a smile fixed on canvas," went on to praise *Le bal au Moulin de la Galette* to the skies: "This is like a shimmering rainbow." [14]

The painters themselves indulged in a little private byplay. Renoir, always good for a down-to-earth comment, looked at the Degas entries, thought whimsically of the painter's incessant criticisms of the Impressionist "color is line" and incessant abjurations "draw, draw, draw," and hit back with "Degas affects to despise color but is a colorist himself. The truth is, he doesn't like color in the work of others, he only permits it in himself." [15]

Degas was as observant and wittier. He looked at one of Lamy's offerings—his expression can be imagined—"and laughed that short laugh of his like the sound of his stinging, whiplash phrases: 'He is imitating Renoir, hein? But Renoir poses butterflies on his canvases, Lamy nails them there, eh, what?' " [16]

The moderately friendly high spirits were needed. For anyone not involved as they were the third exhibition could be seen as justification of Monet's and Pissarro's faith that persistence must break down the public's inevitable suspicion of novelty. There was more abuse than before but more support too, from journals which had discovered an artistic conscience or saw the writing on the wall and from men like Chocquet and Duret who spent hours in the gallery trying to educate the kind of visitors seen one day by Renoir—rich businessmen who stood in front of the canvases and shouted, "They ought to pay us to come in!" [17] There were plenty of unbelievers, plenty of scoffers, including for the first time hostile critics en masse, but they did not have matters all their own way as in the two previous exhibitions.

There was besides a note of desperation, almost of weariness, in the outpourings of these critics; their voices were louder, the abuse more scurrilous but the inner tone had changed; gone was the earlier conviction that these mad painters could safely be left to dig their own graves; indeed the critics were working altogether too hard with the shovel.[18]

More significant still, first the comic papers then the theatre took up the joke in a big way. The comic papers' idea of humor was on the crude side—a pregnant woman being advised by a gendarme to keep out of the exhibition hall if she did not want a miscarriage [19]—but the point was that they still saw the Impressionists as good material after three years of public existence; the joke had not faded.

The theatre provided even more striking evidence that the despised painters had become a Paris landmark. Soon after the exhibition Meilhac and Halévy wrote a farce, *La Cigale*, with an "Intentionniste" painter as clown-hero, whose paintings had the supreme advantage of being admirable either way up. The show was well done—Degas, with great good humor, drew the sketches for a third act skit on himself painting laundresses— and with such established authors and in a good theatre, the Variétés, it was a rousing success when put on that fall. Impressionism had come to stay.

2

It was too much to expect the painters to endure violent attacks for the third time running without some loss of heart. They sold one or two pictures, notably to a new supporter, the stock exchange broker and Sunday painter Paul Gauguin, who was taking the occasional weekend lesson from Pissarro; but in general the surface story of contempt and failure had been repeated, and they could not see beneath or beyond it. There were two possible means of retrieving their position; at the Legrand gallery in rue Laffitte (where the exhibition committee met) some of the unsold canvases were put on permanent exhibition, and on Renoir's suggestion they again decided to hold an auction of the rest.

No record of sales exists from the Legrand gallery, and it may be suspected that the "permanent exhibition" was held in the dark back of the gallery, if not in its basement.[20] The auction did not fare much better. Berthe Morisot's marriage had cut

into her work, and she had no spare canvases for auction, but
Caillebotte came in with Renoir, Sisley, and Pissarro. Forty-
five canvases were sold at an average of just over 150 francs,
Renoir's prices ranging from 47 to 285. Ironically, a Caillebotte
canvas fetched the highest price of nearly 700 francs.

This was discouraging, yet here too a prospect of better things
to come could be deduced. The average price was higher, even
if not greatly so, than at the previous auction. More significant,
the bidding was conducted with the utmost decorum; the
frenzied opposition of two years earlier had disappeared.

The Impressionist painters were too hard hit that fall and
winter to find much comfort in faintly favorable omens. They
were cold, hungry, they had to face illness and antagonism and,
worst of all, the ever present fear of being unable to paint for
want of colors or canvases. Monet's wife was pregnant, Pissarro's
hostile, Sisley was dependent on Duret, introduced to him by
Renoir, and the occasional loan from friends in England. All
were heavily in debt.[21]

Even Renoir was in trouble, but this was probably because
he was helping those worse off than himself. There seems no
particular reason why he could not make ends meet with the
occasional commission and his mother always good for food
and a bed. He was no more inclined to extravagance than in
his workshop days and less concerned to put money by. What
the recent spell of comparative affluence chiefly meant to him
was the chance to work free of worry and to help more people
more generously.

Rivière gives plenty of examples of the way in which he
spread his money about Montmartre. He was always helping
models and their families, particularly when, as often happened,
a model would find a protector, throw up posing with all the
hauteur of the newly rich woman, only to be knocking at the
studio door a few weeks later. Specifically at this time he could
not endure the sight of small children hanging about the streets
all day because the mother had to go out to work as well as the
father, when known. He appealed to Mme. Charpentier to help
him set up a day nursery. She agreed. Typically he chose to

raise the rest of the funds by putting on a music hall evening at
the Moulin, he and his friends doing all the turns. Everyone
enjoyed himself, but having gone to all the trouble of getting
up the show, he practically destroyed the object of it by charg-
ing an absurdly low entrance fee, hating to take even a few sous
from his poor dancing companions.[22] Where the balance of the
money came from when Mme. Charpentier had given her quota
is not difficult to imagine.

So by the winter of 1877 Renoir is in sufficiently low water
to write to Mme. Charpentier, who has sent him an invitation
to one of her soirées, "I thank you very much for thinking of me
and feel very grateful for it. But. Painting is leaving me a lot of
leisure just now, so I have turned house-painter. And having
joined the trade, I dare not ask my patron for time off, being too
new." [23]

He signs this note, "A. Renoir and Company," and students
of his life are left, not for the first time, with the dilemma, is
he serious, is he not? The idea that he would voluntarily give
up painting cannot be considered for one instant; he would
paint something, anything, rather than nothing, and so thoroughly did he follow this insatiable instinct that one of his
oldest friends was to say after his death that he did not believe
he passed a single day of his adult life without painting, except
when he felt too ill to lift a brush.[24]

The explanation in this case is almost certainly that, following his rule in all letters to Mme. Charpentier, he is joking
about the serious. The "patron" he dare not ask leave of was
none other than Eugène Murer. The "dare not" was nonsense,
of course, but the food and wine he was getting from Murer in
return for decorating his restaurant was anything but nonsense.
He had to have it and had to turn commercial to get it.

Murer had that year come up from Moulins, where he had
been a schoolmate of Guillaumin's. He was determined to insert
himself into the art world of Paris. He had a certain talent as
writer—he wrote poems of no special merit and managed to get
published a pornographic novel *La Mère Nom de Dieu*—but
this did not satisfy him; he wanted to paint after the Impres-

sionist manner. Being a practical young man, he began by collecting Impressionist canvases and by having portraits of himself and his sister painted by the men whose work he admired so much.[25]

He was able to do this at little cost. His true gift was not for the arts but for pastry making, and the Murers opened a small shop this autumn of 1877 which soon prospered. He arrived at a favorable moment for the businessman he undoubtedly was, for Guillaumin's Impressionist friends were in distress after the failure of exhibition and auction and eager to earn anything, even a free meal, to keep themselves painting. Murer employed them to decorate his restaurant, then exchanged canvases for meals and, when they were especially desperate, bought some for a few francs. How successful he was in acquiring a collection of his friends' work can be seen by the fact that a few years later when the Impressionists were being salable he and his sister are found managing a hotel in Rouen where he advertised "a magnificent collection of Impressionist paintings" on view free of charge as a bait to encourage both purchasers and hotel patrons.[26]

Murer's character remains in dispute—was he a true friend to these desperate men or was he taking advantage of their situation? Readers can judge for themselves by the evidence of his own words, the opinions of others, and the portraits of him and his sister made by Renoir and Pissarro. The bucolic-looking Marie and the elegant, rather foppish Eugène with the neat beard and mustache and the dreamy eyes are well-known likenesses today.

Rivière did not like Murer. He said that when Renoir could not pay his rent that winter Murer bought a batch of canvases from him for five hundred francs which he sold twenty years later for two hundred thousand. Rivière goes on to accuse Murer of never visiting his friends' studios but waiting for them to come to him.[27] This would mean that they were at the end of their resources and would sell canvases for a song or in exchange for supplies of food which would keep them going for a few days.

Pissarro, on the other hand, speaks of the Murers as being very kind to him.[28]

Perhaps a few words from Murer will clarify the point and, as it concerns this wretched winter of 1877–1878, it is also timely. "I lived in the Boulevard Voltaire," he writes, "in a shop decorated by the Impressionists. Renoir had brightened the friezes with spruce garlands of flowers. Pissarro, with a few strokes of the brush, had filled the panels with country views of Pontoise. Monet, always hard up and on the look out for the odd coin, contented himself by dropping in to see how the work was going on." [29]

Some readers may feel that the true Murer is revealed in the reference to Monet, the one man who refused absolutely to earn money in any other way than painting pictures he wanted to paint. He declined all commissions and would not take part in the decorating. It is worthy of note that Murer was unable to persuade him to make the family portraits.

Murer continues, "Every Wednesday for two years my friends and I met and talked at a friendly dinner presided over by my sister," and speaks of an evening when Pissarro did not turn up. "Over the dessert Renoir told us how he had spent the entire day walking the streets, a canvas under one arm, trying to sell it. Everywhere he went he was greeted with 'You're too late. Pissarro has been here already. I bought a picture from him. I had to, it was only humane, he has such a large family, poor chap!' [30]

"This 'Poor chap!' " wrote Murer, "irritated Renoir, already very dissatisfied by his failure to sell a single canvas. 'This is a fine thing!' he cried in his good-natured-ogre voice, rubbing his index finger nervously along his upper lip in the way we had become used to. 'So because I am unmarried and without children I have to starve? I'm in just as bad a state as Pissarro but nobody ever says "Poor Renoir"!' " [31]

This remark probably implied more than could be read into it. It was typical Renoir, antisentimental, logical, unassailable. Why indeed should Pissarro, who had freely and pleasurably provided himself with a large family, be treated better than a man who had been careful to deny himself such pleasures to save other people from embarrassment.

It was not, however, at all typical of Renoir to grudge Pissarro the first sales, and to understand the reason for this we have to look further, to an event of the utmost importance to him: he had decided to go back to the Salon.

3

There had already been talk of a fourth exhibition in the spring of 1878. Pissarro, Sisley, and Monet all pressed for it, the last most of all, for their position was becoming impossible. Monet's wife had never recovered from the birth of her second child, and the family was living wretchedly at Vetheuil farther downriver. Rents were cheaper there but still more than Monet could pay. Sisley was perhaps worst placed of all because his work, less strikingly original than that of his friends, was even more difficult to sell.

Renoir set his face against another exhibition. He said many times that he was not a fighter but often accused himself of flabbiness too harshly. In the present case his refusal to join the others—for that was what submission to the Salon meant—was made on the grounds of common sense. He had always had reservations about the rule keeping Impressionist exhibitors from the Salon. He had given way three times. As far as he could see the result had been harmful rather than otherwise; they had sold little, always to the converted; they had not convinced the public that they were serious painters; on the contrary they had made themselves a laughingstock.

In fact he was mistaken and allowed the obvious evidence to obscure a very real trend in favor of the new painting. This is a little surprising because he was so much sharper than the others. But given his dislike of unpopularity and public notice it is easy to imagine how he felt when pilloried in the press. Besides, as he insisted, he was not a sticker and was no believer in lost causes. He would not agree to a fourth exhibition; no arguments would move him.

This led to a little hard feeling—hence the petulant reference to Pissarro at Murer's—but Pissarro came round to his way of thinking, not about the desirability of submitting to the Salon but about postponing the Impressionist exhibition to the following year. The reason for his change of front was the great World's Fair of that year. The Fair was to be celebrated as usual by a state exhibition of French painting, an exhibition in which not one modern work was to be shown. Reacting indignantly, Durand-Ruel somehow managed to get enough support to put on a large exhibition of his own, an exhibition confined to the Barbizon painters, so that visitors to Paris should at least be able to see something of what original French painters had been doing within comparatively recent years.

As Durand-Ruel had not the courage to show the Impressionists, Pissarro decided that competition with the Salon, the Barbizon exhibition, and the official one in the Fair grounds would be too severe. He began to withdraw despite the pleas of Monet and Sisley.[32] Then he heard that Duret was at work on a pamphlet, *Les peintres impressionnistes*, which he hoped to publish that spring or summer. It would consist of biographical notices of Pissarro, Sisley, Monet, Renoir, and Berthe Morisot, and the text would try to prove, as Sylvestre had done years earlier, that their work was a natural evolution from French painting of the past. There would be a list of all their chief works and of the collectors who had bought them.

This settled the matter. There was no Impressionist exhibition, and Renoir's decision to submit work to the Salon of that year escaped with no more than a general air of disappointment. Degas, indeed, was sarcastic, but with an undertone of relief; he had never liked Renoir's paintings and took the line that the sooner they were rid of him the better.

There was, in any event, no element of surprise. As far back as the spring of 1877, just before the third exhibition, Renoir made clear that he also wanted to try for the Salon. His announcement brought about what was in effect an extraordinary

general meeting, which Degas urged Berthe Morisot to attend
in a note which added: "A momentous question is to be discussed: is it permitted to exhibit with the Salon as well as with
us? Very important!" [33]

The committee decided to adhere to the rules and to bar any
applicant who insisted on submitting work to the Salon.[34] To
Renoir, this hard and fast attitude cleared the air; he obeyed the
ruling but privately felt free to leave the outcome to the exhibition. If it succeeded, well and good; if not, he knew what to do
in the future. And when, in the immediate practical sense, the
third exhibition failed, he acted. He had had enough of what
Manet was to call "the back door" [35] method of getting into the
Salon. This led him, after the unsuccessful exhibition, to paint
what he considered a suitable picture for the Salon jury and
audience. His conscience was clear; he had given his friends a
full year's warning.

He was not alone in submitting to the Salon this year;
Cézanne tried again and Manet sent pictures as usual. Cézanne's
fate was the customary negative one; he was rejected in 1878 as
in all the previous years. Surprisingly, and to Manet's fury,
both his offerings were rejected. Only the newcomer, Renoir,
was admitted.

There has been much controversy about the merits of Renoir's successful entry *Marguerite* or *La tasse de chocolat*.
Some critics have described it as a chocolate-box picture; others
have seen it as a true Renoir, not Renoir at his best but sufficiently far above the usual Salon entry to deserve success. It is
unquestionably the kind of picture to appeal to a Salon jury
and audience, bright, cheerful and excellently painted; one has
only to study the woman's left hand to see this. Renoir would
scarcely have claimed more for it. And it emphasized his point,
that no painter could afford to neglect the Salon if he wanted
to go on painting, that he was bound to take advantage of every
means of showing and selling his work. The picture was well
talked of. For the first time the name Renoir began to mean
something to the large body of Parisians interested in painting.

He had reason to believe that he had prepared the way for

greater attention the next year and had made his plans for it. Thanks to the reception of *La tasse de chocolat* he had already been given a commission from Mme. Charpentier which he thought would really cause a stir because of her standing in Parisian society and would probably be well hung. This was a composite group of her and her two daughters.

His friends were running into disaster. The Duret pamphlet was followed by two dreadful shocks, the sale of Faure's collection and of Hoschedé's. The baritone put his Impressionist works on the market in the belief that Duret's pamphlet would have helped to make them respectable. He was forced to buy most of them back; the bids failed to reach even the moderate reserve prices.

The case of Hoschedé was even worse. In June he fell into bankruptcy. The forced sale of his paintings resulted in farcical bids, an average of less than two hundred francs for Monet canvases, of just over one hundred for Sisley, of little more for Pissarro. For a time all was despair; even the ever youthful Pissarro declared that he was "done for." [36] Camille Monet was slowly dying and her husband was forced to beg—from Zola, from Charpentier, from Chocquet, offering canvases "at any price you care to name, forty or fifty francs." [37] Sisley was rescued at the last moment by Duret, who found a buyer for a group of landscapes at low prices, but he could not forget what he and his family had had to suffer ever since the war. [38]

Sisley's loss of faith was shown that winter when Pissarro, his optimism rebounding under the encouragement of Caillebotte, began to canvass for another exhibition in the spring of 1879. Sisley, his eye on Renoir, refused to exhibit; he intended to submit to the Salon. "It is true that our exhibitions have helped to make us known," he told Duret, "and to that extent they have helped me too. But I don't feel we ought to stay in the wilderness any longer. We are still a long way from being independent of the prestige one gains by showing at official exhibitions. That's why I have made up my mind to submit to the Salon. If I am accepted—and I believe I stand a chance this year—I think I may be able to sell some pictures." [39]

Renoir was equally adamant; his portrait of Mme. Charpentier and her children had been painted specifically with the Salon in mind; she expected him to offer it there, and he, after the first mild success of *La tasse de chocolat,* had every intention of doing so.

In April, 1879, therefore, the Impressionists opened their fourth exhibition with a truncated list of fifteen exhibitors: Renoir, Sisley, and Berthe Morisot (who was pregnant and had not been working) were not represented. Monet's work was shown but he could not be persuaded to come up to Paris. He stayed, bitter and savage, at Vetheuil by the side of the dying Camille.

By the end of the month the exhibition was clearly being taken seriously. The bulk of the press remained against it, but the public had begun to behave itself and buyers were appearing. For the first time a profit was made—400 francs per exhibitor.[40] For the first time, much more vitally, the name Impressionist was moving out of the realms of fun and abuse into a title for painting to be respected. There was still a long road ahead but the faithful ones, Pissarro especially, could visualize ultimate victory.

When this crucial exhibition closed in the middle of May, the 1879 Salon opened. No pictures by Sisley were to be seen there—they had been rejected—but Renoir's *Madame Charpentier et ses enfants* was the center of attention.

His faith in his powerful *patronne* had not been mistaken, as he said in his own way some years later: "To be fair, I have had one canvas well placed at the Salon. This was, it is true, the portrait of Mme. Charpentier. Mme. Charpentier wanted to be seen in a good light, she knew the members of the jury and gave them a thorough shake up." He added wryly, "But this didn't prevent them, when I sent them the little Mendès children later, from putting it under the roof where not a soul could see it." [41]

For that matter it did not prevent the hanging committee of 1879 from placing the *Jeanne Samary* up on the third row, not precisely out of sight but well out of reach of competition with the Charpentier portrait. Renoir's smile must have been twisted when he first saw it.

Mme. Charpentier had done what she had set out to do. Her portrait always had an admiring crowd before it, and critics fell over themselves to hail the painter's "delicate and original talent." [42] Renoir had arrived.

CHAPTER XII

———

SUCCESS AND AFTER

———

1879-1881

RENOIR'S REACTION to this first considerable success was in character. He made the most of the unusual attention paid to him at the Charpentiers' and their friends', not so much by indulging vanity—his sense of humor kept that well down—as by trying to provide for the future. He knew or suspected that people like Mme. Charpentier were liable to tire of each discovery and move on to the next. More to the point, perhaps, he himself was liable to tire of a life which, however it might titivate him, was not what he had been brought up to. A man who disliked academic discussion and respected art must have found something repellent in society people flickering over the surface. At these soirées cleverness and wit were supposedly the rule, but most of the visitors could muster nothing better than a bright and silly manner, and it is difficult not to believe that Renoir was often bored and uneasy. He was to say later, "Gambetta was the only intelligent man there." [1] He could scarcely have judged more harshly.

So, with eventual escape well within his sights, he followed a guiding principle to take every advantage of the moment and, following another principle, used that advantage to help others. On his wife's advice Charpentier had begun an art journal, *La Vie Moderne*—the title sufficiently describes his aims—and produced a novelty in the form of one-man exhibitions in a gallery attached to the editorial offices, so that readers could see and judge for themselves an artist's work discussed simultaneously in the journal.

Renoir struck two useful blows; he persuaded Charpentier to employ Edmond as manager of the gallery and art critic of the journal and recommended exhibitions of Monet and Sisley, the one because he thought him the best Impressionist painter, the other because he felt responsible for the failure to get into the Salon. He, of course, would obviously be the first exhibitor; the journal was published before the Salon opened, and after the Salon closed he showed a number of pastels. His brother discussed them in detail in the corresponding number.[2]

The attempt to arrange a Sisley exhibition failed—he was the unluckiest of all Impressionists. The Monet proposal was favorably received but with the proviso that he return to the Salon, in which Mme. Charpentier was, of course, a firm believer; as summer had come by the time the Renoir show was over, and Paris began to empty, the question of who would be exhibited next was left open. Renoir celebrated his good luck by taking his first long vacation outside Paris and its suburbs.

His division of time is interesting. At the Charpentiers' he had been introduced by Spuller to two influential friends. One was Deudon the financier, who bought *Jeune danseuse* at a handsome price. The other was a member of the diplomatic corps, Paul Bérard, head of an old French banking family. Renoir and Bérard took to one another, and the result was an invitation to the Château de Wargemont near Dieppe to make a portrait of the eldest Bérard girl.

This was to be the first of a number of summer visits by Renoir, profitable visits in every way; on Bérard's death in 1905 eighteen Renoirs were sold, and this does not take account of the many portraits kept by the family. He liked the Bérards with fewer reservations than usual in this kind of friendship, and they liked him. His work in consequence shows less stiffness and opulence than when he is living up to the rich or well-born or earning his commission as he thinks they would wish to spend it.

He got down to work right away and with quick success; the portrait of Marthe Bérard was so much liked that he painted another, as well as one of Mme. Bérard. He made a study of the famous rose garden and relaxed further: *Les rosiers à Wargemont* is one of the rare pictures of this time without a trace of the human element and is one of the best; the rose trees, delicately brushed in, are skillfully set against a lightly sketched background of château. "Renoir's magnificent rose garden," Vincent van Gogh was to say of it.[3]

After Renoir's death, one of the Bérard family wrote about his visits, how fond everyone was of him and how easy he appeared with all. No doubt he did; his ability to suit himself to his company seldom failed. What perhaps the Bérards did not realize was how much his social ease stemmed from a true democracy. Unlike the present-day democrat, Renoir had no wish to dispossess or humiliate his social superiors. Indeed, he was to make more than one remark before he died which indicated that he foresaw and deplored the misdirected triumph of the common man. His aim, in every way sensible, was self-respect. To attain that, he learned early, it was necessary to be oneself as much as possible. Add a natural wish to please, and Renoir at Wargemont comes into focus.

Faced as he was daily with a conjunction of his hosts and of the army of servants who waited on them, he did not attempt to mask his affinities; though he obviously enjoyed much of his time with the Bérard parents and children, he enjoyed himself even more obviously with their staff. And this, far from causing offense, made him more popular with everybody. The most cordial and most revealing part of the account of him at Wargemont is the picture of a Renoir up at the crack of dawn to hobnob with the servants. Early every morning the Bérard omnibus set off for Dieppe to collect the day's provisions, and every morning Renoir was on it "with the chef and the butler, whom he treated like pals." [4]

He was, not surprisingly, happiest of all when he got away from family and staff, taking brushes, colors and canvases to the nearby coast; he was, after all, a painter, not a professional guest. He walked down to Pourville and made the charming *Maisons à Pourville* and a dramatic cliff study; he visited the little fishing port of Berneval where he made his *Pêcheuse de moules à Berneval*—the contrast between his renderings of the three ragged children and the Bérard children is instructive—and he made many studies of the little beach nearest to Wargemont where the family and their friends went to bathe. *La Plage* is Renoir at his Impressionist best, shimmering in sunlight, a breeze rustling the trees. Everything breathes happiness from dancing waves to frolicking groups of bathers.

A few weeks later he painted another Impressionist canvas, which has a similar appeal but is based on a different outlook, for this canvas was painted on the reach of the river at Chatou just below La Grenouillère where he had joined Caillebotte and his friends for a final open air fling before he settled into his studio for the winter. His choice of companions after the Bérard stay was significant; with them he could open out, talk freely and broadly. *Les canotiers à Chatou* reflects the high-spirited relief. Caillebotte stands negligently on the river bank, a woman friend behind him and the boatman who is just pushing a skiff into the water. The greater part of the canvas is given up to the river, the rippled water beautifully painted with small brushstrokes, the few skiffs, a barge and yacht, but the main interest is firmly placed on the figures in the foreground. Everything shines—it is another sparkling scene—and an atmosphere of carefree holiday fills the canvas. It is dominated by red, a glorious red on the woman's jacket, the sculler's sash, a wild flower, the skiffs, barge and roofs on the opposite bank, which throws up the silver-blue of the water. Renoir had rarely painted better, and it is permissible to see in this work a reaction to weeks on his best behavior.

2

Back in the studio he began to prepare for the next Salon. The progress made by his friends in the last Impressionist exhibi-

tion did not move him. He had begun to make his name and
intended to go on the way he had chosen. His aim was already
clear. It was decidedly not to bask in the smiles of the Charpentiers and their friends and depend on their commissions for a
living. He saw beyond this. A new dealer had set up in Paris.
His name was Georges Petit; he had money and his aim was
avowedly to capture the rich with advanced paintings. He was
prepared to educate the public to a certain extent—he was
trying to fill the void left by Durand-Ruel's withdrawal—but
because he depended largely on snob appeal, he was not prepared to risk taking up non-Salon painters.

Renoir was bent on selling through Petit. He had the money,
he had progressive ideas. He might be persuaded to take canvases that had been painted for the sheer love of it, in which
case Renoir would have reached the position he was after, to
earn a living wage from work he wanted to do. All that was
needed was the cachet of the Salon, not once but several years
running.

Renoir hated business.[5] Since a child he had seen the businessman in operation, beginning with the marking and selling of
china as Sèvres which had nothing to do with Sèvres. He did not
forget. He knew that the dealer deserved some share of an
artist's profits for his foresight and the risk he took. He also
knew that he did not deserve as much as the man who created
the work of art but that he invariably took more, much more, as
much as he could get without losing his milch cow.

Renoir had learned his lesson. He was a man of thirty-eight.
If one goes by the expectation of life one hundred years ago,
thirty-eight then is at least forty-five today. Yet he had only just
managed to rescue himself from penury. He did not miss the
moral. He wanted to go to Petit because Petit paid comparatively high prices for a dealer, but he had no intention of
allowing Petit a monopoly. There was one way and one way
only of keeping the businessman within bounds—to face him
with one or more competitors—and that was Renoir's plan.
Durand-Ruel would be back in action, of that he was sure, and
Durand-Ruel should be offered his work as soon as he was in

the market for it again. So also would Petit and any other reputable dealer who opened a gallery in Paris.

Monet agreed absolutely with him when he explained.[6] They decided to stand together. For this winter of 1879–1880 Renoir won an ally and the Impressionists lost yet another exhibitor. Monet wanted a show at the gallery of *La Vie Moderne*, but that was not the chief reason for his change of heart. He was bitter. Camille Monet was dead and he no longer cared to stick to the principle which had perhaps cost her life. He decided to follow Renoir back into the Salon.

The decision led to a partial break-up of the Impressionist group. Caillebotte and Pissarro behaved nobly. Pissarro's reaction to Renoir's Salon success had been, "I believe he is launched. So much the better! Poverty is so hard," [7] and he was equally generous with Monet now. But Degas was furious. He could spare Renoir with ease but had come to respect Monet's work and still more Monet himself. He accused him of log-rolling. He refused to speak to him or Renoir and asked Caillebotte, "Do you receive people like that in your house?" [8]

This absurdly exaggerated spitefulness expressed, as so often in a man of Degas' strange and difficult character, a disillusionment which was most unwelcome to him. Too critical and clear-sighted for his own happiness, he deeply admired few men. Monet had been one of the few, and Degas could not forgive his treachery, as he saw it.

Caillebotte, struggling to keep the peace and preserve a yearly exhibition, said if any man had the right to complain it was Pissarro; Renoir, Monet, and Sisley (who also withdrew for the second year running) were his friends and not Degas'.[9] But Pissarro knew what hunger and despair were.

When Monet, asked later why he had exhibited with the Impressionists in the first place, replied, "For a long time my friends and I were refused systematically by the Salon jury. What were we to do? One can't paint in a vacuum, one had to sell because one has to eat," [10] he was talking the language of Pissarro. When he gave a similar reason for moving back to the Salon, where Renoir had proved that the Impressionist

untouchables could in fact be admitted, Pissarro understood
that too. He intended to stick to his principles but did not
blame others for weakening. It may be that he was large-minded
enough to understand that Renoir and Monet, supported by
Duret and Duranty, believed that the time had come to carry
the war into the enemy's camp. They argued that if the Salon
admitted them it was an admission of the triumph of the Impressionist cause.

So the split came. The fifth Impressionist exhibition, of 1880,
contained only Pissarro, Guillaumin, and Berthe Morisot of
the true Impressionist painters, and it was little wonder that
the critics were confused. One of the newcomers, Gauguin, the
only one with a hint of greatness, was overshadowed by a
protégé of Degas', Raffaelli, who showed thirty-five works, all
weakly Impressionist. He did the exhibition great harm, and it
may well be that Monet had him chiefly in mind when, asked
if he was no longer an Impressionist since he had stopped exhibiting with them, replied, "I am and always shall be an Impressionist . . . but the little band has become a banal school which
opens its doors to the first dauber who knocks." [11]

Renoir had no objection to naming names. He said of
Raffaelli, "Everything in his pictures is rotten, even the grass." [12]
Then he forgot him. Apart from the coldness of a Degas rapidly
feeling that he had gone too far and whom he rarely saw, all
was as before. He worked hard through winter and spring,
although not so happily as in recent years. He was preoccupied
by technique and the approach to his work, poised between
society portraits, Impressionism, and the rendering of the Montmartre scene in a variety of styles. He did not know how he
wanted to paint except that the pull of the past was as strong
as ever.

The problem is reflected in his work of the time: a circus
study, *Au Cirque Fernando*, faintly Degas in treatment, perhaps
to show he bore no malice, some nudes reminiscent of the
antique painters and sculptors, a pastel of Cézanne, who had
come up to Melun to paint, a still life in the Cézanne manner, a
street scene, *Place Pigalle*, which owed much in layout to the

Japanese vogue then on its way, two society portraits, *Mademoiselle Grimpel au ruban rouge* and *Mademoiselle Grimpel au ruban bleu*, both highly finished after the Italians, and one of the canvases he intended for the Salon, *Jeune fille endormie au chat*, painted strictly in the Impressionist mode.

This last had a story. The model Angèle was a girl after Renoir's heart, cheeky, outspoken, and a good teller of tales about Montmartre bandits, all in rich and pungent argot. She was one of the gay working girls of the time; her conception of seeing life was to sleep with any man who attracted her and offered an evening out. Her mother reproved her in her own way. "You'll tire yourself out," she used to say. Angèle took no notice. The result was that she passed her Sundays in a state of somnolence. When she found herself in Renoir's solitary armchair she fell fast asleep, the cat on her lap. He liked the pose and painted her as she slept.[13]

He offered this and *Pêcheuse de moules à Berneval* to the Salon jury. Monet submitted two landscapes, one his remarkable study of ice on the river at Vetheuil, *La Débâcle*. True to form, the jury rejected it. They accepted Monet's less revolutionary landscape and both Renoir pictures, but all three were so badly hung that the disgusted friends sent a joint letter of protest to the Minister of Fine Arts. Having little faith in action from that quarter, they tried to force his hand—they demanded a fair view for all accepted pictures—by reprinting the letter in a newspaper. They sent a copy to Cézanne and asked him to approach the now very powerful Zola.

Zola agreed to publish the letter with comments of his own. The comments were not always to the liking of his former associates at the Guerbois; he praised Renoir and Monet for their good sense in returning to the Salon, announced that Impressionism as a group no longer existed but that as an influence it was affecting French painting, and ended with a complaint that no Impressionist painter had managed to live up to his program. He repeated what another Guerbois supporter, Edmond Duranty, had said four years earlier in his little booklet *La Nouvelle Peinture*. The intention was to defend Impressionism but when summing up he had allowed himself to write, "The voyage is dangerous and they ought to have set out in larger, stronger ships"—a remark which went far to cancel his praise of the new painting. Now Zola ended his article praising Impressionism as the obvious painting of the future with the remark "not a single painter in the group has managed to apply the new formula powerfully and definitely . . . all remain unequal to their self-appointed task." [14]

Renoir's answer to this sour-sweet condescension was practical as usual. He completed arrangements for Monet's one-man show at the *Vie Moderne* office in June (Manet had had a very successful one in April) and himself looked about for further commissions. The Monet show was decisive. The press reaction was almost unanimously favorable. Duret spoke of Monet as one of the masters, the only truly original landscape artist since Corot; [15] young Paul Signac begged to be taken as his pupil.[16] It was the turning point; Monet was on his slow way to fame, he was never again to go hungry or short of paints and canvases.

Nor, for that matter, was Renoir. The days of struggle for a good meal were over. He was anything but rich and was to have many anxious moments, but for the time being his rich friends ensured him a reasonable income and, if he wished, free holidays in luxurious and beautiful quarters.

"I hear that Monet has sold some of the pictures exhibited at Charpentier's," Cézanne told Zola, "and Renoir has received some good portrait commissions." [17] He was no doubt referring to Renoir's latest conquests. As if to emphasize how well he was thought of by his society connections, Renoir met yet another great French family, the Cahen d'Anvers, and was given a commission to make a portrait of the eldest daughter. He was also introduced by Bérard to the banker Ephrussi, wealthy, lively, a powerful friend and, when Renoir was in the mood, a companion rather after the style of Lhotte and Lestringuez (with whom Ephrussi quickly became an intimate), but with the advantage of a fortune behind him.

Renoir seemed at last to be on the point of achieving the state he had aimed at for so many years. In theory he ought to have been content. Yet there were many signs this year of 1880 that he was going through a spiritual crisis or, if that sounds too dramatic for him, through a long bout of uncertainty and uneasiness. He was discovering that the policy of drift had disadvantages as well as delights. It could lead a man into several paths at once, all of which might be dead ends. He was also having to reckon with the passing of time and the effect of conscience.

To take the passing of time first. He was in his fortieth year. He was one of those people who are eternally young at heart, but this does not mean that he could accept silliness indefinitely. The life of Montmartre was charming, it was also frivolous. Nothing in this world is simple and his position was not simple; he could spend part of the time telling himself that he was getting too old for that essentially young people's world and the rest of the time feeling the charm of it with all the old magnetism. The changes of address tell their own story; in the next year he was to move studios three times as if hoping that a fresh street in the old Montmartre quarter might begin life again for him.

This was asking for disillusionment. Other difficulties arose. The moment he began to make money fairly handsomely, it was hard to avoid asking himself what he thought of the way he was making it. Was it not coming altogether too easily? His mind was not wholly clear about the commissioned portraits—the canvases demonstrate this clearly—nor could he have been completely happy about leaving the Impressionists. Pissarro was too nice a man, Caillebotte and Berthe Morisot had been too good friends, for him to be able to jettison them, even from the painting point of view, without a pang, especially as they all remained as friendly as ever.

Add the fact that he was worrying increasingly about the various styles in which he was painting—as if he said to himself, experiment is all very well at twenty or thirty but at forty one ought to have made up one's mind—add his very real modesty which made him doubt at times whether he could draw or paint at all, and it will be seen that he had cause for thought.

Then there was Cézanne in Paris. He had just set up house in the southern suburb of Plaisance after his year at Melun. To make a portrait of Cézanne, as Renoir had recently done, was an experience not to be forgotten; to talk to him, to listen, to look at his work was chastening. No one knew what Cézanne was in terms of group classification. He had shown for the last time with the Impressionists. He no more knew where he was going than Renoir, but it was to be his way and nobody else's way. He knew, as Renoir knew, that he had far to go, but he had confidence in his worth as Renoir had not. Five years earlier he had told his mother, "I begin to think myself better than all those round me and you will know that this good opinion I have of myself has only been arrived at after long and careful thought. I must go on working but not so that I can give my pictures the finish which wins the admiration of fools. . . . I must try to perfect what I do for the pleasure of reaching greater truth and knowledge. And believe me, the time will inevitably come when I shall force people to recognize and admire my work and they will be more ardent and more convinced than those flattered simply by surface appearance." [18]

It is improbable that Cézanne repeated this noble affirmation to Pissarro, Monet, or Renoir, the three painters he preferred as men after Guillaumin, but it was not necessary to speak; his faith and determination to live up to it shone out to the observant. Renoir had seen genius in Cézanne the moment he met him. In the Impressionist newssheet during the exhibition of 1877 Cézanne was hailed, nominally by Rivière, but a Rivière primed by Renoir, as a great painter: "His still lives, so precise in their relationship of tones, possess the solemn quality of truth. In all his work he evokes emotion because he himself feels strong emotion in the face of nature." [19]

There were many in Paris who saw in Cézanne only the "farceur" of Manet,[20] a foul-mouthed, antisocial hobbledehoy. Renoir, with his love for the working people, would never make this mistake; he understood Cézanne's wish to keep the pretentious at a distance and to test his new friends to the uttermost. If he wished to speak and act like the lowest of Midi peasants,

Renoir sympathized. But Cézanne could speak in quite another fashion when he met a man who treated him as a fellow explorer. Renoir heard, admired, and his doubts mounted, doubts of Impressionism, doubts of the wisdom of continuing with commissioned portraits. Some years earlier he had moved from Left to Right Bank, in part to escape the possible effect on his work of too much hobnobbing with the romantic painters of the Fantin school. He saw a greater danger ahead, if he was not wary, of becoming the modern Bonnat, society portraitist.

To a man in this mood Cézanne was a portent, a disturber of the peace, and perhaps a savior too. Renoir listened to: "The painter possesses two things, an eye and a brain. The two must work together. Both must be developed to meet the painter's needs, the eye by looking at nature, the brain by logically organizing the sensations which lead to the form of expression." [21] Was he really looking at nature, the human kind? Was he organizing his sensations?

3

Renoir's answer to all this was to remove himself from everything with the power to unsettle and to go back to what he considered his beginnings as a serious painter. He returned to Mère Fournaise on the river between Chatou and Bougival and spent summer and fall there with his mother and sister. He sailed and painted with Caillebotte and as often as possible saw Monet, his companion and leader in those unforgettable weeks at La Grenouillère.

When he came back to Paris his mind was made up; he must get right away. Symbolically, he changed studios; he still kept rue Saint-Georges as base but left the Montmartre rooms. He had money in his pocket and knew how to get more for the journey he had in mind. The portrait of the eldest Cahen d'Anvers daughter had delighted the illustrious family, as well it might. Renoir had taken great pains with it and his artistry is everywhere apparent, in treatment of hair, background, pose.

He was never to paint a better commissioned portrait. As with the Bérards, the eldest daughter was used as a guinea pig; only if the painter succeeded with her was he invited to proceed with the more costly family group. Renoir was not so much invited as besought to paint the daughters together. The fee alone would give him the vacation he wanted, in Algeria.

Renoir had no sooner begun to make money and Monet to escape from starvation diet at Vetheuil than Durand-Ruel struggled back into the picture market. The recession was not over but relaxing, and Durand-Ruel's powerful friend Feder of the great Union Générale helped to put him on his feet. One of Durand-Ruel's first thoughts was of the men he had had to abandon six years earlier. He began with Sisley, now the chief sufferer, but bought from them all.

Renoir received this new approach with caution. He declined offers of money. He had all he needed for the moment and suspected that the dealer had an ulterior motive, as he had; it was Durand-Ruel's aim to get the Impressionist painters away from the Salon and into an exhibition of their own which he would back. He had one weakness, as Renoir was to say later: he wanted to own his painters. He had cornered the market in the Barbizon painters; he wanted to do the same with the Impressionists. Renoir disliked monopolies, having noticed that they invariably ended in reduced prices. He was always to be grateful to Durand-Ruel but always wary of him too.

Before the question could come to a head, he was off; by March he was in Algiers. He left two portraits for submission to the Salon, left them with Ephrussi, whose name and wealth might sway the jury and hanging committee. He went to Algeria because Delacroix had painted there—he wanted to discover the source of his luscious greens, purples, blues—and because he had never forgotten Monet's description of the translucent atmosphere which brought out the colors.

He began badly, with all the frustrations of the tourist arrived in a southern country he fondly imagines is bathed day by day in sun blazing from a cloudless sky. "It is a fine country," he told Mme. Charpentier after days in which he had not touched a brush, "but it seems that I've been unlucky, which doesn't surprise me. Everybody told me it never rained here but up to the present every time I've put my nose out of doors I've had to change my clothes immediately, all of them." [22]

He added, consolingly, "But what a wonderful countryside when the weather's fine, incredibly rich and with such thick vegetation!" He found consolations (and distractions) in the persons of Lhotte, Lestringuez, and Cordey whom he met in Algiers. They had no doubt been seduced by his descriptions before he left of the marvels he would paint there.

Before he could return to France he had dealt with Durand-Ruel's pleas that he rejoin the Impressionist fold and contribute to the sixth exhibition Pissarro was organizing. The dealer reproached him for causing hard feeling and joined himself with those who said that he was betraying his friends and his cause by submitting to the Salon.

Renoir did not change his mind, and the sixth exhibition was held that April without him, Monet, Sisley, and Cézanne. But he did not relish the role of renegade, and tried to make his position clear to his old backer and associates. "I will try to explain to you why I submit to the Salon," he wrote to Durand-Ruel. "There are scarcely fifteen collectors able to appreciate a painter outside the Salon. There are eighty thousand who wouldn't buy even a nose if the painter hadn't shown it in the Salon. That's why I send two portraits every year, poor though they be. Besides, I don't want to fall into the absurdity of thinking that a thing is bad or good just because of the place in which it is seen. In a word I don't want to waste my time inveighing against the Salon. I don't even want to look as though I did. I simply want to paint as well as I can and that's all. Ah, if I was accused of neglecting my art or of going against my principles for the sake of some idiotic ambition, then I could understand my critics. But as there's nothing in this, no one even suggests such a thing to me, quite the contrary. At this minute I'm busy as I always have been in trying to do good things. I want to paint outstanding pictures for you that you can sell at high prices. I shall reach this point soon, I hope. I have gone away far from all painters, to think hard under the sun. I believe I've got somewhere and have found what I was after. I may be wrong but I shall be astonished if I am. Have a little patience and I hope to give you proof that it is possible to submit to the Salon and to do good painting.

"I beg you to plead my cause with my friends. My submissions to the Salon are purely commercial. In any case it is like certain medicines, if they don't do you any good they won't do you harm either.

"I believe that I'm pulling myself together again. I am going to work hard and save myself.

"I wish you excellent health and lots of wealthy collectors. But keep them till I get back. I shall be here another month. I don't want to leave Algiers without bringing back something from this marvellous country." 23

The canvases he brought back with him in April must be counted a disappointment. He made studies of one or two Arab types—*Jeune Arabe* and *Fillette au falcon*, for instance—but it is difficult to believe that he could not have made them without going outside Paris. There is no sign that he understood anything about the people he was painting, nor could he be expected to understand them. He was six weeks in Algeria. The greatest genius in the world could not assimilate a race strange to him in such a period.

His landscapes also disappoint; *La Mosque* and *Le Ravin* are rich in unbridled color but seem less Renoir than a painter determined to work close to Delacroix; they are indifferently composed and do not suggest Algeria in anything but picture-postcard sense. In one canvas alone did he strike a new note. In *Les Bananiers* the plants have obviously fascinated him sufficiently to demand careful study; he carries his fascination into a well-constructed picture with colors skillfully applied to suggest the climate in which they flourished.

He came back happily enough, feeling fitter and less torn between the various ways open to him. He had not found himself but was clearer-minded. What he could not have imagined was that his life was on the point of taking another and decisive turn.

CHAPTER XIII

———

MARRIAGE AND REAPPRAISAL

———

1881-1882

Renoir's age had a considerable bearing on a more important matter than doubts of his fitness to enjoy youthful foolishness and determination to cash in on his painting. Within limits he had decided to settle down and had found the woman with whom he wanted to settle.

Renoir says next to nothing about Aline Charigot—he was always reticent about himself and never more so than in his courtship—and Rivière contents himself with generalities. Jean Renoir has reconstructed the love story of his mother and father with tact and tenderness. Here it is necessary only to give the bare outline.

Renoir met his future wife when he was lunching at the crémerie opposite his rue Saint-Georges studio. The owner of the little shop—a dairy which, in Paris fashion, also provided simple meals for a few regulars—came from the Aube. This district just above Burgundy is often regarded as part of that region; the river Aube rises less than thirty miles north of Dijon, the Burgundy capital. For the purpose of this story they might be one and the same, for the people of the Aube sound just like the Burgundians, who speak slowly and deliberately and roll their r's gutturally; they can always be picked out of a crowd of Frenchmen.

Provincials living in Paris are clannish. One day Mme.

Camille heard the Burgundian accent in her crémerie. She at once questioned the speaker and discovered a Mme. Charigot from the Aube who lived in the same Paris street. They became friendly, and when Mme. Charigot's daughter began to earn her living she lunched regularly at the crémerie, as Renoir did.[1]

It is not certain when Renoir first met Aline there. At the time he settled at rue Saint-Georges in 1873 she was only eleven, twenty-one years his junior. Like her mother and Renoir's mother she became a seamstress, but whereas Mme. Charigot sewed at home, Aline was taken on by a Dijonnaise dressmaker on the Butte. Girls went to work young in those days, and Aline probably began to lunch at the crémerie when she was fourteen.

She and Renoir took to one another quickly; she seems to have posed for La Tonnelle that same year and certainly posed for Sortie du Conservatoire the year after, when she was fifteen. Rivière remembers Renoir's despair when he could not reproduce her face to his satisfaction as he saw it in front of him. He was seeking as always to perpetuate the youthful brightness of eye and skin and the suggestion of unawakened femininity that enthralled him.[2]

Aline Renoir must be the most frequently painted wife in the history of the art. Every lover of French painting knows her face as well as he knows his own and understands why she interested and then fascinated the painter. She is the essence of what is known as the Renoir girl; she had the "catlike" face he loved—rounded, with small nose, large and slightly almond-shaped eyes, and creamy complexion. She looked domesticated, nothing of the blue-stocking, and this too he must have liked, for he did not think women should have to earn a living. He believed they only developed fully in the home.

For some years there was no question of marriage—she was too young, he too poor—but they saw a fair amount of each other. She became a good dancer and swimmer and accompanied him to dances and to the river, although she danced mostly with the experts Cordey and Lestringuez; Renoir was rather heavyfooted. They do not seem to have discussed an engagement. Apart from her youth and his poverty there were two obstacles—Renoir's fear of committing himself and a woman to the kind of life he had seen in the Monet and Sisley homes, and the objection of Mme. Charigot, who considered a painter a bad match.[3]

What soon emerges is Aline's good sense; she was a true daughter of her province where the virtues of thrift, moderation, and pride in housekeeping are preeminent. In days when women affected many airs, she remained placidly herself; she had a good appetite unlike Renoir and did not attempt to hide or suppress it. She knew her own mind and how to deal with her mother; maternal complaints she thought unreasonable were countered with a threat to withhold money earned by her needlework and posing.[4]

When Renoir went off to Algeria she had reached nineteen, a marriageable age, and it is probable that part at least of the struggles about which he tells Durand-Ruel were not due to painting but to a contest between his wish to settle down and his wish to travel, broaden his mind, and perhaps arrive at a style of painting all his own. The forties are often a difficult time for unmarried men, particularly so when, as in the case of Renoir, lack of money has hindered them from seeing anything of the world beyond their own close circle of friends. He had only just begun to feel the lure of ready money to spend, and he was curious, energetic, young at heart, ambitious. The conflict between this restlessness and his love for Aline with the kind of domesticity she would expect must have been prolonged and severe.

It seems that some part of that reflection under the sun of which he speaks must have settled his thoughts on the matter. This became apparent when he returned to France in time for the 1881 Salon. Duret, then on a visit to England, wrote to Renoir and urged him to come over. He knew his proclivities and tempted him with a pen picture of English feminine beauty.

Perhaps somewhat to his own astonishment and certainly to Duret's, Renoir declined. He could not bring himself to make the journey, he said, even to see "charming English girls." He was apologetic: "It is a misfortune to be forever hesitant but then that is the basis of my character. And as I'm getting older I fear there's no chance that I can alter myself." He added, "The weather is very good here and I have models. That is my only excuse." [5] He meant, the only excuse he was prepared to give or to enlarge on.

He was at his beloved spot, the reach between Bougival and Chatou, once more, boating, bathing, dancing with a crowd of old friends, and he was expressing his feelings as always with a painting which, perhaps more than anything he was to do, immortalized these happy days under the sun. *Le déjeuner des canotiers* showed these friends on the balcony of La Grenouillère just after they had finished lunch. On the tables are bottles of wine and dishes of fruit. Around them, sitting, standing, talking, young, happy, at ease, are the friends. Among the men are Caillebotte, Lhotte, Lestringuez, Ephrussi, and one of the few nonartistic people of Renoir's large acquaintance, the harum-scarum Baron Barbier, introduced years back by Bibesco and relished greatly by the painter for his eternal youth. Among the girls are Angèle, the model for *Jeune fille endormie*, and Mlle. Henriot. The presence of sunshine is everywhere felt and a delightful freedom of action which matches the holiday surroundings. The men's clothes range from top hat and morning dress to straw hats and a singlet, the girls' from Mlle. Henriot's smart outfit to the simplest of summer dresses and flowered hat.

The picture is in a direct line from *Le bal au Moulin de la Galette* and *Les canotiers à Chatou*, yet one senses extra joyousness in it, for the girl in the foreground of the picture, arms on table, hands propping up a little dog, was Aline Charigot.

If further cause for cheerfulness was needed, Berthe Morisot and her husband Eugène Manet with their small daughter Julie were at Bougival for the summer. Renoir loved to visit this versatile and hospitable couple and they were charmed by his unpredictability, so enlivening after the formality and rectitude of middle-class Paris gatherings. "You know, I never know what I shall do next," was a frequent apology of his when he was late or did not turn up at all.[6] The Manets were civilized people and she, as painter, knew that painting had first call. They were patient with Renoir and were rewarded; he could be amusing in his dry way, he was often refreshingly down to earth, and his manner with the little Julie (whom Berthe determined there and then he must paint) was altogether charming. Julie doted on him and so, soon, did they.

This summer of 1881 he would be at his most unpredictable and exciting. He was in love. Jean Renoir thinks that he spoke to Aline then.[7] But she was a sensible girl. She saw that he wanted to marry and have a home, but she did not believe that he yet wanted the kind of home on which she would insist, one in the full sense of the word, with children. He was still restless. Algeria had merely inflamed the long suppressed wish to see something of the world. He must have told her often of his longing to study the work of the Italian masters in Italy. Partly because of his own doubts, partly because of Cézanne's insistence on the fundamentals of painting, he wanted authority from the past to direct him.

This girl of nineteen, who knew nothing of painting except what she had seen of Renoir at work, somehow deduced the importance of the Italian journey to him even when he was proposing to her. Jean Renoir thinks, again, that they decided to postpone the question of marriage and that she advised him to make the journey and think matters over.[8] That fall, after he had paid a promised visit to the Bérards at Wargemont, Renoir duly went off. He departed so abruptly that one wonders whether his final talk with Aline was held the day before he caught the train.

2

The first thing Mme. Charpentier knew about his journey was a letter from Venice. "I have unexpectedly become a traveller, the fever to see the Raphaels has swept me off. So I have begun to gulp down my Italy. Now I shall be able to look a man in

the face and say, Yes, Monsieur, I have seen the Raphaels. I
have seen Venice the beautiful, etc. etc." [9]

He wrote penitently; he was supposed to have made a pastel
portrait of a Charpentier daughter that winter. "So I hope that
in spite of my ingratitude you will receive me when I come
back. A man who has seen the Raphaels! What perfect painting!
Do you want me to tell you what I have seen in Venice? All
right. Take a boat and go to the Quai des Orfèvres or opposite
the Tuileries and you will see Venice. The galleries? Go to the
Louvre. To see Veronese, go to the Louvre. Except for Tiepolo
whom I didn't know. A rather expensive method of acquiring
knowledge all the same.

"No, it's not true, it is very beautiful, very beautiful, the
lagoon—when the weather is fine, that is. San Marco astonishing,
the Doge's Palace, everything astonishing. I'd rather have Saint-
Germain l'Auxerrois." [10]

He had made a study of the Doge's Palace, he told her, adding, "That's never been done." [11] He also inevitably painted
Saint Mark's and a gondola on the Grand Canal. The Saint Mark
has become one of the world's most famous pictures. In *Venise*
we see one of the last flickers of the Impressionist Renoir on his
way to an experience which would lead him into other paths.
It is a fine study with a glorious spread of stormy sky, not at all
the Venice of the tourist. The study of the gondola has been
acclaimed for its color; certainly it conveys the effect of the light
on a northerner and follows Manet, the first of that generation
of French painters to visit Venice and paint there.

Opinions on these Venice canvases have differed widely;
Eugène Manet was soon to tell his wife, "Renoir's views of
Venice are hateful, absolute failures"; [12] other men have praised
them to the skies. They are perhaps a special taste. What is
clear is that this city has an immediate and powerful effect on
a painter used to the subdued colors of Paris.

By the middle of November, Renoir was in Naples and from
there told Durand-Ruel (who had paid him two thousand
francs before he left France) how the Raphaels in Rome had
affected him. "I've been meaning to write to you for a long

time but I also wanted to send you a heap of canvases with the letter. But I am still in a kind of research fever. I am never satisfied and I scrub out, scrub out again and again. I hope this mania is coming to an end, that's why I give you my news. I don't think I shall bring back much from my trip but I believe I shall have made progress, the kind of thing that only occurs after long research. One always goes back to one's first loves but with a hint of something more."

He enlarged on his struggles to find a new style or, more precisely, a true one. "I am like schoolchildren. The blank page must be filled with fine script but, ouf!—a blot. I'm still making blots—and I'm forty!" Then he explained the cause of them. "I have seen the Raphaels at Rome. They are very beautiful and I ought to have seen them long ago. They are full of knowledge and wisdom. He's not like me, he doesn't seek the impossible. But how beautiful he is. I prefer Ingres in oil painting but the simplicity and grandeur of the frescoes is admirable." [13]

The reference to Ingres is significant. Renoir looked at Raphael and thought of Ingres. The reference shows how far he had gone in repudiation of most of his recent work; probably he had not given Ingres a thought for the past ten years. The full result of this Rome visit following on his year or more of self-examination was not to be seen at once, but the *Baigneuse* he painted at Naples showed the way he was going. Already it revealed the influence of the ancient frescoes, which a second canvas, *Baigneuse blonde,* was to bring into the open.

From Naples he crossed to Capri, which he praised ecstatically to Chocquet, in an end of year letter, adding, "Greet Cézanne for me when you meet him." [14] At Capri, too, he heard news from Paris that brought a spontaneously ungrudging letter from him to Manet. Gambetta had formed a government, had appointed Manet's old friend Antonin Proust as Minister of Fine Arts, and Proust had recommended Manet for the Légion d'Honneur. That staunch Impressionist collector, the Rumanian doctor De Bellio, whose partisanship led him astray, was furious when he learned about it: "Why only Manet?" he de-

manded. "Monet, Degas, Sisley, Renoir, and Cézanne should
have had the cross too!" [15] Renoir had no feeling other than
pleasure that a painter so much greater than himself and who
had suffered so much calumny should at last have what mattered
a lot to him, public honor. "So at last we have a cabinet minister
who suspects that painting exists in France! . . . When I come
back I shall have pleasure in saluting you as the officially recognized painter everyone loves. . . . You are like a Gaullois of old,
the happy fighter with hatred for nobody. I admire you for your
gaiety which you have kept alive even at the height of injustice." [16]

Before he could come back to France an unexpected commission was offered him, to make a portrait of Wagner, then finishing *Parsifal* at Palermo. It is difficult to know whether Renoir
did or did not want to paint the man whose music he had spent
so much of his time debunking in the Paris discussions with
Maître, Bazille, at Lejosne's, and in his own Montmartre
group. He seems to have agreed because an old Lejosne acquaintance and Wagner enthusiast, Judge Lascoux, begged him
to. He was curious to see Wagner, yet when he reached Capri,
he hesitated. Edmond, always anxious to advance the reputation
of his brother, pestered him to do it. So "after having resisted
my brother a long time I finally sent my letter of introduction." [17]

It is difficult to think that Renoir was repaid for his efforts
or that his reputation was advanced by what he did. Yet this
was scarcely his fault. He began by feeling seasick on the voyage
from Capri. At Palermo no one seemed to have heard of
Wagner. When at last he tracked him down to the Hôtel des
Palmes he was turned away once by the footman and put off a
second time by Wagner's wife, who said that her husband had
just written the last note of *Parsifal*, was suffering from a bad
attack of nervous strain, and could not eat.

On his third visit Renoir was lucky; he was greeted graciously
by Frau Wagner and her small son and, after being "plunged
into an immense armchair," was eventually joined by the master
"in velvet with great black satin sleeves. He was very handsome

and friendly, offered me his hand, told me to sit down again, and began the most foolish conversation, punctuated by 'Hi! Ah! Ho!' half in French, half German with very guttural endings to his words.

" 'Je suis bien gontent. Ah! Oh!' followed by a guttural 'vous venez de Paris?'

"We began to talk about everything—that is to say I only had to repeat, 'Dear Master, certainly dear Master.' And when I got up to go he took my hands and put me back in my armchair. The nonsense I had to say! I blush as red as a turkey cock to think of it."

Eventually Renoir escaped, having made an appointment to paint the portrait the next day. Wagner said he could give him only half an hour. When Renoir arrived, the composer "was very cheerful though he seemed very nervous. He regretted that he was no Ingres. In short, I think I spent my time well—thirty-five minutes isn't much—but if I had finished even earlier the portrait might have been more beautiful because my model ended by losing some of his cheerfulness and becoming stiff."

When Renoir had done, Wagner wanted to look at the canvas. "Ah! Ah! I look like a protestant preacher."

The one good thing Wagner had said during the interviews was a blunt, "You French take too much notice of critics." [18] As for Renoir, he managed to sell the portrait to Robert de Bonnières when he got back to Paris so did not consider the time wasted.

At Marseilles on the way home—it was January, 1882—he ran into Cézanne and at once changed his plans. Instead of going back immediately to Paris he went to L'Estaque with Cézanne and began a series of painting excursions with him. He was carried away by the climate and the views and set to work in great fettle and in the spirit of what he had seen and admired in Italy.

He tried to explain himself to an impatient Mme. Charpentier, who felt this reluctance to return to Paris a sort of slight on herself. When working in the hot sunshine, he now said, he could scrape off again and again if not satisfied. This was a splendid way to learn as well as being a method the painter could not use in the north. He used the word "learn" in spite of his age, forty-one, and his growing reputation, and he meant it in every sense of the word. He was seeking the new as well as the right technique to convey it.

He made one discovery of moment at L'Estaque and told his patronne about it. "I studied in the Naples museum a great deal; the paintings of Pompeii are very interesting in every way. Now I am not working in the sunlight to make portraits but to warm myself and to observe at the same time in the hope that I shall discover the secret of the simplicity and grandeur of the ancient painters. Raphael, for instance, did not work out of doors but studied sunlight all the same—his frescoes are full of it. I have already benefited from studying out of doors; I no longer worry about small details which tend to extinguish the effect of sunlight instead of enhancing it." [19]

Cézanne as well as Italy had something to do with this search for a return to classical simplicity. After a few weeks, Renoir was sending his first batch of canvases to Durand-Ruel with an ecstatic letter; he thought Cézanne a wonderful painting companion and contrasted the sun of the south with the kind of weather he would have had to endure if he had gone straight back to Paris.

Two weeks later, he was begging Durand-Ruel to send him five hundred francs. The delightful climate had changed abruptly; he had been caught painting in the open, drenched, chilled, and sent to bed with influenza. Within a few days the influenza had turned to pneumonia.

Cézanne and his mother rescued him, and he saw a new side of the supposedly flinty-hearted and unapproachable man. "I have been ill," he wrote, "and am convalescing. I can't tell you how good Cézanne has been to me. He wanted to take me into his house. We are going to have a farewell dinner there with his mother, for he goes to Paris and I am obliged to stay in the Midi for a while—doctor's orders. But I don't want to stay alone at L'Estaque, so shall probably turn back to Algiers for a week or two, an idea which bores me, for I'd much rather be at home. Mme. Cézanne made a *brandade* of cod for my lunch and I think I have rediscovered the Ambrosia of the gods. One should eat it and die." [20]

When Cézanne went off Renoir felt low, and even Mme. Cézanne's cooking could not save him; he had been very ill, his recovery was slow, and he fretted. He had never been notable for patience, and scarcely knew what it was to be ill. The after-effects of pneumonia gripped him hard, and he felt in the depths. At this moment Durand-Ruel, knowing nothing of his state, innocently wrote to beg him to exhibit with the Impressionists at a seventh exhibition he was arranging for that spring.

3

Durand-Ruel was still determined to get the true Impressionists together. He was thinking of them and of himself, for he had a considerable stock of their canvases. He found himself treading a thorny path. The original exhibitors had broken into three loose groups: Degas with his protégés Raffaelli and the American Mary Cassatt; Pissarro with his protégés Gauguin, Guillaumin, and Vignon; Monet and Renoir with Sisley and Caillebotte. During long and complicated negotiations each of the leaders objected to the protégés of the others. Manet reported a call by Pissarro, who, gamely sticking to his last, still had hopes of persuading the ailing painter (Manet was in the early stages of locomotor ataxy) to join an Impressionist exhibition. "That terrible man Pissarro has just paid me a visit about the forthcoming exhibition. These gentlemen don't seem to be of one mind. Gauguin plays the dictator. Sisley, whom I have also seen, wants to know, before he decides, what Monet is going to do. Renoir is not yet in Paris." [21]

Manet declined—a decision his brother said he afterward regretted—and repeated his refusal at a dinner Caillebotte tempted him to. "I shall never exhibit in a side-show," he declared. "I believe in going into the Salon by the front door and facing all the competition." [22]

There was nothing more to be said after this, and for a long time it seemed that, lacking the celebrated figure of Manet to hold the disparate sections together, the exhibition plan would fall to the ground. Monet demanded that Raffaelli, Gauguin, Vignon, and Guillaumin be left out as not true Impressionist painters or simply not good enough for him to exhibit with; like Manet he referred to them as "these gentlemen," their identity being understood by all. Pissarro replied with a demand for the jettisoning of Caillebotte, who was no stronger a painter than Vignon. Degas would not consider dropping Raffaelli or Mary Cassatt.

Monet struggled for justice. "If I am forced to separate myself from Caillebotte, who is my friend, then Pissarro must separate from his." He was even firmer about the Degas adherents. "If I am expected to take part with certain persons, then I must regretfully refuse to go any further in the matter." He added, "In any case it is understood that I exhibit only if Renoir does." [23]

This placed the onus on Renoir, and Durand-Ruel undertook to persuade him. He could not have struck an unhappier moment. When his letter arrived at L'Estaque, Renoir was still in bed, weak and deep in the misery following the pneumonia and influenza. He returned a, for him, savage letter, refusing to have anything to do with the hangers-on. "With Monet, Sisley, Mlle. Morisot, Pissarro, I would accept but with them only. We five—or six if you include the incomprehensible Degas—could make an exhibition which would be an interesting manifestation of art." [24]

Durand-Ruel persisted and met with even plainer words from the sickbed in the south. Renoir's view of Raffaelli is already known. By this time his views on Gauguin were almost as scathing. Cézanne had told him of his summer painting holiday the previous year with Pissarro at Pontoise, how they were joined by Gauguin and how Gauguin tried to steal his "petite sensation." [25] Gauguin was not in fact serious but Cézanne, whose sense of humor was not his strong point, took the jest in deadly earnest. This was enough for Renoir. He did not care for Gauguin's nude study, which had been so highly praised in the previous year's Impressionist exhibition. He also objected to the fact that Durand-Ruel had not invited Cézanne to the exhibition he was now trying to arrange. He overlooked the fact that Cézanne had no wish to be linked with the Impressionists.

All in all he was unnaturally excited, and his replies, by telegram and in a letter written for him by Edmond (who had come down to replace Cézanne as nurse), were the reverse of conciliatory. "It must be understood that I won't join in any shape or form the combination Pissarro-Gauguin. . . . You'll know that this decision doesn't refer to you personally because you are not making this exhibition—Monsieur Gauguin is—and please believe me as always your devoted and faithful artist. I am trying to defend our joint interests because I consider that to show in such an exhibition would halve the price of my canvases." [26]

If he had left the matter there, Durand-Ruel would have had enough to think about. But having dictated this and much more to Edmond, the sick man snatched the paper and scrawled, "Unhappily I have only one aim in my life, to see that my canvases are shown. The means I use are not good, perhaps, but they please me. To exhibit with Pissarro, Gauguin, and Guillaumin would be like exhibiting with some social rabble. The next thing will be that Pissarro will invite the Russian Laverov or some other revolutionary. The public doesn't like the whiff of politics and at my age I don't want to be a revolutionary. To show with the Jew Pissarro would be a revolution.

"What's more, these gentlemen know that I have taken a big step forward at the Salon. They are trying to deprive me of what I have gained. They neglect nothing to make sure I come a cropper once more. I don't want it, I don't want it. Get rid of these people and give me artists such as Monet, Sisley, Morisot, etc., and I'm yours, for then it wouldn't be a case of politics but purely of art." [27]

Of course, he regretted this tirade when he was on his feet and feeling himself again. "I wrote too strongly to you during my illness," he was saying a month later. "My reply wasn't very wise." [28] But by this time the exhibition was on. He had given Durand-Ruel a loophole in his telegram: "The pictures of mine you have are your property. I can't prevent you from doing what you like with them but it will not be I who am exhibiting." [29] The dealer took this as permission and announced to the still arguing painters that Renoir would exhibit. This brought in Monet and Sisley. Berthe Morisot had already agreed. Degas refused to drop Raffaelli and, with Mary Cassatt, they retired from the exhibition. Monet kept Caillebotte and accepted Gauguin, Vignon, and Guillaumin. Renoir submitted to the Salon as usual, another woman's portrait, which was accepted. He had a new companion there in Cézanne, admitted after nineteen years, as "pupil of Guillemet."

Renoir did not see this seventh Impressionist exhibition; as soon as he was fit to travel he went over to Algeria to recuperate and paint. This was a pity, for the exhibition was the only one that can be called wholly Impressionist; for the first and last time all the original painters were represented, most of them by masterly works, and their 123 canvases dominated the show. Degas should have been there to complete the band, deny Impressionism though he did, and Manet, perhaps the finest Impressionist painter who ever refused to consider himself one— only that winter he had made his superb *Un bar aux Folies-Bergère*—but with these reservations the gathering at 251 rue Saint-Honoré in a gallery rented by Durand-Ruel fully came up to his expectations, both the collection as a whole and its reception.

Renoir's twenty-five canvases were the least representative of all the friends, but they included *La Loge, Les Canotiers, Jeune fille endormie*, several river studies between Chatou and Bougival, and the sunny luncheon party at La Grenouillère. They give some idea of the way in which Durand-Ruel had been snapping them up since he came back into circulation; he had bought sufficient Renoir pictures to put on a private show that same year.

This seventh exhibition was not only the end of the Impressionists as a body, it fittingly marked the end of their long struggle against misrepresentation of the most malicious and stupid kind. Their first exhibition was eight years back, and for most of those years they had suffered in mind and body, from public abuse to private misery. Now at last they were accepted. They might have been excused for cynicism; their work had not changed materially over these years; all that had changed was the taste of the people who looked at it. Yet it seems that they were too much relieved to feel anything but pleasure. Eugène Manet wrote happily to his wife down at Nice. He had attended the hanging, was there on the opening day. "It is sure to be a success," he wrote, and quoted the most shameless volte-face as proof. "Wolff was there showing the exhibition to his friends. He was full of praise." [30]

Then came the critics' articles, also sent to Nice with the news "The Impressionists are doing very well, especially Sisley and Renoir. Durand-Ruel gets 2000 francs for a Sisley. The very first day the admission money came to 950 francs. . . . Duret, who knows what he's talking about, says this is the best exhibition the group has ever had." [31]

In Algiers, Renoir was also supplied with cuttings by Durand-Ruel. His reaction was cool. He was glad of the money—he was already drawing on the dealer as on a bank—but his mind had moved far from Impressionism since that visit to Rome. So he says, "I am thankful I didn't send you my last batch of canvases, for you would have put them in the exhibition and I see clearly from Wolff's article, which follows the usual bourgeois pattern, that it's no use showing my pictures until they've been bottled at least a year. In three or four years Wolff will discover that my views of Venice are very beautiful. But what do you expect? When a man is in the habit of judging pictures which have not been painted more than three months he isn't able to see very clearly." [32]

By the time he at last got back to Paris—he had been away a full six months—Renoir had had his fill of travel for the moment. He had also clarified his mind about marriage. He now wanted it as Aline wanted it. Soon afterward they were married and, following a honeymoon in Sicily, settled in the rue Saint-Georges studio both knew so well.

CHAPTER XIV

"MA MANIÈRE AIGRE"

1883-1887

RENOIR HAD FOUND one form of peace but was still searching for another. Soon after entering his happy marriage his long-standing doubts about his way as painter came to a head. "Round about 1883," he said later, "a break came in my work. I had reached the end of Impressionism and came to the conclusion that I did not know how to paint or draw. In a word, I had reached an impasse." [1]

The steps leading to this conclusion were many: his never waning sense of kinship with the eighteenth-century painters he had discovered in his youth, the words and example of Corot and Cézanne, the Raphaels in Rome, and the Pompeii frescoes. All this, joined to his lifelong tendency to underrate himself, brought him back to those Beaux-Arts lectures on drawing when "I thought I should never learn to draw a head." [2] He still, he felt, did not know how to draw a head and, infuriatingly, had for years been following a will-o'-the-wisp which actually diverted him from acquiring the knowledge.

The final straw seems to have come from Lamy. Peering into the boxes of the bookstalls along the quays he came across an old copy of Cennini's famous treatise on painting and brought it back to Renoir's studio. Cennini's insistence on the prime importance of draftsmanship was perfectly timed. Renoir looked back with something like disgust to Pissarro's "linear form is not necessary . . . in the act of painting one draws; accuracy of tone reveals the light and shape of the object." [3] He now saw this theory, with its insistence on *plein air* painting and emphasis on the effect of light, as a drag on his emergence as a properly integrated painter. He questioned it and the rest of the Impressionist doctrine with its avoidance of black and the bounding line. "I understood," he said later, "that Impressionism was too complicated a business altogether, the kind of painting that makes you compromise with yourself. There is a greater variety of light out of doors than in the studio . . . and just because of this, light plays far too important a part; you have no time to work out the composition. . . . When the artist paints directly from nature he reaches a point when he no longer composes but looks wholly for the momentary effects of light. That soon leads to monotony." [4]

He at last decisively rejected Monet's teaching in the Fontainebleau forest, a teaching he had been flirting with on and off for the past twenty years, and came firmly down on the side of the Barbizon painters Monet had criticized. "Corot," he now said, "made his studies in the open air but his compositions were done in the studio. He *corrected* nature. . . . I was lucky enough to meet him once and told him of my difficulties with *plein air* painting. He said, 'That's because you can never be sure what you are doing out of doors. Always paint over again in the studio.' And this much-criticized studio work did not prevent him from interpreting nature with a realism no Impressionist painter has been able to match!" [5]

In this dramatic rebound he went further back than Corot, to follow a master for whom he had hitherto had little time. This was Ingres, who proclaimed the superiority of line over color and had advised Degas many years earlier, "Draw lines, young man, and ever more lines, from life and from memory. That is the only way you will become a good artist." [6]

Degas had taken the advice to heart. He passed it on to Gauguin and anyone who would listen; Renoir must often have heard his battle cry, "Draw, draw, draw!" [7] at the Guerbois and Nouvelle Athènes whenever Pissarro or Monet extolled the

Impressionist method. It can be assumed that Renoir held his usual watching brief during these inconclusive arguments. But now he plumped firmly for Degas and his master. Once again he began to live in the museums, with Raphael and his beloved eighteenth-century painters. He studied antique statuary. For three years he struggled to master his drawing.

These years, from 1883 to 1885, exhibit what he was to call "ma manière aigre." They are crystallized in a work which absorbed the greater part of his creative time throughout this period, *Les grandes baigneuses.*

2

The years were devoid of spectacular incident just as they were devoid of spectacular painting. In April, 1883, Durand-Ruel gave a one-man show for Renoir—the second of four such exhibitions to feature the work of Monet, Renoir, Sisley, and Pissarro—as well as showing some of his canvases in his London gallery. In the catalogue, Duret praised the progress Renoir had made, in stronger color, more supple figure work, and increased mastery of light and air, but in spite of this and of generally good notices, the sales were disappointing. The dealer, erring as always on the optimistic side, had pushed the prices too high.

In September, Renoir went for a painting holiday in Guernsey which produced nothing memorable in outdoor studies, and two months later he and Monet joined forces to travel slowly along the Côte from Marseilles to Genoa, two weeks of gentle traveling, which ended with a visit to Cézanne at L'Estaque. Monet had not been to the Riviera before and reacted as Renoir had done earlier, during that stay of mixed fortunes with Cézanne; he too was excited by the colors. Monet planned another visit to Bordighera, the place he liked best, this time alone, to paint seriously. Monet begged Durand-Ruel, "Please don't tell *anyone* about this journey, not that I want to make a mystery of it but because I want to make it by myself. Much as I liked the tourist trip with Renoir it would be embarrassing if both of us went there to work. I always work better by myself alone and from my own impressions. So keep the secret unless I tell you otherwise. If Renoir knew I was just about to go off he would undoubtedly want to come with me and each of us would be a bad influence on the other. You will think the same, I'm sure." [8]

Monet was a very sensible man. When he and Renoir painted together at Bougival and Argenteuil and in Paris, Renoir followed him cheerfully and uncritically. He was unlikely to be so obliging now, and the conflict of his impulse to paint after Monet and his newfound wish to be himself could lead to differences. That would affect the work of both. Better they avoid painting together, therefore, and remain good friends, which they did.

The effect of the December excursion on Monet was to send him back almost at once to painting. The effect on Renoir was powerful, too, but not immediate. "We are enchanted with our journey," he wrote in a letter which explained Monet's slightly acid "tourist trip." For Renoir continued, "We have seen some marvellous things though we shall probably not bring back anything of moment because we are always walking. But what walks!" [9] This enthusiasm for Midi scenery was to lead him eventually to Cagnes.

In May of the next year, 1884, Renoir produced a surprise for Durand-Ruel in the shape of the outlines of a plan to establish a Société des Irrégularistes. This was an attempt to form a corporate union of artists and craftsmen pledged to the use of original handwork. "Its aim," wrote Renoir, "is to arrange as soon as possible exhibitions for all artists, Painters, Decorators, Architects, Gold and Silversmiths, Embroiderers, etc., who believe in irregularity.

"Among other conditions of admission the rule expressly states for architecture: All ornaments must be made after nature, and no motif, flower, leaf, figure, etc., etc., is to be repeated exactly; profiles, contours, etc., however small, must be carried out by hand and without any use of precision instruments. In all plastic art, the gold and silversmiths and others

will have to exhibit by the side of their completed work the
drawings or paintings from nature which they used during the
making of the work; no work containing copies of details or
groups taken from printed books will be accepted." [10]

Renoir was to explain his feelings on this subject much later.
"In a row of Gothic columns, for example, with a cabbage leaf
as motif, I defy you to find a single leaf opposite the other or
carved in the same way. And this applies to the columns themselves; they are never precisely opposite to one another nor are
they ever precisely the same. Not one of the modern architects,
beginning with Viollet le Duc, has grasped the fact that the
very spirit of Gothic architecture is irregularity; instead, they've
decided that the old architects didn't know what they were
doing. I once said, in the presence of architects, that the Parthenon was the very essence of irregularity. They were tickled to
death. Actually I had made a guess because I felt sure it must be
so, and later I discovered that I was right. That new church at
Rome called Saint Paul's is simply atrocious because all the
columns were turned out on a lathe. When you glance at the
columns of the Parthenon you are astonished by their regularity
but take a closer look and you'll find they are all different. The
same irregularity is to be found in all the primitives and even
in China and Japan. It is the professors of our day who have
invented regularity by compass." [11]

It was this belief that had made him attack the work of Haussman in his letters printed in Rivière's newssheet during the
third Impressionist exhibition.[12] He saw old Paris, irregularity
itself in building and planning, pulled down and modern
regularity put in its place. To him this meant one thing, the
triumph of the machine over the handworker, and he wanted
to fight the trend by forming a body pledged to the kind of
work he had done as a child, where no painted flower on a tea-
cup matched another. This, he claimed, pleased the man who
made an object and the man who bought or looked at it; the
one obtained the satisfaction of handwork that no machine
labor could give, the other satisfied the instinctive demand of
the visual sense for a sight that repetition could not stale.

Nature abhorred regularity as much as a vacuum; no two eyes in a face were alike, no two ears; no mouth, no nose was absolutely straight or placed dead center, just as no two leaves on a tree were identical. If nature took care to avoid monotony and boredom, craftsmen should follow it. And not just craftsmen; Renoir realized that painters would need protection, too, because even in painting, measuring devices were being used increasingly, and eye and hand were no longer trusted to make a work of art.

This gallant attempt to put back the clock was stillborn, and no more was heard of it. Renoir never showed his wisdom more plainly than in his insistence on the necessity for handwork and creative relaxation after it and in his gloomy visions of a world that neglected them. All he prophesied has come true; every mechanized country today is filled with millions of discontented machine-tenders.

All this Renoir foresaw, yet he did not succeed even in getting his proposal printed; unknown to him he chose the worst possible moment to offer it to Durand-Ruel. The dealer's great backer, the Union Centrale, suddenly collapsed, and for the second time within a few years he found himself on the verge of bankruptcy. He was in no condition to support a new movement. He had to cut purchases from his advanced painters once again, and there was general gloom among the men who had begun to think themselves free from money worries at last.

Monet and Renoir reacted well to the bad news, and Renoir's letter makes good reading: "There's not much I can do for you just now but if you need me I beg you to consider me completely at your disposal whatever happens. I shall always be your very devoted friend." [13]

He added a consoling "As for my pictures, if you are forced to make sacrifices to get rid of them, don't worry about it at all— I shall make more and better ones for you." [14]

Nevertheless the news was disturbing to a newly married man who, partly because of the marriage and partly because of his change of heart about painting, had to face a falling away in lucrative commissions. One picture only was accepted by the

Salon, in the first of these years, 1883, then nothing more for seven years—and by that time he no longer needed the cachet of a Salon showing.

Little more is heard of Mme. Charpentier after the long delayed pastel Renoir made following his second visit to Algeria. For her, he had become *vieux jeu* and was subject to criticism for failing to paint pictures pretty enough to get into the Salon. With the loss of her patronage went most of his profitable connections.

He had already lost the Daudets after an attempt to help poor Cabaner. He took him along with the score of a set of songs he had just written. Mme. Daudet, who fancied her voice and had considerable influence in musical circles, opened the score at Cabaner's setting of Richepin's *Les Chansons des Gueux*. The first line on which her eye lighted was "Merde, merde, joyeux merde!" [15]

The Bérards were among the few influential people who stuck gamely to Renoir and ordered portraits. But the loss of the Charpentier and Daudet soirées meant in effect that the run of lifesaving commissions was a thing of the past; he had to rely in future on friends such as Chabrier (just making his name with *España*), Catulle Mendès, and those with plenty of goodwill but limited means.

Durand-Ruel made considerable efforts to monopolize Renoir and Monet—he tried to give them money when they asked for it—because he foresaw that they would be driven to a rival. And this was what happened; the plan to use Petit, which had been in abeyance since Durand-Ruel's return to circulation, was soon to be put into action: Monet exhibited with him the next year and both he and Renoir the year after.

In general this was a worrying time for Renoir—worry, of course, within the context of a happy home life. Aline proved herself an excellent hostess and cook, and invitations to Renoir dinners were sought after by painters and writers. But with happiness came added responsibility; he now had not only himself to think of, money was short, and he was not painting with his former speed or certainty because of his preoccupation with line.

This may account for his restlessness during these years of experiment. He was perhaps trying to stir himself to greater productivity by change of scene and discovering, as others have discovered, that an unsettled mind makes nonsense of every effort at outward stimulation. Early in 1884 he was telling Monet, painting on the Côte d'Azur, "I'm stuck here in Paris and very bored. I'm always chasing after the unfindable model. I'm a figure painter. Alas! this can sometimes be a pleasure but only when one finds figures to one's taste." [16]

He turned from his figure problems, which did not consist merely in finding the right model, to a triumph that pleased all but one of the old painting friends. At a great sale of Manets at the Hôtel Drouot the receipts totaled 115,000 francs. Berthe Morisot thought the individual bids too low,[17] but Renoir looked beyond the money to belated recognition of a great painter. Perhaps remembering Wagner's advice, he laughed at the incoherence of Wolff, forced to alter his opinion: "He's beginning to talk a new kind of nonsense, not through spitefulness but because he has become incomprehensible." [18]

A summer visit to Wargemont was preceded by a stay at La Rochelle. He went there on impulse after seeing a Corot canvas inspired by the town. He liked what he saw but painted little that pleased him; however far he removed himself from his studio he seems to have been haunted by the long meditated picture of bathers—still no more than a large sheaf of sketches.

3

His numerous retreats from Paris during summer and fall of 1885 were a continuation of the worried pilgrimages of the previous years. He remained far from a style of his own, imprisoned within the narrow limits imposed by the determination to base his work on draftsmanship. The "manière aigre" was still with him, though this year was to see the beginning of the end of its extreme phase.

In June he discovered a new riverside retreat, the picturesque village of La Roche-Guyon. This was a good twenty miles downriver from his parents' cottage, it was very much quieter than Argenteuil, Chatou, or Bougival, more beautiful, and had the advantage of nearness to Monet. Upriver a mile or two was the Vetheuil of Monet's magnificent maturity as painter; downriver a similar distance was Giverny where Monet had settled with the widowed Mme. Hoschedé.

After a month there Renoir moved to Wargemont. He returned the next month to La Roche-Guyon and during September went with his wife and baby down to Aline's birthplace, Essoyes in the Aube. He rounded off the season's visits with a further stay at Wargemont in November.

Cézanne had spent a week with him at La Roche-Guyon in June, and it is scarcely a coincidence that it was here, two months later, that Renoir first saw a gleam of light in the gloom of his uncertainty. He wrote Durand-Ruel, "The only positive thing I have to tell you is that I don't have to seek any more. I only have the trouble of beginning." [19]

Little more than a month later he was writing happily from Essoyes, "I think I shall give you pleasure this time. I have recovered, never to leave it, the old painting, sweet and light. . . . It's nothing new but follows the pictures of the eighteenth century. I don't mean the good ones. I say that simply to explain my new and latest work to you as closely as possible—Fragonard or even less good." And he emphasized again, "You understand, I don't compare myself with an eighteenth-century master but I have to tell you the kind of mood in which I'm working—of those people who reproduce nature with the air of one who doesn't know more than we do." [20]

With this jibe at the man he had been, he got to work with vigor and enthusiasm for the first time in nearly three years. It cannot be said, for all his relief at having found his path, that he had found himself; he had a very long way to go before the mature Renoir, rich and assured in his work, came to the surface. In 1885 he was simply expressing relief at release from the bonds of a theory.

How restricting a theory can be is shown clearly enough in his work over these three years; there was very little of it and

it fell far below his best. He was closest to himself in the joyous
trio of dance canvases, *La danse à Bougival, La danse à la
campagne,* and *La danse à la ville.* The first of these is by far
the best known, but there is a strong case to be made for the
last. In this the model is almost certainly Mme. Renoir, in the
others Suzanne Valadon. The man in all three is Lhotte. Renoir
succeeds in conveying movement, grace, and youthful pleasure
in what one is tempted to call the old style, although the drawing is greatly improved. But the improvement has not reduced
the picture to aridity as with *La Coiffure,* the study of a bathing
girl pushing back her hair. This, curiously enough (Renoir
would have been greatly displeased), is not unlike a similar
canvas by Gauguin in his early period when he too was
struggling to master drawing.

Then there is the strange *Les Parapluies.* Renoir seems to
have begun this canvas in the late seventies and abandoned it.
After he took it up again in these years of devotion to the
principles of Ingres the result was that half the canvas is drawn
much more carefully than the other half and is besides in
another world, women's fashions having changed in the meantime. This famous picture is original in thought and layout,
the colors are intriguing, much of the drawing apt, and the use
of black can be seen as a definite rejection of Impressionism.
Whether the picture can be called successful is another matter;
there is something slightly repellent, a rigidity about it as
about almost all Renoir's works in these years because he was
denying what gives life to his finest pictures. The effect left by
most of the work of the early eighties is of a preliminary study,
exceedingly careful but dry. He used the word sharp to describe
it.

Apart from a few bathing studies and some Wargemont
commissions which have little to commend them, his only other
significant work of this period is *La mère et l'enfant,* the well-
known canvas of Mme. Renoir suckling her first child. Berthe
Morisot was much impressed by the work he had done on this
picture. She had come to know Renoir well, seeing quite a lot
of him at Bougival (where she still rented a cottage each sum-

mer) and visiting his studio in Paris. Since the coming of the
baby the Renoirs had taken rooms in rue Houdon for living in
while he worked in his old studio, and it was here that Berthe
Morisot (who had yet to meet his wife) saw one of the many
versions of the pose. Her comment is interesting because it
accentuates a Renoir all too little known to those who judge
him by his Impressionist years. "A red pencil and chalk drawing
of a young mother nursing her child," she writes in her diary
when she returns home. "Charmingly subtle and graceful.
While I admired it he showed me an entire series made from
the same model." [21]

Her final judgment comes in the next entry: "He is a first-
rate draftsman. How interesting it would be if all these preliminary studies for a painting could be shown to the general
public which still thinks that the Impressionists work casually.
I do not see how one can improve on the rendering of form in
his drawings. I thought two drawings of women entering the
water as delightful as Ingres." [22]

If she told Renoir what she thought—and it is reasonable to
suppose that she did—he must have been gratified. This was the
first month of 1886 and he remained in the grip of Ingres
worship. That it was beneficial, even essential to his art is no
doubt true; that it was no more than a stage to the complete
painter he had still to demonstrate.

4

The history of a creative artist is seldom one of steady advance
toward recognition and financial security. Most often it re-
sembles Renoir's, a series of what seem to him blind alleys. It
is not a career for a man with unsteady nerves or wavering
faith, and Renoir proved, the hard way, that he had neither.
Many times in his twenty years and more as painter he had
apparently been within sight of success: when his two Salon
pictures of 1870 were praised; when Durand-Ruel first took
him up after the war; when Chocquet began to commission him

in 1875; when Mme. Charpentier and her friends did the same the following year; when the Charpentier family group became a Salon favorite in 1879; when Durand-Ruel came back into business in 1882. And this includes only the major landmarks in the life of one struggling painter.

Yet every one of these promising leads had faded out after a bright beginning, and by 1886 he, husband and father, was much less financially secure than the carefree bachelor of a few years earlier. And his efforts to establish a style of his own meant, practically, more pre-painting studies and sketches and fewer finished pictures to sell.

The opening months of the year did nothing to encourage him. Just before the close of 1885 he and Monet had been honored by an invitation to exhibit with the Vingt of Brussels, a society formed in 1883 to forward the cause of modern art. Both accepted and were shown early the next year in Brussels. The compliment of the invitation remained their only satisfaction; the Belgian press proved just as obscurantist as the French press and not less insulting.[23] A few weeks later the tide began to turn; both were invited to join Petit's Exposition Internationale, which ran from May to July.

The way to Petit was made unexpectedly smooth for them by Durand-Ruel's voyage across the Atlantic in an attempt to retrieve his fortunes. This left them without dealer backing and free, as they chose to think (he did not agree), to find the best possible market in Paris. There was no doubt in their minds about this market; Petit had established himself strongly during the past few years. Nor was there any doubt about the manner in which their works were received during the exhibition; they were highly praised, they sold and, perhaps most important in a long-range view, they were for the first time sought by other dealers. It is an axiom only too well known to the artist that when a dealer comes to him instead of him going to the dealer, success is not far away. Petit was impressed, began to buy their canvases, and talked of another exhibition the following year. Two up-and-coming galleries, Boussod and

Valadon (for whom Theo van Gogh was working) and Knoedler, made flattering advances.

Over in the then faraway United States, Durand-Ruel at the same time introduced Impressionism to what was potentially the largest and richest market in the world. He came in response to an invitation from the American Art Association and collected no fewer than three hundred canvases to take with him. The bulk of these were Impressionist works with a few of the even more daring Neo-Impressionist paintings of the young Georges Seurat, leavened by some Boudins, and even one or two academic paintings to lessen the shock.

There was criticism, of course, but the kind of criticism that put to shame the ravings of Wolff years earlier and the Belgian critics that same year in what were supposed to be two of the most civilized capitals in the world. There was also praise, not overwhelming but sincere, for all the Impressionist painters.

The test of the exhibition soon came. It was due to run one month. At the end of the month the throng of visitors remained so large that the show was transferred to another gallery and a very important one, the National Gallery of Design, for a further month. Some pictures were sold and the publicity for both shows warranted a promise by Durand-Ruel that he would return with another exhibition. He arrived back in Paris in July, just when the Petit show was in its final days, with the welcome news that although he had not made much money for his painters he had prepared the ground for the future, maybe a very near future. There was every hope, he thought, that the Americans would prove appreciative and generous collectors of Impressionist pictures.

Renoir, who had demurred at the risk of allowing his canvases to be taken across the Atlantic,[24] must have been glad that he had given way. All were convinced that the dealer had begun to tap a source of sales which could dwarf French reception. They were convinced too easily; Durand-Ruel was an unduly optimistic man, and painters who have suffered over the years for their principles need little encouragement to see triumph ahead.

Within a few months Renoir's prospects seemed to have changed miraculously for the better. He began that summer at La Roche-Guyon then went on to new territory, St. Briac near Dinard in northern Brittany, where he spent two months.

Yet neither the good news nor the fresh countryside stirred him to his full stature. He was still preoccupied with the technique of drawing, and good though his sketches often were at this period, the finished work remained tentative, thin, and, strange word to have to use of such a sensuous painter, severe.

So it was with his canvases of this year. They were few—at St. Briac, for instance, he made only sketches and watercolors "so that I shan't be short of notes this winter." [25] But in most cases they were not used or not finally worked on to a canvas; he had become highly self-critical. The completed canvases now known are only the studies of his wife and child painted after many preliminary sketches, *La blanchisseuse et son enfant,* brilliantly drawn, and *Le banc dans le jardin.*

This last shows signs of greater freedom, but over it is felt the shadow of *Les grandes baigneuses.* Most of the work of this and the years immediately succeeding—work still limited in quantity by Renoir standards—has considerable charm, but the sculptural effect due to insistence on line remains a clog on the painter's true nature and clouds his vision. This insistence might have been necessary at that time—Renoir obviously thought so—but it could be a means to an end, no more. The lover of life, the bold colorist, the master of generous curves of the brush and of rich modeling remains in abeyance.

Pissarro, one of the best of judges when he could overcome prejudice, saw this restriction plainly in the following year of 1887 when at last *Les grandes baigneuses* was finished and took the floor in a second Exposition Internationale at Petit's. Pissarro admittedly was not in the best position to speak without bias; he had, he thought, moved far ahead into the Neo-Impressionism of Seurat, and looked back contemptuously at pictures of the past painted by himself and his old Impressionist friends. Romantic Impressionists, he now called them. Yet he did not accuse Renoir of romanticism when he studied *Les grandes baigneuses* at Petit's; his criticism was all in the other direction. "I understand," he told his eldest son, "what he is trying to do. He is right not to want to stand still. But he has chosen to concentrate on the line and his figures are all separate entities, detached from one another without regard for color." [26]

Many would agree with Pissarro today, though not perhaps with his subsequent judgment: "Without the gift for drawing and his old instinctive feeling for beautiful colors, Renoir becomes incoherent." [27] It might be nearer the truth to say rather that, well drawn though it is, this picture remains no more than a chilling series of entities, wooden ones, and that the color, once the great and individual joy of the painter, is anemic and applied without regard for one of its main roles, to give unity to the design. The canvas carried out the teaching of Ingres to the letter; it is a colored drawing. It leans besides, and heavily, on Girardon's bas relief *Le bain des nymphes*, which Renoir studied minutely at Versailles during the years of his "manière aigre" period.

These were not views held by the visitors to Petit's or by the critics. With the exceptions of Huysmans (who had hailed Gauguin's nude study at the 1881 exhibition with rapture) and an old Guerbois companion, Zacharie Astruc, friend of the tragically dead Manet, all reactions were favorable. Vincent van Gogh, just arrived in Paris from Antwerp, may have visited the exhibition—certainly he saw some Renoirs of this time—and was recalling them two years later when he was in Arles and still trying to acclimatize himself to the pellucid atmosphere of the Midi. "I often think of Renoir here," he told his brother Theo, "and of his pure, clean line. That is just what objects and people look like in the transparent light down here." And when he looked at the Arlésiennes he again thought of the painter: "Some women here remind me of Fragonard—and of Renoir." [28]

The many favorable critics at Petit's and the people crowding before Renoir's picture were possibly relating the painter to Fragonard as he had done. Evidently it did not occur to them that he was not Fragonard and could not be and that a man cannot go backward and survive as an independent artist, though this was to occur to Renoir increasingly during the next few years. Possibly the Paris enthusiasts reacted with delight to the spare delicacy of the picture after looking at so much thick paint and complicated designs. Tasteful it was, yet the true lover of Renoir pines for a snatch of vulgarity; the pleasure of seeing a horse reined in pales before the sight when he is given his head. But the elegant crowds at Petit's were quite carried away by this ancient novelty; once again Renoir caught the fugitive favor of the Parisian art public.

His reaction had all the caution of a man who has been in sight of success too often; he told Durand-Ruel, then back in New York with his second Impressionist exhibition: "People say that I haven't done badly. It's always difficult to know for oneself just how things are going. I think I've taken a step in the public estimation—a small step. It's always like that. Monet is still going strong. In short, the public has the air of coming to us. I may be wrong but that's what I hear on all sides." [29]

Then came the comment that showed what he truly thought of the canvas which had taken most of his thought and time over the past three years or more—by May, 1887, when he wrote this letter, it was nearly four: "But why this time and not the others? It's incomprehensible." [30]

CHAPTER XV

STRUGGLE FOR A STYLE

1887-1895

A T THIS POINT, the rapturous reception of *Les grandes baign-euses* at Petit's, Renoir was still far from the opening of his long final period. Not for eight years did he begin to paint in the manner most people now recognize as the mature Renoir— warm, opulent, and above all sensuously aware of the beauty of the human body. Of course he did not stand still at any time— critics of his work distinguish many changes—but the man in the street usually sees either the pictures of the seventies and early eighties or, more often, of the mid-nineties to the end of his life, and thinks of both as typical Renoir. He rarely considers the work of the intervening period, which indeed is not often shown, and Renoir would be the first to sympathize with the omission because he thought he painted little worth preserving during his middle age.

Eight years is a long time in a man's life by any standard. When it follows immediately on four years of intensive effort to master drawing it seems even longer. Yet there is reason for seeing this stretch of time as one of the most remarkable epi-sodes in Renoir's career. For more than half his lifetime he had consciously drifted with the tide. He enjoyed painting so much that he followed any style that pleased him at the moment. He painted many superbly good pictures. Then, at an age when most men are settling into a rut, this supposedly easygoing

Renoir decides, in spite of the commitments of a wife and child, that all he has done is useless, that he has not once painted as he was meant, as all his genuine instincts bid him to do. He could easily have worked as he pleased, sat back, listened to the applause, and raked in the commissions. Instead, he determinedly went to school again.

To study as he studied, to sketch and sketch again, to restrict his output of finished work, to force himself to be dissatisfied with pictures he would have gaily knocked off a few years earlier, to see his income dwindle, his old customers fall away, and still to battle on—all this is so uncharacteristic of Renoir from youth to middle age that one feels incredulous that he could keep it up. He had many difficulties to meet apart from the search for his style, long worries about money followed by ominous signs of a breakdown in health just when money began to come freely. But he stuck to his principles. It took him the best part of four years to get beyond his "manière aigre." More than once he thought he had come to the end. He said so joyously. Then another turning in the road disclosed itself and the prospect of more years of technical practice.

Renoir enjoyed painting. Whether he enjoyed the mass of preliminary sketches he drove himself to make before painting is another matter. He scarcely made one outstanding canvas during this decade and more of experiment. But he would not be beaten, he would not be satisfied with second best. It is an inspiring story.

2

This prolonged struggle was worked out against a background of much traveling which it would be confusing and tedious to relate in detail; he stayed several times in the south of France, revisited Italy, went to Spain, painted in Brittany two years running, was the frequent guest of Berthe Morisot on the riverside, crossed to London, and spent some time in Holland. He was to leave rue Saint-Georges, to see the birth of a second son, Jean, to meet the dealer Ambroise Vollard and to see, with relief mixed with dissatisfaction, his work widely accepted. His health was to deteriorate.

At the end of the period, in 1895, he was still nine years from the time when he could no longer walk unaided, but the writing was already on the wall. He was not to give up painting to the day of his death, but the pressure of these years of the eighteen eighties and nineties to reach self-expression demanded good health and energy, and he must have suspected that he might be deprived of both at any moment, and was fighting against an incurable malady.

This suspicion explains his frequent journeys to the south. They did not merely gratify a longing to travel, nor were they merely the hope of a much worried man that new places would act as incentives to whip his work into final shape and give it the original creative impetus it needed; both these elements were present, but his main preoccupation was that southern warmth would keep the enemy at bay, keep him going at full stretch until he reached his goal.

His paintings of 1887 all show the faults of *Les grandes baigneuses*. His final Bérard commission, *Mademoiselle Lucie Bérard*, and the portrait of Mme. de Bonnières remain stiff, and the two figure studies against a country background must be accounted failures. In *Jeunes filles jouant au volant* and *La femme, la vache et la brébis*, he tries to fit modern types into a classical composition, but the effect is dry and even slightly ludicrous. *La Natte*, with the formidable Suzanne Valadon as model, is a powerful piece of drawing but conveys a general tone of severity wholly out of keeping with Renoir's true gifts. It is admirable but it is not Renoir. It demonstrates clearly what he might have become if he had continued rigidly with his Ingres worship.[1]

The most successful canvas of 1887 is his portrait of Julie Manet, Berthe Morisot's little daughter, dressed in an embroidered English frock and holding a cat in one arm. The humanity of this painting reflects Renoir's reaction to the free and easy hospitality of the Manets', or, to be exact, to the free and easy atmosphere he imposed on this family. As Berthe Morisot was accustomed to painting in short bursts, giving her models frequent rests, Renoir agreed to paint before and after lunch, and this break of a couple of hours no doubt affected the portrait considerably. Over the meal he was most amusing, as so often with sympathetic listeners, and made Berthe Morisot and her husband laugh at his stories of his other sitter of the moment, Mme. de Bonnières. When she went to a ball, he explained, his face preternaturally solemn, she used to stand upright all the way in the cab so as not to crease her gown. And her sittings for him were interrupted in very different fashion from those in the Manet house; her maid used to arrive with a most appetizing chop, leaving the painter, his mouth watering, to watch her demolish the succulent dish. All he had to digest was her explanation that the chop was essential to build up her strength to continue the pose.[2]

He laughed at Mme. de Bonnières, but had almost done with this type of sitter. He laughed, but not as he had laughed twenty years earlier. Up to a point, he had always painted society portraits with his tongue in his cheek, but his views had changed with his position. As a young man he wanted money, he enjoyed painting, even painting that did not pretend to advance anything but technique, and he was youthful enough to appreciate the piquancy of the contrast between the elegant Boulevard St. Germain salon and the rather scruffy gatherings at his studio on the other side of the river. But the middle-aged Renoir had his own home and family; he had not, even though far from prosperous, to look far for the essential franc, and, above all, he had become conscious that time was closing in; enjoyment of painting as such, he now saw, came a bad second to the long task of finding himself as painter.

So by 1887 the effort to turn the complimentary phrase to a wealthy sitter and to endure her essential silliness with a smile, had become too great to be borne; in future Renoir was to accept commissions only to carry him on financially until he could live wholly off the kind of work he wanted to do.

The Julie Manet portrait was in another class from his purely moneymaking work, hence the charm and lack of restraint. Yet this lack was still only comparative, for Berthe Morisot, watching, commented that he remained "in his Ingres period," and had very mixed feelings as she saw him painting the canvas punctiliously section by section after the master's instructions. She thought that the preliminary sketch was painfully reminiscent of a struggling student.[3]

Subconsciously, Renoir felt this too, and after another change of scene—some fall weeks at Auvers [4] where so many painters, his old champion Daubigny in particular, had found themselves—this feeling led to a visit to Cézanne in January of the next year, 1888. Old M. Cézanne had died two years earlier, and Paul lived at Jas de Bouffan with his mother and elder sister. They were not in harmony, but at first Renoir seems to have noticed nothing; he was too much enraptured with Cézanne as mentor and with the house: "that beautiful eighteenth-century building." [5] Years later he remembered his weeks in it with typical emphasis on the good things: "Ah, in those days they knew how to build houses fit to live in, with fireplaces at which one could really warm oneself. In fact the great salon with its high ceiling would have been glacial, but my goodness, when one sat by the fire with a folding screen at one's back, what a fine heat one felt! And the excellent fennel soups Cézanne's mother made for us! I can still hear her giving me the recipe as though it were yesterday: 'Take a branch of fennel, a small spoonful of olive oil . . .' She was a fine woman!" [6]

This continued attempt at intimacy with Cézanne is instructive. Cézanne's formidable reserve did not daunt Renoir, he knew the man beneath it. He understood the black moods, too, and the foul language. Cézanne was a seeker, greater by far than he, but a seeker nevertheless, a man who had not found his path. Whether Renoir realized that their paths would prove so far apart does not matter; he was in daily contact with genius, with utter absorption in painting, with grim endurance through years of neglect from almost everyone of moment in the world of painting. It was comparable to his earlier relationship with Monet, but with the essential difference that now, in 1888,

Renoir too was trying to find himself as painter. And if he was tempted to weaken as he had weakened with Monet—and how much more severely tried he was now in these long years of experiment!—who better to be with than the ironly determined Cézanne? This new meeting did not visibly change Renoir's work—his version of the Mont Sainte-Victoire could not be mistaken for a Cézanne—but undoubtedly gave him strength to struggle on.

Renoir's appeal to Cézanne is not difficult to understand. Cézanne was very conscious of his ostracism by the Paris dealers and critics and of the insults he had had to endure for years. He brooded about it. He was bitter. In Renoir he had that rare pleasure, a man whose work he thought well of who admired him without reservation and believed in his future triumph.

Renoir's visit ended abruptly in February, and it is clear from a letter to Monet that one of the frequent storms in the Cézanne ménage had blown up out of the blue, taking him and Cézanne with it. "We have been obliged to leave Cézanne's mother suddenly because of the black avarice which reigns in the house." [7]

One wonders whether, in the end, they were given nothing but soup to eat. Whatever the cause, they went down to Marseilles and along the coast to Martigues, which Renoir describes as "the Venice and Constantinople of Ziem and Swedish painters. On every side I see lots of crapulous pictures. However, it is a very beautiful place and I hope to make something of it. We are fed and lodged extremely well for five francs a head." [8]

Renoir was sufficiently pleased with his situation and company to stay on until March when he heard that his mother was ill. When she recovered he selected some canvases for a Durand-Ruel exhibition that May. This was yet another attempt by the dealer to harness the old Impressionist painters to his chariot. He was only partially successful. His second exhibition in New York the preceding year had been disappointing. He decided nevertheless to continue to try to open up the American market by establishing a New York branch. Monet did not agree with this attention paid to America, which he considered so much money thrown away that might have gone into efforts nearer home; he dropped out of the exhibition and soon gave the agency for his work to Boussod and Valadon. He maintained vigorously—and was seconded by Renoir—that he wanted to show the public that Impressionist painters were not the creation or child of one dealer but could be bought anywhere.[9] The May exhibition shrank to a small showing by Renoir, Sisley, Pissarro, and Berthe Morisot—small but encouraging.

Renoir could not follow Monet, however much he sympathized with his stand. He was very short of money; how short will be seen by the fact that throughout his trip south he was forever asking Durand-Ruel or his son to send hurried reinforcements. At the end of his trip, he even had to ask them to pay his hotel bill at Martigues.[10] So there could be no question at the moment of trying to send some of his work to another dealer.

His shortage of money through this long period was to be shown clearly the following year, in 1889, when Monet appealed to all friends and acquaintances to subscribe to a fund he had opened to buy Manet's *Olympia* from his widow and present it to the nation. He had persuaded the government to place the picture in the Luxembourg with a possible transfer envisaged later to the Louvre, and was hopeful of killing two birds with the one stone, to honor Manet in the way he would best have liked and to help his widow to live in comfort. All that remained was to collect the purchase price.

Few gestures could have appealed more to Renoir, to his kindness and to his increasing admiration for Manet's work, yet he was forced to respond to Monet's appeal with a rueful "Impossible to find the money. I am desolated. But I can't wait any longer without replying to you. Manet will get into the Louvre without me. I can't do anything but wish all success to your efforts." [11]

Not for another five months, in January, 1890, was he able to send anything, and then no more than fifty francs.

It may well be that this chronic money shortage sent him to

Essoyes with his wife and child in the fall of 1888; life was cheap there. But he was fascinated too by the people as models— cheaper by far than his Paris models and with all the interest of the unfamiliar, as he was soon to say. The prospect of painting there cheered him, as a note from Berthe Morisot makes clear. She was off to Nice for the winter, saw him just before each went their different ways, and reminded him that there would always be a spare room waiting for him in their house at Cimiez. She found him "not at all downcast, but very perky and reason- ably satisfied with his work; he said he would come to visit us on his tricycle!" [12]

The reference to depression of spirits is illuminating; the struggle to earn money plus the uncertainty about his work (the first an inevitable result of the second) was preying on Renoir's nerves. Pissarro met him that fall of 1888 and after- ward told his son that Renoir had admitted being attacked by everyone, especially by Durand-Ruel and the collectors of his Impressionist pictures, because of his incessant efforts to change his romantic style.[13] The "romantic" can be disregarded (it was merely a Pissarro under Seurat's sway) and "attacked" is too strong a word for what was actually happening to Renoir; never- theless, there is plenty of evidence that almost all the men who had admired and bought his earlier work were puzzled and dis- appointed by the new phase he was taking so long to get through. They did not like his recent pictures and they did not buy them.

Pissarro naturally sympathized with Renoir; Seurat was a first-rate draftsman, and the dotted technique of Neo-Impres- sionism was based on accurate drawing. They thought they had discovered the answer to the problem of linear form, Renoir did not, and that was all the difference Pissarro could see between them. Even when, just about this time, Pissarro began to modify his technique yet again, following Seurat less faithfully, he still proclaimed Neo-Impressionism as the only possible method of advance in painting.[14] He was incapable of understanding that one man's truth was not necessarily another's, but he went so far as to say that "the search for unity is the end to which every

intelligent artist must direct his efforts, and even if one's work
has great faults it is more intelligent and truer art to search
for unity rather than remain enclosed in romanticism." [15]

He ended with a practical note on Renoir: "He doesn't get
any more portraits to do now." [16] This was true and must have
struck Renoir as unjust; the men who had helped to keep him
painting when his work was conventional turned their backs on
him precisely when he was trying to make himself a better
painter. Whether he was really less depressed when he spoke to
Berthe Morisot or, which is always possible with him, was showing her the side of him she liked to see, his letters remain consistently bright. Yet his one major painting of the Paris months
previous to the move to Essoyes certainly could not have convinced him that he had reached the end of the long road. *Les
filles de Catulle Mendès* is very much the work of a man in the
grip of a theory which restricts all the natural artist, and his
experiments in color are unhappy because the color is not an
integral part of the composition.

At Essoyes he unmistakably began to recover spirits. "I am
painting peasant women in Champagne," he told the Manets,
"to avoid the cost of the Paris models. I am making studies of
laundresses, or women washing clothes I should say, on the
banks of the river here." [17] He promised to be with them in
Nice in January.

There were, in fact, faint signs of better work. He made a
charming study, *Arbre plongeant dans l'eau,* a nude with more
freedom than he had allowed himself for years, *La sortie du
bain,* and, most encouraging, *Femme en robe rouge s'essuyant
les pieds.* In this last, glimpses of the Renoir of the future, as
well as the best of the past, are clearly visible. The first was
painted at Bougival before he left for Essoyes, the others by the
river at Essoyes.

Yet the Ource was to repay his work by its side with a wicked
blow. Just before the end of the year, when he and Aline were
getting ready to go back to Paris, he was seized by acute
rheumatism. He saw his promised visit to Nice disappear. "I
am a prisoner," he told Eugène Manet. "I caught cold in the

country and have paralysis of the face, local, rheumatic, etc. In short, I can no longer move one side of my face and for diversion am promised two months of electrical treatment. I am not allowed to go out in case I catch another cold. It is nothing serious, I think, though so far there has been no improvement." [18]

To Durand-Ruel he was more frank. One wonders whether he dreamed what this attack was to lead to. "I hope to come back Thursday evening if my neuralgia permits. It's caught me good and proper. Half my face is paralyzed. I can't eat or sleep." [19]

3

The electrical treatments succeeded, but Renoir was worried as anyone would be who has had the shock of facial paralysis. He may have suspected what is well known today, that rheumatic complaints owe much to the psychological state of the patient and that facial paralysis in particular can be almost wholly emotional in origin. He was a highly strung man—the way he walked, the mobility of his facial expressions, and the amount he smoked every day proclaimed that—and the worry of the last few years must have tried him hard. At any rate, as soon as he was fit to travel he went where he felt sure of getting calm and strength. Firmly disregarding the hurried flight of the previous year he returned to Aix, rented the Montbriand house of Rose Cézanne's husband, and stayed there several months.

They do not seem to have been happy months except that they helped to confirm his love of the Midi. A story went the rounds of the painting fraternity in Paris that Renoir and Cézanne had had a difference. The only definite record of any misunderstanding comes from Pissarro some years later. He tells the story of Cézanne's quarrel with the minor painter Oller, who was forbidden Cézanne's house in a stern letter, and adds, "This incident is simply a variation of what happened to Renoir." [20]

Apparently Cézanne's elder sister or mother brooded as
Renoir did not, and kept alive resentment of the previous
year's plain speaking in Jas de Bouffan. If it is true that the two
painters differed in 1889 when Renoir was unwell, it would
help to account for his long bout of unfinished work. In this
year and the next he completed only a handful of canvases; the
rest he destroyed.

How strongly he now felt about his work is shown by a
letter of this time to Roger Marx, who was arranging an exhibition of French painting to be shown in a great World's
Fair in Paris that summer. The ever enthusiastic Chocquet,
eager to get his favorite painters into an exhibition seen by
millions of foreign visitors, began to praise them fulsomely to
Marx. Renoir heard of it through Cézanne and at once wrote
to Marx, "I should be most grateful if you would decline to
listen when M. Chocquet talks to you about me. When I have
the pleasure of seeing you I hope to explain the reason for this
request. It is very simple—I dislike everything I've done, I
think it bad, and should be horrified to see it exhibited." [21]

Such a stand must have gone some way to placate Cézanne,
whose work, unknown to him, was to be smuggled into the Fair
by an amusing ruse of Chocquet's. Cézanne's stringent artistic
conscience had been taken over by Renoir; not even Cézanne
could outdo the younger man in self-criticism and, whether
angry or pleased with him, must have looked on him as a brand
plucked from the burning. As far ahead as 1902 he is saying
with typical forcefulness, "I despise all living painters except
Monet and Renoir." [22]

If any one person is to be seen as the motivating force behind Renoir's astonishing change of heart it is unquestionably
Cézanne. There is evidence that after their first meeting
Cézanne regarded Renoir for some years with his usual suspicion of Parisian artists. Renoir's recognition of a phenomenon
Paris had not seen for a hundred years or more, one of the
world's great artists in the making, a recognition so charmingly
shown, was too obvious to be gainsaid. Yet his work and attitude
toward it in those early days could indicate only one thing to

the southerner—a nonserious man. Cézanne remained on the defensive.

Not until 1882 did he relax guard when Renoir painted at L'Estaque, fell ill and was nursed by him. These February weeks of 1882 changed the whole course of Renoir's life as a painter. For the first time he worked by the side of Cézanne and, when he went down with pneumonia, saw for the first time that this supreme artist of his time was also a man with a gentle and kind heart.

The change was seen at once, in Renoir's unnaturally brusque refusal (Cézanne could not have been blunter) to show at the seventh Impressionist exhibition. A few months later came the discovery of Cennini's treatise, a sort of echo of Cézanne from the far past, and Renoir began his long and hard fight, wholly against the grain, to make a Cézanne of himself.

This late meeting with Cézanne in 1889 and the difference with him led inevitably to the raising of an already high standard of self-judgment. The years 1889, 1890, and 1891 are notable in painting only for Renoir's last Salon showing in 1890, the portrait of Catulle Mendès' daughters round the piano which was badly hung and received little attention; he could find little to cheer him in his work, which often seemed to stand still.

This may be why he took such pleasure, during this dreary period, in the Manets, Berthe and Eugène, who were anything but dreary when he was with them. He got into the habit of dropping in to their Thursday night dinners in winter.

The atmosphere of these dinners, which had begun a few years earlier, was quite different from the superficial glitter of the Charpentier soirées or those of Alfred Stevens and Edouard Manet, carried on by his wife Suzanne after his death. At these last there was a lot of gossip, and visitors and hosts were expected to show their paces, Bosc singing his songs to his own guitar accompaniment, Chabrier playing *Danse Macabre* fancifully, Cros reciting "Le hareng sec, sec, sec," and the inevitable Suzanne Manet's meaningful rendering of Chopin. Mme. Morisot's description of one Manet soirée was probably not far wide of the mark. "I found the Manet salon as before, nauseating," she told her daughter Berthe. "The heat was stifling, the drinks warm." [23] And her chief hope of relief seems to have been similarly affected: "M. Degas was there but this is not to say that he bestirred himself; he looked sleepy and older than your father." [24]

By contrast Berthe Morisot's dinners were quiet, exclusive, and on the precious side in conversation as in food—the guests were offered dishes such as rice prepared in Mexican fashion and chicken with dates. Henri de Régnier, a typical Parisian dabbler in the arts, recalls: "I met Renoir at Berthe Morisot's house. Mallarmé first took me there, then we used to go often on Sundays too, after the concert. It was a curious and distinctive circle. Eugène Manet, Berthe Morisot, and their daughter Julie lived in the best type of middle-class surroundings which mirrored a very fine taste. Eugène Manet was eager and excitable. Berthe Morisot, elegantly aloof, had a cold and rather haughty affability and gave one sharp, sad glances from under her white hair. Little Julie was a shy, quiet child with red cheeks and beautiful slanting eyes." [25]

Berthe Morisot tried hard to be a serious artist, and the names of her guests—Degas, Mallarmé, Renoir, Monet, Astruc, Fantin, Puvis de Chavannes—show that she was also trying hard to surround herself with the kind of men who would appreciate her talent. By the late eighties and early nineties the chief guests had established themselves as Degas (one of Berthe Morisot's first painter friends), Mallarmé, and Renoir, and they ensured plenty of discussion over the table, for three more different men would be difficult to find.

Renoir always professed himself terrified by the moody, sharp-tongued Degas but relished his brilliant *bons mots*. He thought Degas a wonderful draftsman and painter, although he must sometimes have felt the realism too strong for his taste. With Mallarmé his appreciation was for the conversation only; he could not understand the poetry. He contributed a humor and good sense of his own. He and Degas were always a little edgy with one another—the Salon submissions still cast a shadow

—but an outwardly improbable comradeship sprang up between the other-worldly poet and the down-to-earth painter, possibly because Renoir also took a roseate view of life in his work, possibly because they were at opposite poles in so many ways, as one incident recounted by their hostess makes clear: "Renoir said last night that talent, in literature as in painting, revealed itself only by the way women are treated. This was said, I believe, à propos of the charming Natasha in *War and Peace*. Mallarmé sees greater beauty in men than in women. He says this in innumerable roundabout ways. I reply that I am absolutely indifferent to all that kind of thing." [26]

Berthe Morisot came to rely more and more on Renoir, who must have stood out in such company. He no doubt managed a little high-class gallantry from time to time—he had had plenty of practice at the Charpentiers'—but his real strength lay in his democratic tastes and contacts and his avoidance of circumlocution. She would envy him his freedom of speech and the charm that carried it off. He possessed another merit too, and it was for this that she encouraged him to stay at a new summer home they had found at Mézy, some miles further downriver from what is known as the Renoir area of the Seine. He came unannounced as always, carrying the lightest of gear, and they painted together or apart as their whims took them with Julie an interested and sometimes critical spectator.[27]

It was no wonder that Berthe Morisot loved his company. Everyone who worked with Renoir or watched him at work, from his brother in his youth to his son in his old age, has commented on the joy he radiated. He could be witty at a dinner party in his blunt way, gay at a dance, stimulating at a conversation between friends, but he really came to life when a brush was between his fingers. To see a man loving his work and never willingly parted from it is heartening and even inspiring, particularly to a woman like Berthe Morisot, with feminine doubts of her gift, who relied on a man's lead.

Renoir gave her a lead. He openly admired her work—"she was the last elegant and feminine artist we have had since Fragonard, not to speak of that virginal something she conveyed in high degree in all her painting," [28] he was to say after her death—and in consequence she worked more confidently with him. His value to her came out even in these riverside visits in the early nineties when he seldom got beyond sketches; unable to please himself, tearing up the sketches, he still managed to communicate pleasure in his work.

He perhaps first met the Polish writer Theodore de Wyzewa at the Manet dinners. De Wyzewa admired the work of his hostess and was eager to write about it. When he met Renoir he wanted to write about him too. Renoir evidently appreciated this championship when his creative faculties were at a low ebb and somehow managed to turn a blind eye to the Pole's obvious affinity with Mallarmé. One point in De Wyzewa's favor was his ability to penetrate to the painter as he wanted to be rather than what he was. He told Berthe Morisot, "I believe more and more strongly that since Manet's death only you and Renoir have preserved the qualities of painters of the past, that you and Renoir alone are true artists amidst a generation of teachers and pupils." [29]

He confessed, "I still dream of an article or book in which I could express my feelings about the art of yourself and Renoir in a way which would give you pleasure." [30] He was to write this book—a collection of essays on painters he admired [31]— though not in Berthe Morisot's lifetime, but he began his essay on Renoir that same year of 1891. Soon after new year De Wyzewa and the painter went off to the tiny resort of Tamaris-sur-mer, close to Toulon, where De Wyzewa had the idea of watching Renoir at work before writing about him.

As these regular winter flights to the south indicate, Renoir was trying to be cautious. His susceptibility to rheumatic complaints was too obvious to be ignored, and he was terrified that his painting might be curtailed or even brought to an end before he had found himself. When he was satisfied, he would be able to relax, or so he liked to think: "I want to have done with all my exaggerated waverings and come back with plenty of pictures," he told Durand-Ruel.[32]

He also went south for the reason which made Cézanne

return to Aix again and again and finally never leave it, the reason why Vincent van Gogh (then not one year dead) left St. Rémy for the north with such sorrow; he was fascinated by the clear atmosphere and the colorful models.

That, at least, was how he felt when he once again reached the Midi. Although he had wonderful weather at Tamaris and an excellent choice of local models, he commented, "Nothing is finished except two studies and I've given myself a lot of trouble to get even as far without more gropings." 33

He wrote this at the beginning of March and added dolefully, "Four days ago I was fifty and that's a bit old for a man to be still seeking the light. But I have done what I could, that's all I can say." 34

Two weeks later he was announcing that he had sent off a box of canvases, but his satisfaction did not last long enough for Durand-Ruel to receive them. One week afterward he was writing, "I am very much worried by the stuff I've sent you, it's a hotchpotch of styles. I shall soon send you another lot of things more likely to last. I think I'm making progress and don't want to come back until I'm satisfied with myself." 35

This was not to be; as at L'Estaque he was caught in a rainstorm, went down with influenza, and soon afterward moved along the coast to Le Lavandou. By the end of April he was in Paris again after breaking his journey to see the Maison Carrée at Nîmes. He was still very much where he had been when he left the city at the beginning of the year. In terms of true originality the whole year's output could be reduced to two canvases, the better of which was *La leçon de musique*. It is possible to see in this work—one of many attempts to paint girls at the piano—some hints of the Renoir to be. The drawing, excellent though it is, does not dominate the picture, the color is used to heighten emotion and tie the figures and objects together, the painting is luminous, and the old Renoir gift of conveying the essence of femininity is cleverly used in gesture as well as face, figure, and fold of gown.

He again spent some time that summer at Mézy with Berthe Morisot and her husband and daughter. For once Renoir did

not come alone, arriving, unexpectedly as usual, with his wife
and son. At first the visit seemed likely to flounder. Neither of
the Manets had met Aline before and must have felt that
Renoir had placed them in an invidious position. His faith in
them was rewarded—by the end of dinner all were at ease—but
Berthe Morisot did not forget the visit for some time to come.
Later that summer she told Mallarmé, one of her most cherished
friends, "Renoir has just been with us for a few days, this time
without his wife. I could never manage to convey to you my
astonishment when I first saw that ungainly woman. I had
imagined, I can't say why, that she would be like her husband's
paintings. I shall introduce you to her this winter." [36]

Like many women, she instinctively reacted against the wives
of men who attracted her. Some years earlier she had called the
wife of Manet, who appealed to her for much the same reasons
as Renoir, "that fat Suzanne." [37] Berthe Morisot was, of course,
slim and elegant. But she was a civilized woman too and, after
the first reaction, kind; she and her husband were to dine with
the Renoirs that winter and to discover all the merits of the
Renoir home.

4

The next year, 1892, was no more distinguished by the quality
of Renoir's painting than the previous one. Although the
number of completed canvases was larger, not one was up to the
standard of *La leçon de musique*. The year was noteworthy
chiefly for an invasion of Gauguin territory in Brittany, a first
journey to Spain, and a substantial exhibition at Durand-Ruel's
designed to cover the entire period of Renoir's work from the
beginning of Impressionism. This last was by far the biggest
showing of any of his contemporaries. Helped by extensive loans
from collectors, Durand-Ruel managed to include no fewer
than 112 items in his catalogue.

These collectors provided a panorama of loyal souls from
early days—Duret, De Bellio, Chocquet, Dollfus, Caillebotte,

Rouart (whose son was to marry Julie Manet), Chabrier, and Bérard. Monet lent portraits given to him by Renoir; and among the newer names were Robert de Bonnières, Jacques-Émile Blanche, and Paul Gallimard, owner of the Variétés Theatre in which the Impressionist skit had been staged, man of the world, and proprietor of a beautiful Normandy estate.

Blanche was a significant addition to Renoir collectors. He was a typical intellectual of his time, trying his hand at poetry, the novel, painting, criticism. He had just become friendly with Toulouse-Lautrec and was in the first stages of a fervent admiration for Jane Avril, latest star of the Moulin Rouge, the Montmartre dance hall then all the rage—an admiration which was to culminate in her appearance as the heroine of his new novel. He was a contributor to Natanson's *Revue Blanche,* which was advanced in a decidedly precious and pretentious style and attitude, and he belonged to a generation which might have been expected to regard Renoir and his friends as somewhat passé.

That he did not was no doubt due to his friend and master, Alexandre, who wrote the introduction to Durand-Ruel's catalogue of the Renoir exhibition. This introduction was what is now known as a "rave" notice. Yet it judged the feelings of fashionable art lovers accurately. After many false starts, Renoir was at last established as a serious painter. Confirmation came in the usual manner; *La leçon de musique* was bought by the government for the Luxembourg, an event that must have caused the painter mingled gratification and concern, humorously expressed concern, maybe, but concern nevertheless real. With the irony of life he knew so well by this time, this worldly success came when he could not feel pleased with his work, when he was still groping. His progress toward self-realization as a painter was dragging horribly for a man not endowed with overmuch patience. He had been sitting for nearly ten years at the feet of Ingres, the old masters, and the eighteenth-century painters; he was over fifty, and he had not yet escaped the thrall of the copyist.

But for all his fifty-one years, Renoir had not lost his youthful buoyancy. What the exhibition chiefly meant to him at that moment was money to spend in the right and only way, to get away from it all and again free his mind. With the proceeds from the canvases Durand-Ruel had sold, he went off with Gallimard (another regular at the Morisot dinners) to Madrid, the Prado, and its Goyas.

He was enthusiastic about the Goyas—"his *Royal Family* is worth the trip by itself" [38]—but worshipped Velásquez, whose greatness all the other painters he studied at the Prado merely made him feel the more. All he could find to say of El Greco was, "His faults only strengthened my natural preference for Velásquez . . . the whole art of painting is in the little pink bow of the *Infanta Margherita*." [39] He admitted that "Titian has everything, first mystery, then depth. Rubens is a shell beside him, nothing but surface, whereas you almost feel like trying to open Philip II's cuirass to find out what's inside. . . ." [40] Even this, however, led to "You see how I love Titian, but I always come back to Velásquez. . . . I almost feel like kissing the horses in *The Surrender at Breda* . . . his painting radiates the joy he felt in making it." [41]

This joy, of course, was the great attraction of the Spanish master, this and his fluency, the fluency Renoir was trying so hard to recover. His final comment was significant: "Only the painter who knows his business from A to Z can give the impression that a picture was done in one and the same breath. His work looks easy, but think of the experiments he must have made before it looks so!" [42]

He was obsessed by Velásquez and made short work of Gallimard, who had the admittedly irritating habit of interrupting a long stint before a canvas by coming up behind him with a reproving, "Yes, but I prefer Rembrandt." Renoir's patience soon snapped. "You and your damned Rembrandts make me tired. While I'm in Spain let me look at Velásquez as long as I like. There'll be time for Rembrandt when I'm in Holland." [43]

Holland was not next on the list, however, but an effort to combine work and a family holiday, first at Pornic beyond

Nantes, then on the island of Noirmoutiers, which he could see plainly from the Pornic shore. He complained humorously to Berthe Morisot; he had been meaning to write to her for a long time but had restrained himself "because I'm in a very bad temper. I have ended up by getting stranded at Pornic where I'm teaching my son to swim. That's fine as far as it goes, but I ought to be making landscapes. The country round here is quite attractive and that's what annoys me. Landscape painting is becoming increasingly painful to do, the more so as I feel it to be my duty. Clearly, landscape work helps one to learn one's craft a bit, but somehow I don't feel able to hang about outdoors like a tramp any more the way I used to do." [44]

He added that he wanted to write "Come!" when the beauty of the country particularly struck him, but forebore "because I don't want to play a dirty trick on you by bringing you to a place that bores me, a place I should soon be out of if I were alone." [45] When he had to break the holiday to attend a funeral in Paris, and met her there, he was equally frank, as she told Mallarmé: "His wife and son are enjoying the bathing tremendously, but he is bored to death." [46]

How much was said and written as a matter of tact is not clear. Berthe Morisot had lost her husband that spring, and Renoir would be the last man to tell a recently widowed friend that he was enjoying a summer at the sea with his wife and child. He would tend to lean over backward to give the impression that he found domestic life tedious when he wanted to paint. But it is true that he painted little he thought worth preserving until Aline and the boy went back to Paris en route for the usual summer stay at Essoyes and he moved over to Pont-Aven in Brittany.

The choice of a place made famous by Gauguin, and in which he could not avoid hearing much of Gauguin—not a man he thought well of in any sense—is a little curious. He stayed at the large Hôtel des Voyageurs, not the auberge of Marie-Jeanne Gloanec further down the street where Gauguin had reigned as monarch of all he surveyed, and he stood no risk of running into Gauguin, in Tahiti for the past eighteen months, but the choice remains odd. One result of it is that comparisons are unavoidable. Although he and Gauguin are very different painters, when they paint similar scenes the canvases cannot escape analysis. Renoir was stirred by Pont-Aven, too, and for the first time in years began to paint freely. He brought back to Paris that winter a number of Pont-Aven studies, but it would not be easy to argue that any one of them stood favorably beside Gauguin's best work in the same countryside.

Some critics have claimed that Renoir recovered his touch more quickly in landscape than figure, and quote these Brittany canvases—particularly *Près de Pont-Aven*, a study of the church of Riec-sur-Belon, and *L'embouchure de l'Aven*—as proof that the painter is approaching his final manner. But the question surely is, not so much whether this is a fact, as whether it is relevant. For all his recent deprecatory words to Berthe Morisot, Renoir's landscapes were showing less sign of strain than his figure studies simply because they did not call for such attention to draftsmanship. Yet as he was preeminently a painter of people, this new ease in landscape does not appear of great moment. Besides, many will think that he had long since painted his finest landscapes in such works as *La Grenouillère, La Canardière, Printemps,* and *La Prairie*. Even in those early days he did not treat landscape very seriously except when actually working with Monet; now, in the nineties, his development as a figure painter had become all important to him, and such landscapes as he painted were almost all made deliberately as a form of practice.

In this year of Pont-Aven, 1892, he did in fact paint two figure studies which suggest that he is on the way out of his difficulties. One is *Le Croquet*. He did not play games and deplored the growing fetish for them, and if he deigned to take notice of croquet and shuttlecock it was only because they allowed a painter to reproduce novel poses of the feminine body.[47] *Le Croquet* is a remarkably free study of a woman bending to pick up her ball, and *Baigneuse allongée de dos* (one of a series of bathing studies made during an excursion to the sea) likewise indicates that the stringent rule of Ingres is loosening into the mature Renoir, in which the line is allowed to flow and the color plays a creative part in the composition.

He, of course, was not at all satisfied, and was off again that winter in search of a stimulant. He revisited the Martigues district and hurriedly wrote to Berthe Morisot from Saint-Chamas: "I have been thinking specially of you just now, because if you want to be in the most beautiful countryside in the world, here it is. Here you have Italy, Greece, and the Batignolles all rolled into one, plus the sea." He drew a map on the letter showing a round trip from Marseilles to Port de Boue with a note: "I think this is the most beautiful excursion in France; beautiful and inexpensive too." [48]

There is no sign that the beauty led to better work, so he went down to Beaulieu, where he is found in April, 1893, apologizing to Durand-Ruel: "I don't speak of what I have done, that's why I haven't written you earlier. I find my studies sometimes good, sometimes bad. . . . For fifteen minutes I'm contented with what I've done; the next day my opinion is likely to be quite different." [49]

That summer he spent a few days at the Gallimards' country place in Calvados, which he found "beautiful but cold—I am going to take a walk to try to decide whether it is any use for painting." [50]

The walk was evidently unfavorable, for he was soon off on a tour of Normandy, finding many beauties but no inspiration, crossed the country to Burgundy to visit his wife's relatives, then carried Aline and his son to Pont-Aven—a restless zigzag which expresses his state of mind more effectively than any letter. He was at Pont-Aven, he told Durand-Ruel, "solely to escort my family, though I have begun one or two things. I must finish them and this is a good place for it, with plenty of models." [51] But he came back to Paris with very few finished canvases.

5

He stayed in Paris for the winter of 1893–1894, caught influenza, and had only just recovered when he heard that Caillebotte was dead. For the past years he had kept in touch with this good friend and fervent admirer at monthly dinners at the Café Riche, where a few of the companions of Impressionist days talked over old times. Pissarro was often there, Sisley occasionally, Monet rarely, but Caillebotte, Duret, and De Bellio scarcely missed a dinner, and Duret brought with him the young and enthusiastic critic Gustave Geffroy whose portrait Cézanne was soon to begin. Geffroy has left a record of these gatherings.[52]

How much Caillebotte not only liked Renoir but relied on his business sense in preference to any other man was shown when he made him his executor insofar as his priceless collection of Impressionist paintings was concerned. When Renoir accepted this duty the last thing he could have thought was that he would live to carry it out; Caillebotte was seven years the younger. The shock of his friend's sudden death (he had cerebral paralysis) followed quickly on the news of two other losses, first of Tanguy, then of De Bellio.

The disappearance of two of the staunchest Impressionist supporters in Caillebotte and De Bellio brought to an end the Café Riche dinners and, indeed, the history of Impressionism. It also involved Renoir in trouble, years of it. Caillebotte had left his collection to the state and the bequest threw Renoir into the kind of publicity he loathed. All the reactionary forces in painting, politics, and journalism fought hard and foully to prevent Impressionist paintings from being hung in the Luxembourg. Gérôme threatened to resign from the Beaux-Arts if the government accepted the bequest, and spoke for the leaders of the Institute when he described the pictures as "filth"[53] and declared that their appearance in the Luxembourg would denote "a deplorable moral degradation in high places."[54] The academicians and the journals supporting them were equally abusive; "this heap of excrement" painted by "anarchists and madmen" [55] was a typical sample of their language and of their desperation in this last-ditch action by the old guard of the Beaux-Arts.[56]

Renoir, far from well and anxious to get on with his work, was obliged to spend much of his time in this distasteful attempt to carry out the wishes of his dead friend. He tried hard, although he disliked controversy more than most men, and in consequence became the special target of Gérôme and his allies. Pissarro, the "anarchist," told his son in London what was being said of his old friend: *"L'Éclair* publishes an interview with Gérôme. He blackguards Renoir and says he must not be confused with Renouard, who can draw and has talent!" [57] The conservative *Le Temps,* which might have been expected to use some restraint, went further by pillorying him as "A real malefactor who has led astray the youth of our time." [58]

The Minister of Fine Arts, the man who had to make the decision, was the Roujon who went back on his predecessor's promise to help Gauguin. When the painter left France for good early in 1895, Roujon told him, "I don't understand your painting. It disgusts me and I shall do nothing to encourage it." [59] Such an attitude did not bode well for the fate of the Caillebotte legacy. Renoir and the Minister had many discussions, mostly abortive: "Roujon and I could never agree on anything," Renoir recalled afterward. "Not that he is unintelligent or unpleasant as a person. But to avoid quarreling with him I had to be careful never to speak of the painters I really admired. . . . I can still hear him saying, 'If that Cézanne only had the first idea how to paint!' " [60]

Month by month, year by year, the argument and abuse went on. Not until 1897, three years after Caillebotte's death, did Renoir compromise. To ensure that some part of the collection was taken by the state, he at last agreed to withdraw certain canvases which the obscurantists had vilified with particular ferocity. In the end, only half the sixteen Monets found their way to the Luxembourg, less than half the Pissarros, two of the four Cézannes, two of the three Manets, six of the eight Renoirs, and nine Sisleys. The seven Degas canvases alone were taken without serious demur.

Between the various phases of this long struggle, Renoir continued to entertain at his home and tried to work. The company he kept and the way he gathered it is seen in a note to Berthe Morisot at the end of March, 1894: "Next Wednesday, Mallarmé will give me the pleasure of coming to dine at Montmartre. If such a climb is not too much for you in the evening, I am sure he would love to meet you here. Durand-Ruel is coming and I intend to ask the above-mentioned poet to ask Regnier on my behalf. I would have liked to invite Degas but must confess that I can't scrape up the courage. I don't speak of my sweet and lovely Julie; her presence is taken for granted. I believe that Mallarmé's daughter will come with him." [61]

Soon after this dinner he began another portrait of Julie Manet in the new and smaller apartment on rue Weber taken by Berthe Morisot since her husband's death. The painter then begged to be allowed to change it into a double portrait, of mother and daughter, and to paint it in his Montmartre studio. He promised to finish it in six sessions of two hours, an indication of his growing confidence. He was not often refused a favor by Berthe Morisot, and she and Julie duly climbed to his latest studio, in rue Tourlaque, up against the great Montmartre cemetery, a street in which Toulouse-Lautrec had preceded him some years earlier. Renoir had changed studios more than once since leaving rue Saint-Georges, partly because of dissatisfaction with his work, but he had chosen the rue Tourlaque studio for a definite reason; it provided more than just elbow room for the making of large canvases such as *Les grandes baigneuses*.

He had no need to promise the Manets a good lunch after the morning sittings; they had long since sampled Aline's cooking and were anxious for more. Renoir's home address had changed as well as his studio and was within walking distance of it. The new Renoir home was in a block of buildings on the slope of the Butte, at the far end of rue Girardon. They had the romantic name of Château des Brouillards, romantic and ominous, too, for a man liable to rheumatic complaints. Most of the romance seems to have disappeared before the Renoirs moved in, but the house still had atmosphere. It also had a hedge, gardens, an orchard, and some good trees, the remnants of what had once been an estate of some importance. As a result the family had a sense of privacy unusual in Paris, especially in Montmartre, yet they also enjoyed superb views from the Butte.[62] The house was roomy and was to become more historic in the eighteen-nineties than any Montmartre squire had made it a century earlier, for here Renoir was to find himself as a painter.

6

Not many weeks after the Manet portrait was done, Aline took Pierre to Essoyes for the summer as usual. The boy became ill there, Renoir was summoned, and this forced him to refuse Berthe Morisot's invitation to Brittany. He did not wish to go far out of Paris that summer, he explained, so as to keep in touch with Essoyes. The farthest west he would go was Trouville.

He ended his refusal note with the kind of amusing post-script he was often writing to those of whom he was fond: "So enjoy yourselves and bring back to Paris some of those glorious views of the sea, which are particularly splendid in Brittany, where the sea is opaque to the very edge of the sand, with white-clad Julies against a background of golden isles. What a sentence! But then I wrote it, of course, to madden Mallarmé." [63]

Berthe Morisot's pique—she had come to rely on Renoir as some sort of fond family jester—was expressed to the poet, her other faithful friend of these years. "Renoir could not come to join me, to my great regret. His too, I believe—at least he says so. He is consoling himself with Gallimard at Deauville." [64]

When Renoir came back to Paris from Normandy he found a change in the family that was to go far toward putting him finally on his feet. His wife had invited a fifteen-year-old cousin

from Essoyes to stay with them. Gabrielle Renard was to become world-famous as a Renoir model and must take some of
the credit for the final dismissal of the shadow of Ingres. She
was a big girl, dark and with a strong profile. She was precisely
what Renoir needed in his house at that time, something chal-
lengingly new, a gypsy type always on call, the perfect model
in appearance and, as he soon discovered with exultation, in
disposition too. She would pose indefinitely and hold the pose.
It had been one of his many problems that models did not stand
up well to the long painting sessions he preferred, sessions
elongated as far as possible so that he did not lose concentration
and inspiration. Gabrielle never caused him a moment's worry
in this direction. She was strong, healthy, placid, and seemed as
fresh at the end of a sitting as at the beginning.

The girl had not been asked to Paris for this purpose, or at
least not primarily. Her real function in the Renoir home was
announced to Berthe Morisot that fall by a rather crestfallen
Renoir: "I have a quite absurd piece of news for you . . .
namely, the arrival of a second son. He is called Jean. Mother
and baby are both in splendid health." [65]

Berthe Morisot, amused—he had evidently been prophesy-
ing—replied that he would have to think hard for another ten
years, then he might be favored with a daughter. When the
winter season closed in, he and Mallarmé continued a practice
they had taken up since the death of Berthe's husband, escorting
her to the operettas all loved.[66] The year had scarcely ended,
however, when Renoir came down with influenza. This sent
him south once more, to the warmth.

He did not go alone; with him went the sixteen-year-old
Jeanne Baudot and her parents. Jeanne, godmother of the baby
Jean, was the daughter of the chief doctor of a railway company.
The Baudots were friends of the Gallimards. Jeanne had
studied the Renoir canvases in the Gallimard collection, begged
Gallimard for an introduction to the painter, and, having had
her way, declared that she too must be a painter and that Renoir
must be her teacher.

She persuaded her doting parents easily enough; to persuade

Renoir was another matter. Renoir wanted to paint, not to teach. He placed her with an American woman, another admirer of himself and his work who had sat for him and then taken up painting. This plan collapsed quickly; the two women did not see eye to eye. Renoir then advised the École Julian. Jeanne attended a few classes, was criticized as being unduly influenced by the Impressionist technique (an interesting pointer to the backwardness of the Paris schools), swept out, and once again besieged the Renoir studio. Renoir accepted his fate. Jeanne began to come to his studio regularly, ostensibly to learn, mainly to watch and worship.[67]

But she had a gift of a kind—her work exists—and she was young and pretty in a slim, dark fashion. She soon joined forces with Julie Manet and her two Gobillard cousins, and Renoir found himself backed by a female chorus of youth, liveliness, and admiration. He made the most of them when he happened to be in the mood to use models with youthful charm and stimulating variety.

By the winter of 1894 Jeanne had become a recognized favorite, as Renoir demonstrated when he decided to introduce her and her parents to his beloved Martigues area. He did not forget old friends, however, and wrote enthusiastically to Berthe Morisot from the little seaside village of Carry-Lerouet, urging her to join him. In spite of his previous recommendations, she had not yet seen this part of the coast, and he once more gave her minute directions—the hotel to stay at, the best floor to choose, the price she should pay, and the easiest way to get there.[68]

It was not to be; these appeals of February, 1895, failed in their turn. This time, Julie was down with influenza and her mother could not leave her. No sooner had Renoir put the latest of his calls to the beautiful south in the hotel mailbox than the beauties vanished in winter storms. He and the Baudots hurriedly moved to Marseilles in search of warmth. What he had in mind beyond this is not known. Perhaps he was bound for L'Estaque, to show his friends the countryside in which he first painted with Cézanne years ago; perhaps he was bound for a reunion with Cézanne himself, a Cézanne with whom the rift (if there ever had been one worthy the name) had been healed. It may even be—the gesture would be typical—that he intended to console Cézanne for the farcical prices paid for his canvases at the sale of Tanguy's remarkable collection the previous year, prices that seemed cruelly to underline the fate of this long-neglected painter.

But whatever his plans, they were shattered at Marseilles; a telegram told him that Jean was seriously ill with bronchitis. He took the first train home.[69]

When the child had recovered, Renoir, according to his son, went off again, this time definitely to Cézanne.[70] If paid (there are doubts about it), this visit must have been very short; up in Paris Berthe Morisot caught influenza from Julie, it turned to pneumonia, and she died in the first days of March.

Renoir had not been able to paint seriously for months. One thing after another—his child's birth, his own influenza, the hurried returns to Paris (for, of course, he was at Berthe Morisot's funeral), his subsequent efforts on behalf of the bereaved girls (Berthe Morisot's elder sister had predeceased her, leaving two daughters in her care)—kept him from making the final assault against the barrier of the student-draftsman. Yet at this moment in 1895 he was within reach of what he had so long struggled for. After Berthe Morisot's death his interest turned ever more toward his own family. The domestic life in the Château des Brouillards charmed him, and the two new models there—the baby and the girl who looked after him— lured him almost imperceptibly out of his preoccupation with line. He painted *La famille de l'artiste*.

CHAPTER XVI

VOLLARD

1894-1895

RENOIR WAS OFTEN TO SAY that he had done with Impressionism. As he had. Yet there were aspects of Impressionist painting which expressed him as well as any man who followed that particular technique. One was the abolition or softening of the bounding line, another the use of pigment to obtain a surface texture that shone and gleamed. These he now began to return to, bending them to his individual purpose.

Everyone who has studied Renoir's paintings knows that the key to his work is intense feeling for life and movement. They know, too, that the great bulk of his work in the long "Ingresque" period fails because it goes contrary to the painter's nature. It was not in the true Renoir to use a strong bounding line, for this isolated the figure from the movement he loved, made it static instead of fluid. Nor was it in him to be satisfied with a statuesque nobility at the expense of mobility, in the wake of the ancients. Nor, again, could he persist indefinitely with the use of the delicate colors of his "manière aigre"; for him life was synonymous with color, and the pastel shades of *Les grandes baigneuses* were a negation of all he stood for.

One thinks, of course, of Rubens. Like Rubens, Renoir reveled in the human body, in the sheen of a woman's skin, her full breasts and plump buttocks. Like Rubens he was a colorist and a sensualist, the one complementing the other, and *La famille de l'artiste* recalls Rubens in color and style. It has not entirely thrown off the long legacy of stiffness, but the beginning of the smooth and generous brushstroke rhythm characteristic of Renoir's final work is clearly seen.

In succeeding canvases of these first years of freedom Renoir expressed himself with increasing confidence. *Dans la prairie*, the study of two girls sitting in a meadow, is gloriously colored, and obvious attention to draftsmanship is giving way to his gift for the use of strong color to reproduce a living image. *Jean Renoir jouant avec Gabrielle et une fillette* and *Les enfants de M. Caillebotte* are in another world from the commissioned child studies of his earlier years, and their truthful and vivid representation of life is brought about by inspired use of color. *Femme au chapeau* has often been described as one of Renoir's finest pictures; in drawing, composition, and unexpected color combinations it gives rare pleasure. Two years later, in 1897, came *Joueuse de guitare* with its dazzlingly rich effect—one wonders how many painters would have dared put such colors side by side on canvas—which shows an almost perfect integration with drawing, masterfully used in the service of feeling. Unmistakable signs of the later preoccupation with red are seen in Gabrielle's dress, the chair and child's dress of *Joueuse de guitare*, as well as the background of another 1897 canvas, *Baigneuse endormie*.

2

It was at this time that Renoir met Vollard. Before quoting Vollard's now famous account of this meeting it might be well to see Renoir as Vollard must have seen him. He had aged greatly. His hair, mustache, and beard (worn a little longer now) had turned almost white; his face was if possible more bony than ever. He wore invariably a tweed double-breasted jacket and trousers, occasionally a stiff gray hat, but more often what was then known as a cycling cap. He still smoked interminably, still spoke pungently and to the point when driven to it, still loved life as youthfully as ever, still had all the charm of the man innocent of pretension.

Vollard was a creole from the Isle of Réunion, like the Parnassian poet Léon Dierx whom Renoir had met at the Nouvelle Athènes and was to meet later in the south. He was a thin, bearded, bright-eyed man, a man of sudden enthusiasms who combined a strong business sense with an ability to take the wildest of risks. He had opened a small gallery in rue Laffitte at the beginning of 1894 and was first discovered, in what may loosely be called the Renoir circle, by the indefatigable Pissarro, who was forever touring the galleries in search of sales for himself and his friends.

From the beginning Vollard was quite clear that he could not compete with established galleries for the work of painters already well known. He looked for the comparatively unknown, hoping to discover an unusual painter he could boost. He has been accused of lacking judgment; this may be so, but he possessed a flair for his work which comes to much the same thing as judgment. When Pissarro first called at his gallery he found "some very fine early Gauguins," [1] and this haul (obviously at low prices) was typical of Vollard. He saw possibilities in Gauguin. Further than that, he saw that although he had returned from Tahiti, Gauguin would never rest in Europe once he had tasted the life of the tropical islands. He would again be forgotten by the Paris art world and would be glad to sell canvases cheap to the first dealer who took the trouble to get in touch with him.

His hunch proved profitable. Not long afterward he was to buy the entire Gauguin collection of the disgruntled Émile Bernard. This made him at one blow the most important Gauguin dealer, a position he was to clinch by arranging (for a scandalously small yearly payment) to obtain from the South Seas all the pictures painted by that great but neglected man.

This was to be his second remarkable coup. The first was already in process before he met Renoir; both Pissarro and Degas had spoken favorably to him early in 1894 of the work

being done by Cézanne in his isolation at Aix, and to a man like
Vollard a hint was enough.

He could have been in no hurry to meet Renoir for business
purposes because the painter was well established and known in
the trade to be specially friendly with Durand-Ruel. But Vollard took the long view—one never knew what might happen.
He was insatiably curious, and unlike most people had no fear
of injuring his dignity. He wanted to meet every good painter
he could find.

It is clear from his references to nude studies of La Boulangère (the Renoir servant) and Gabrielle hanging on the wall
of the Renoir house that this first visit must have been some
time after Gabrielle's arrival at Château des Brouillards and
Renoir's return from his summer and autumn painting excursions. This would place it sometime in the winter of 1894–1895.

Vollard was never to become one of Renoir's main dealers in
the sense of staging exhibitions of his work; his part in the
Renoir story was different. The two men took to one another
at once—Vollard was just the type of original to amuse and
fascinate Renoir—and their friendship led to at least two
masterly portraits and two books about Renoir by the dealer
which, whatever their shortcomings (Vollard was incurably
naïve, often trivial and not firmly wedded to truth), will always
remain valuable to anyone who wants to know more about the
man behind the paintings.

Besides, Vollard soon began in his rather devious way to pick
up Renoir canvases whenever he could get them cheap—he was
a great haunter of by-streets—and after the painter's death was
able to produce hundreds. These alone would have made his
fortune. More importantly the world discovered itself richer
than it had supposed, for many of these canvases had been forgotten or were assumed to have been lost or destroyed.

Vollard was to begin his best-known book on Renoir with
their first meeting, which Berthe Morisot had encouraged. "I
wanted to find out who had posed for a Manet in my gallery . . .
had been told that Renoir would know and went to see him. I
found him living in an old house called Château des Brouillards

in Montmartre. In the garden was a servant dressed like a gypsy. She told me to wait. At that moment a young woman appeared, as buxom and friendly as a pastel by Perroneau of one of Louis XV's ladies.

"It was Mme. Renoir. 'Didn't the maid ask you in? Gabrielle!'

"The rebuke took the girl by surprise. 'But it's so muddy outside and La Boulangère has forgotten to put back the mat at the door.' " [2]

In truth Gabrielle had taken one look at Vollard's shabby clothes, dusky skin and gleaming eyes, put him down as an Algerian rug seller (they swarmed in Paris then as now), and told him they wanted nothing—an incident that even Vollard's elastic pride would tempt him to suppress.[3]

He continues his story: "I was shown into the dining room while Mme. Renoir went to fetch her husband. On the walls were the finest Renoirs I had ever seen.

"The painter soon arrived. I had never seen him before. He was thin, bright-eyed and very fidgety, as if he could never stay still.

"I explained why I had come. 'Your man is M. Brun,' he said, 'a friend of Manet's. But we can talk better upstairs. Come up to the studio.'

"He ushered me into a commonplace kind of room with two or three pieces of furniture which did not go together, a heap of colored stuffs and a number of straw hats which looked as though Renoir used to scrabble them between his fingers when posing the model. There were canvases everywhere stacked one against the other. Near the model's chair I saw a pile of copies, unopened, of La Revue Blanche, an advanced magazine very popular with certain sections of the public. I remembered reading much praise of Impressionist painting in it.

" 'That's an interesting magazine,' I said.

"Renoir agreed, adding, 'My friend Natanson sends them to me but I must admit I've never read the thing.'

"When I stretched out a hand to glance at the top copy he cried, 'Don't touch them! That's for my model to rest a foot on.'

"When he sat down and opened his color box I was astonished how clean and tidy it was; the tubes were all squeezed flat and carefully rolled up as they were used. It reminded me of the neatness of women.

"I said how impressed I was with two nudes hanging in the dining room. 'Studies of our maids,' he explained. 'Some of our girls have splendid figures and pose like angels. But I'm not hard to please, I'd just as soon paint the first old crock who comes along. All I ask is that a woman has a skin that takes the light.' " [4]

At this point Renoir must have recalled his sufferings—the "penitential act" [5] he spoke about when Chocquet first commissioned him—during those long years of society portraiture, for he went off into a diatribe. It is a diatribe many will welcome from him. " 'I can't understand how men can paint those overbred females called society women. Have you ever seen one of them with hands worth painting? The hands of a woman who does housework are beautiful. Look at the marvellous hands and arms of Raphael's *Venus Supplicating Jupiter* at the Farnesina in Rome! His Venus looks like a fine, strong housewife borrowed from her kitchen to pose! That, of course, is why Stendhal thought Raphael's women fat and common.' " [6]

The interview was cut short by the arrival of a model. Vollard, much intrigued, asked if he could come again. Renoir said he could, but not until evening when work was done. Vollard took him, as he thought, literally. The next time he arrived fairly late in the evening and found that Renoir had gone to bed. After that the dealer began to understand his host's habits, called earlier, and the men became good friends. But the naïve Vollard, who liked to think of a painter as a man apart, could never get over Renoir's clockwork division of the day. The neatness of his painting gear, the dealer discovered, was emblematic of his whole life. "He lived like a bank clerk!" [7] he complained. Renoir, who always worked to set hours even in his youth, had by the nineties pared away inessentials so that he should have the longest possible time, feeling at his best, for his work. He allowed himself a few theatres, dinners, soirées at friends', that

was all. "He arrived in his studio morning and afternoon like
a man in an office," sighed Vollard, "and in the evening he
usually played chess or dominoes with Mme. Renoir before
going to bed early." [8]

In November, 1895, Vollard scored his first substantial success; encouraged by Renoir he collected a large number of
Cézanne canvases, going down to the Midi to find many of
them, and put on an exhibition which astounded Paris art
lovers. Cézanne had been at Aix so long that he had become a
legend, his work unseen or forgotten. One day Pissarro was
admiring these pictures when Renoir arrived in the gallery.
"My enthusiasm was nothing to Renoir's," wrote Pissarro.
"Degas himself is seduced by the charm of this refined savage,
Monet, all of us. . . . As Renoir said so well, these paintings have
that indescribable quality of the things at Pompeii, so crude
and so admirable!" [9] When Pissarro came back another day
Vollard told him that Degas and Renoir had been so anxious
to buy a Cézanne sketch of fruit that they drew lots.[10]

It is by way of Vollard that we hear Renoir's comments after
he had visited London and the museums of Holland, journeys
notable chiefly for the fact that they were almost his last pleasure trips outside France.

The London visit was a disappointment and produced some
frank talk. When Vollard asked him what he thought of the
English school of painting, the reply was, "It doesn't exist. The
English copy everything. One moment they're making Rem-
brandts, the next Claude Lorrains. There is only one interesting
English painter, Bonington, and one never hears of him." [11]

Renoir explained that he went to London chiefly to see the
Turners; he had no doubt heard much about them from
Durand-Ruel, Pissarro, and Monet, who all studied them in
London during the war. Pissarro and Monet were both critical,
but Renoir liked to judge for himself. He had also seen a reproduction of *Portrait of Turner as a Young Man* and was
intrigued by the fact that it looked like himself. When he saw
the original in London he was shocked: "It was dreadful. What
a difference between him and Lorrain, whom he tried so hard

to imitate! Turner had no idea of construction. And as for his so-called daring canvases—gondolas under a London sky!—there isn't a sou's worth of sincerity in the whole lot of them. Give me a primitive who crudely copies a piece of drapery." [12]

He ended with the devastating "Luckily the Claude Lorrains in London made up for the Turners, the Lawrences and even the Constables." [13]

The Dutch visit was not such an anticlimax, but Renoir remained critical and his comments on Rembrandt are of a piece with that on the nonseriousness of Boucher; he had not moved from his youthful beliefs. He loved the *Betrothed Jewess* and said of the *Night Watch*, "If that picture was mine I'd cut out the woman with the chicken and sell the rest as wastepaper." He much preferred Rembrandt's *Holy Family* and *Carpenter's Wife* in the Louvre and added a typical comment on this last picture of a woman nursing a child. "A magnificent ray of light shines through the bars of the window and turns the breast into gold." [14]

In general, he said that although he loved Rembrandt he found him a bit stifling. "I prefer paintings that make a wall shout with joy." He added, with comic despair, "people are forever telling one that Rembrandt is greater than Watteau. As if we didn't all know that! But beyond this is the pleasure a picture gives you, a pleasure no one can measure." [15]

To make his point Renoir told Vollard of a conversation between Maurice Joyant, one of the many dealers beginning to buy Renoirs, and a client. "Oh, that man Renoir!" said the client contemptuously. "He's never serious."

"How right you are," agreed Joyant, not without sarcasm. "Painting a woman excites him more than going to bed with her." [16]

CHAPTER XVII

———

SEARCH FOR HEALTH

———

1894-1903

I N 1899 Durand-Ruel mounted an Impressionist exhibition.
It contained forty-one Renoir canvases dating from 1874 to
1898. This representative collection created a sensation, and
the demand for Renoirs became so persistent that from this
moment until his death twenty years later scarcely a year went
by without a Renoir exhibition in Paris, New York, or one of
the other great art centers of the world.

Five years later one room at the Salon d'Automne was devoted entirely to the showing of thirty-five Renoirs. He was
hailed by every Parisian critic of note as one of the greatest
living painters. Only Monet and Cézanne were more highly
thought of.

These were years of triumph. He need worry no more about
money; he could sell whatever he cared to paint at prices which
twenty years earlier he would have thought unbelievable. He
lived up to his vow to Rivière, to make himself independent of
dealers and of change of public taste. Throughout the new
century he painted only what he wanted to paint and as he
felt like painting it.

He was not without critics. He has them still. But he had one
advantage over them all, that not one could be so critical of his
work as he. "Unlike me," he had said after seeing the Raphaels in

Rome, "he doesn't chase after the impossible." [1] He was still searching.

Materially and morally, however, he had won his long fight and, unlike most famous artists, had won it comfortably within his lifetime. Few will think his success undeserved. His life had not the drama of a Gauguin or a Van Gogh; he had not suffered physically as much as Monet, Pissarro or Sisley. Yet, though temperamentally less suited to the struggle than they, he too had gone short of food, warmth, comfort. He had sacrificed much that he liked and had lived for years in an uncertainty peculiarly repugnant to a man of his upbringing and nature. Where he rose above his companions was in his ability to ride the struggle with an air; he had a jest for the myriad unpleasantnesses, not in the least romantic, which bedevil an artist who is not prepared to give the public what it wants.

This showed spirit of a high order, but was as nothing to his feats in later years. In middle life he forced himself to become a serious artist rather than a man who painted for the love of it. Now, in his final two decades, he fought the worst enemy a painter can meet; no sooner had he found himself after the long years of experiment than his health began to fail.

It is a melancholy story, made bearable only by the spirit with which Renoir fought a losing battle; he knew that he was doomed but would not give up. [2]

2

People may wonder why Renoir settled in a house ominously named Château des Brouillards when he was liable to severe attacks of rheumatism. The answer probably is that he loved Paris and worked well there, loved Montmartre especially, and did not want to leave his good friends—friends in every grade of social life, from the nobly born concierge to the milkman, from the poet next door to the brilliant Natansons of *La Revue Blanche*. Besides, the air on the hill at Montmartre was reputedly healthy. [3]

It seems likely that his end would have been the same wherever he lived; even today, when medical science is considered advanced, the treatment of rheumatic complaints remains haphazard. In Renoir's day doctors scarcely had an idea how to deal with them. Their usual advice was to take the waters in one of the numerous European spas. Renoir obeyed but suspected his future as far back as 1894 when he went down with rheumatic attacks and told Julie Manet "I'm caught; it's going to get me slowly but surely." [4]

But if there was one man in the world who would work to the end it was Renoir. Recovered, he continued to paint every day, continued to see his friends, to visit his beloved theatres, continued to travel. In 1897 he was at Berneval in Normandy to see the Bérards, painting vigorously, but as so often produced his best canvas in Paris, the fascinating *Jeune fille au métier*. He returned to Berneval the next year, the year of the family study *Le déjeuner à Berneval*, with its highly original layout, and the superb *Jean Renoir tenant un cerceau*. Never had he painted with such certainty, never had his coloring been so rich and individual.

In 1897 he bought a house at Essoyes, a step that indicated the change in his position. For the first time in his life, at the age of fifty-six, he was able to have a house of his own. He was to spend fifteen summers there, and it was during 1897, before it had been enlarged to contain a proper studio, that he had the accident which, his son thinks, led to the final years of pain and deformity. As so many people then, Renoir was a keen cyclist. One rainy day he skidded, fell, and broke his right arm. The arm was put into plaster. [5]

He continued to paint. He was, said Vollard, the only painter who had ever painted as well with the left hand as the right, and Pissarro encouraged a disconsolate son with "Didn't Renoir paint delightful pictures with his left hand when he broke his right arm?" [6] Renoir was in fact ambidextrous but this cannot take away greatly from the feat. A broken arm is not painless, nor can it be forgotten when in plaster, but he refused to be intimidated and painted on as if nothing had happened. He was not one to complain of physical pain, and did not do so now.

Back in Paris his doctor gave him a clean bill of health. Not until Christmas did he have the first indication that the doctor was mistaken, and it was nothing more alarming than a minor shoulder pain. His son tells how that same day, at a Berthe Morisot Christmas party, when Renoir spoke of the ache Degas cracked jokes about the aftereffects of fractures, especially attacks of dreadful muscular rheumatism, and the horrors of arthritis. Everyone laughed, Renoir too. Soon afterward he learned that arthritis was incurable.[7]

The following autumn, of 1898, the Renoir family moved again, to a corner apartment where rue La Bruyère crossed rue La Rochefoucauld. The move was made no doubt to shorten the walk from the painter's main studio, which he still kept, and to give him less of a climb. The new home saw the worst attack he had yet suffered since the facial paralysis of ten years earlier; he was unable to move his right arm and was in such pain that he could not paint.[8]

From this moment everyone knew that it was to be a fight against time. As always he had one thought, his work. He wanted to go on painting until he died. He was determined to continue. He had his Burgundy home for the summer; he now had to find a more southerly one for the worst of the winter. Early the next year, 1899, he began the search. In February he was in Nice, went along the coast road the few miles to Cagnes, liked it and stayed there two months.

His reports to Durand-Ruel make cheerless but inspiring reading. By this time his legs, particularly the ankles, were badly swollen and his hands had begun to stiffen and curl up. From the Hôtel Savourin in the main street of Cagnes he told the dealer in February, "I am outside the whole day and the sun has baked me like leather, a thing I can't enjoy in Paris. I can't get about because my legs won't unswell themselves. When they make up their minds I think I shall recover more quickly." [9]

A week or so later he is saying, "I haven't spoken about my

health because it's difficult to tell. One day bad, the next better. I think I shall have to get used to living like this. My legs simply won't get unswollen." [10] He preferred to talk about his painting, but here too he was realistic. "I predicted a long time ago that until my attitude toward my painting matured I shouldn't get any further. I'm not complaining; it might be worse." [11]

By April: "I haven't much to tell you. I'm always the same in spite of great heat and wonderful weather. I am properly caught. The doctor here foresees that I shall have at least eighteen months of it before I'm really cured. You can imagine my hollow laughter." [12]

After a short spell in Paris he decided to take the waters of Acqui above Genoa. This was the first of many spa treatments. The result of all was much the same: "I am very tired and the treatment has made me even more nervy than usual. All the same I think I'm feeling a bit better." [13]

The improvement, such as it was, did not last and by December he was back in the south, this time at Grasse where he settled for a time in Magagnosc, a village down the Nice road where his wife and Jean (the elder boy was at boarding school) joined him early in 1900. He busied himself with a portrait of Jean which he offered to Limoges—an interesting gesture from a man who had not seen the town since he was four years old. One wonders, did he think that Jean had a look of his Limousin grandfather?

His health did not improve but his spirits remained wonderfully high for a man who suspected that he was fixed for life with an incurable ailment. When Jeanne Baudot persuaded her parents to Spain that spring in her master's wake, he wrote the family a "Spanish" letter: [14]

Chero Mademoiselle et Amica et chero Dottoro Baudotti
Chipa si majenta tableauto di Velasquez representato l'Infanta Marguerita. Si, si boune, boune sous un daito griso, en roba brodetto d'argenta aveco uno rubano rougo dans las cheveaux tas, i un mouchoivo bianco a la maina. Dottoro let-

trato tableauto dans le fondo de son sombreros et rapportas a
Parigi, 33 rue La Rochefoucauld.

Amico Renoir
silva da rheumatismos
Grassa 24 avrillo 1900

By June he was taking his second cure, this time at Saint
Laurent-les-Bains. This too had only a temporary effect, but
he was stimulated out of awareness of rheumatic pains when
he took a house for the summer at Louveciennes. Before his
mother's death four years earlier the Lerays had moved with
her to Louveciennes where they were joined by Victor. This
next elder brother to Renoir had had an exciting life; carried
off to Russia by a Grand Duke impressed by the cut of the
clothes he made, he had become one of St. Petersburg's fashionable tailors only to bankrupt himself by a succession of love
affairs.[15]

The Baudots had a summer house at Louveciennes, and the
studio they built for their daughter had brought Renoir down
to the river to stay with them more than once. In spring two
years earlier Jeanne had appeared in the kind of muslin hat and
dress Renoir loved. He had already made several studies of her,
but to the end of her life she remembered the picture he insisted on making when he saw this dress because he posed her
on the grass in the garden backed by flowering bushes and she
was able to see his method of dealing with the blank canvas.
The study itself is of no importance—he did not finish it—but
her description shows that he was beginning to settle into his
final period, that period of luminous canvases relished by the
world ever since. "He covered the canvas with a scumble made
up of carnation oil and turpentine mixed progressively with
color as he painted. In this way he indicated the values and
harmonies and made his figures, landscapes and still lifes appear in a kind of festive spirit which interpreted his joy in
painting." [16]

In the summer of 1900 when he rented a house for the
family he used to walk into the Baudot house (the gardens

adjoined) to paint in Jeanne's studio. He painted to some purpose, he made *La sortie du bain* with the faithful La Boulangère as model, and Durand-Ruel bought it for ten thousand francs.[17] This was by far the highest price a picture of his had ever fetched and emphasized the standing he had reached.

Further indication of his reputation came at Louveciennes on July 14. Jeanne ran into his house brandishing a newspaper with the page open at the honors list. There followed shortly a letter from Durand-Ruel which Renoir confirmed typically. "Yes, I'm guilty. Now I hope the house of Durand-Ruel will club together to award me a decorated chair of honor!" [18]

His position in modern French painting had been officially recognized; he had been made Chevalier of the Legion of Honor. The award brought unexpected embarrassment. It had been offered to Monet also and brusquely refused; he was not interested in honors twenty years too late.[19] Renoir therefore had the task of telling his old companion why he had not refused it, too. Monet was astonished and did not hide the fact.

Renoir, obviously agitated, attempted to explain. It was difficult, if not impossible, because he believed in accepting life as it came. Probably he had never given the matter a thought until he heard from Monet. "My dear Friend, I have let myself be decorated because I didn't think it was for me to say whether it was right or wrong. But a piece of ribbon musn't endanger our old friendship. So tell me what you like, that I'm a fool, use the nastiest words you can think of, it's all the same to me, but seriously, whether I have made an ass of myself or not, I rely on your friendship. I don't care a rap for any other." [20]

Three days later, extremely dissatisfied with himself, he wrote again. "I realize today, and before that, for that matter, that I wrote you a stupid letter. I was in pain, nervy, all over the shop, and one ought never to write at such a time. I now ask myself what difference it makes whether I am decorated or not. You have taken a splendid stand, but as for me, I never know today what I shall do tomorrow. You must know me better than I know myself just as I probably know you better than you know yourself. Don't let's speak of it any more. Love forever!" [21]

Monet's reply was simple: "Ah, it's sad!" [22]

By November, Renoir was back at Magagnosc with his family, feeling better and hopeful of painting well. All went well—that is to say, he was rarely out of pain but could walk and work—until April of the year 1901, when he went down to St. Raphael and immediately caught influenza. "How many times?" he asked Durand-Ruel in despair. [23]

Once more he recovered, resumed work, and as usual spent the summer in Essoyes, then some weeks in Paris. And it was in this year that his third son, Claude (known always as Coco), was born.

3

The arrival of another child once again gave him a renewal of life. Here was a new model to be painted in any number of fascinating poses. Coco, following Jean and his mother, was to instigate many good domestic canvases.

He had already painted *Jean Renoir dans les bras de Gabrielle*; in the next year or two he was to make, outstandingly, *Portrait de Coco, La leçon d'écriture de Coco*, and, a little later, in 1910, *Coco et les deux servantes*. The first, one of many portraits of the child, is an uninhibited forecast of the future, red, striking and free. The second is a worthy mate for that earlier study in tenderness, *Jean Renoir dans les bras de Gabrielle*, and the third is Renoir at his most assured, rich and wholly pleasing. Never was he to show that much-painted model Gabrielle to better advantage, and one understands from this third study why he could not tire of asking her to pose.

It is curious that although Coco provided the impetus for this rush of family portraits and groups, Jean posed for the finest of them. *Le pierrot blanc* was painted the year after Coco's birth. It was made after the *Gilles* of Watteau, but Watteau could not have painted it. Everything about it pleases, and the pierrot costume is rendered with dazzling skill.

In all these canvases Renoir succeeded in portraying the

homely expressions and attitudes of everyday life as he had failed to do in his society groups; they give the pictures a warmth and verisimilitude that satisfy because they express the painter's true tastes.

Yet if the birth of the third and last of his children gave him new life as painter, it seems also to have marked the beginning of a definite deterioration in his health. Jean, then seven, says that he dates the serious extension of his father's illness from this year.[24] One wonders whether any man could have lived a greater irony than the sixty-year-old Renoir. He had almost everything that life could offer, an extremely capable wife who looked after him with great care, three children and two devoted servants who were also splendid models. He could sell every picture he painted, sell it immediately at his own price—Durand-Ruel, Petit, Vollard, all the dealers were ready buyers. He liked nothing so much as to paint, but just when his great love in life coincided with the making of money, when he had thrown off the last effects of the years of struggle to find himself, he was increasingly hampered by pain. During those long years from 1883 to 1895 his production of pictures had been small because of doubts about the worth of what he did—his letter to Marx puts his feelings precisely; now that he felt himself on the right road an incurable physical ailment prevented him from painting more than a tithe of the canvases he wanted to make. It is a marvel that he did not grow into a cynical old age, the cynicism that so often accompanies a man young in heart but physically old.

There was plenty to complain about if he had had that kind of disposition. In 1901 the effects of the facial paralysis began to return; the optic nerve in his left eye was partly paralyzed and gave it a fixed look.[25] The joints in his feet became so swollen that he could only walk with a stick. His hands were growing so twisted that he must have wondered how much longer he would be able to grip a paint brush. He caught cold after the slightest exposure to cold or damp.[26] As for his perpetual discomfort, the mind refuses to take it in; perhaps no healthy person could imagine the nights he must have passed.

Yet to him all this added up to one thing. He had little time for self-pity, fear for his painting absorbed him. He was anxious that his family should continue to live in the comfort they had been accustomed to. But there he parted company with the ordinary conscientious man; he was an artist, and the artist's first loyalty and love are given to his work. It would be impossible to exaggerate his dread that he might be halted when everything that was strongest in him cried out for expression by painting and when he was just beginning to feel his power. To himself he still had very far to go; he was desperately anxious to get there.

In these years it must have seemed that only a miracle would do it. But the miracle could perhaps be aided; he must find a home in the south. For some time he hesitated between Magagnosc and Cagnes, the one close to Grasse high above the sea, the other close to Nice and virtually on sea level. In 1903 he chose Cagnes. He settled in the Maison de la Poste, close to the hotel in which he had stayed, and shared the house with the post office. It was a fine old building and he liked the bustle of the post office business. His humor remained as gay as ever. He had scarcely settled into the house before he was telling Durand-Ruel, "As I write I am in the middle of an attack and my legs are in a pretty poor way, but I think things will improve soon. While waiting for the improvement I am indulging in a spot of Midi laziness." [27]

He was not without company when he wanted it; during his spells in the south he had made many friends, as he always did, and one of the best was a chronicler of his final years, the painter Albert André.

CHAPTER XVIII

MARTYRDOM AND TRIUMPH

1903-1919

RENOIR HAD sixteen years to live. To the artist striving after perfection this was not long enough; to the man, his life made one long physical misery, it was, in his darker moments, too long. These moments inevitably lengthened the more crippled he became; what he felt when he saw his precious painting time being remorselessly eaten into is best not imagined.

The pattern of these final years scarcely varied: the winter at Cagnes, first in the Maison de la Poste, later in the house Renoir built in an olive grove halfway up the hill, where doctors told him the air was healthier; summers at Essoyes; a week or two in Paris between the removals from one headquarters to another.

This was not at all the kind of life Renoir would have wished to live. He liked the warmth (in reason) and the clear light of the south, but his love for Paris did not lessen, and this will be understood by anyone who has come from a northern capital to live in the Midi. He missed the theatres, the good conversation, the old friends, the feeling of a place throbbing with life. But he tried to make the best of the change just as he tried to minimize the rheumatism which was steadily attacking all the joints in his arms and legs, and he did both as he had done most things in the forty years since joining Gleyre's studio, because he put his work first.

He dreaded the long journeys between south and north, tiring for the healthy man, torture for a man obliged to shift position every few minutes, and expressed his feelings vigorously: "I shall rejoin everyone Tuesday or Wednesday," he told Jeanne Baudot from Cagnes in August of 1903. "Up to then I shan't have a clear head. Altogether too much moving about. What a devilish idea, the invention of railways. I am one of their numerous victims but I get about all the same." [1] Arrived at Essoyes after the usual halt in Paris, he delayed a letter to his old pupil, "having nothing cheerful to tell you. For a whole year I've messed everything I've done and I'm feeling about as friendly as a watchdog." [2]

This was the combined result of the Cagnes-Paris-Essoyes trips and what greeted him when he settled into his Essoyes house: "We've had such weather that one would drown trying to cross the street. Let's see if a spot of sun brings me back to sanity. When I'm more satisfied with myself I'll let you know." [3]

His sense of humor returned before the sun, when he heard that De Wyzewa, who was of the precious school of writers, had at last published his long-promised *Peintres de jadis et aujourd'hui*. "It ends with me and I'm afraid it will make me a lot of enemies. It is admirably written as always, but what a pity it has to be on me!" [4]

Then the sun came out and he made *Le jardin d'Essoyes*, a study, very free, very atmospheric, of Gabrielle and Coco, and its companion picture *Jean et sa bonne*. He was active enough and lively enough to growl to Rivière (who had spent many years in the wilderness of marriage to an invalid), "If these rascals go on with their massacre there won't be a tree left round Essoyes!" [5]

Throughout that winter and the following spring, of 1904, he worked on at Cagnes, then at Essoyes again in summer, but with increasing difficulty. His perpetually swollen feet often kept him awake half the night; his knotted hands could barely hold brush and palette. In August he tried another spa, this time at Bourbonne-les-Bains. It was his fourth "cure." The third, at Aix-les-Bains three years earlier, had been a failure: "After three weeks of massage and baths," he told Vollard, "I shall come back without any result, completely stupefied." [6] But he tried again in 1904 and cheerfully, too. He wrote to Durand-Ruel soon after getting to Bourbonne, "I see heaps of people here pleased with these waters." [7]

After the first week he was still optimistic—"if my improvement continues I hope to get back to work soon" [8]—but with a haunting doubt: "What hinders me most at this moment is not being able to sit down for long because I'm so thin. I weigh 97 lbs. That's not exactly fat. The bone stands out of the skin, and after a time I just can't sit down any longer." [9]

He went back to Essoyes virtually a skeleton and almost too weak to lift his arm to paint. But he felt less pain and that was enough for him. By the end of September he was informing Durand-Ruel joyfully, "I have done lots of things." [10] He brought them to Paris a few days later on his way to Cagnes and the dealer was astonished. No one has been able to explain how this crippled man managed to paint in such quantity and with such fire. Among the batch of 1904 canvases were *La Boulangère*, a nude study of the Renoir servant, one of the finest nudes he was ever to paint, and the scarcely less fine *Grande baigneuse au chapeau*, sometimes known as *Grande baigneuse aux jambes croisées*. He also made further studies of Jean and Coco. His canvases were becoming more and more transparent, the white of the canvas appearing through the glaze. This gave his pictures a watercolor purity and threw up his individual colors impressively.

His return to Paris was something of a triumph; he was feeling, after that bout of work at Essoyes, that all was not yet lost, and his great success in the Salon d'Automne seemed to be a good omen for the future. He went back to Cagnes for the winter in great form, and at once began to paint with all the éclat of a young man oblivious of mortality.

Fate seems to take a malicious pleasure in testing almost beyond endurance those who make supreme efforts. Renoir had not been back in Cagnes many months before he was laid low with stomach trouble, followed by such fierce rheumatism that he could scarcely hold the pen to write a letter. This was at the end of 1905, a year notable for another *Grande baigneuse au chapeau* and *Gabrielle à la blouse entr'ouverte*, with its green background, unusual in a painter who was soon to concentrate more and more on red.

Renoir battled on and was rewarded by two better years, 1906 and 1907, as conveyed in his notes to Durand-Ruel: "Wonderful weather and I'm at work," [11] and "Health good and I work a lot." [12] When he said his health was good, he meant that his pain was sufficiently tolerable to allow him to concentrate wholly on painting. Most men would have been on their bed or in a clinic and feeling very sorry for themselves. But Renoir was an artist, and to the artist whose work is threatened even a bearable pain is a blessing.

He knew, if he cared to think about it, that his feet and hands were growing more deformed every month and that the time must come when he could walk no more and perhaps paint no more. He did not choose to think about it.

Another change in his life was beginning to come between him and work. He was growing famous. Not only did he have to entertain friends—Vollard, Durand-Ruel, André, and many others—but to deal with young worshippers, painters seeking guidance, journalists seeking interviews, celebrity hunters. He was patient with visitors up to a point. As André, watching, said, "He welcomed his friends joyfully, but when he thought someone had come to see him out of sheer curiosity he drew himself in, would not speak and became quite disagreeable." [13] When he did choose to speak he developed a short way with the impertinent. One, for instance, wondered with tasteless astonishment how, with a hand so cruelly bent, he was able to paint such voluptuous pictures. Renoir smiled crookedly and shocked him out of the studio with a "But I don't paint with my hand, I paint with . . ." And he motioned downward.[14]

His many paintings of these two years include a series of studies of his home. The best, *La maison de la poste à Cagnes*, was the only one painted at the back of the building, looking down on it through an old olive tree. This study conveys the sense of sunlit buildings shining white, and the olive tree—that so often painted subject—is a work of art. The whole picture breathes confidence. One would not imagine that it had been painted by a man scarcely able to hold his brush and never free from pain, from the occasional twinge to the morale-shattering ache deep in the bone.

2

By this time the famous Renoir, who had too many callers for his liking, had become a lonely man. At close on seventy he had outlived most of his old friends. Berthe Morisot, Caillebotte, Chocquet, Mallarmé, Sisley, Pissarro, Cézanne, to mention only the most notable, all were gone. He had lost touch with some before their death. Soon after the 1882 exhibition, bitter with the treatment Sisley had received from critics, collectors, and public—at one moment he seemed to have made his name, at the next he was ruthlessly dropped—he withdrew from society, avoiding even his friends.

The year before the exhibition, he moved to the village of Moret near the Fontainebleau forest he had painted often. He stayed there for the rest of his life and seems scarcely to have left it, first because of a growing misanthropy, then because he was too poor. Years of poverty ended in the loss of his wife in dreadful circumstances (she had cancer of the mouth) and his own painful death soon afterwards from cancer of the throat. Renoir and Monet both saw him from time to time (Monet was at his deathbed), but Sisley's pride seems to have hardened with his fortune, and there was little they could do. And they had to see, after his death in 1899, the inevitable demand for his work; Sisley canvases began to fetch prices that would have kept him and his family in comfort for the rest of their lives had it come earlier. It is one of the most senseless martyrdoms in the history of art, and an indictment of a society in which such martyrdoms were, and are, possible.

His death brought Monet and Renoir together. Monet arranged a sale of canvases donated by friends for the benefit of the two daughters, a sale to which Renoir gladly contributed. The two old friends corresponded again after Cézanne's death in 1906. Neither had seen Cézanne for some years,[15] but both revered his dedication to painting and saw him as the great master of modern times. To Renoir, he was also the great exemplar, the man who had led him out of aimlessness into serious painting. They heard with dismay of the local preparations for a grandiose memorial to the painter who had been consistently ignored and insulted by his townsfolk. Renoir, who was close to Aix as Monet had been close to Moret where Sisley died, tried hard and long to influence the people there, but without success as he finally reported. "This monument," he wrote, "began as a bust. Now it is a nude woman. I simply don't understand. They'll have to shift for themselves. At the beginning of the business I suggested this: a bust of Cézanne in one of the Museum galleries (the Aix Museum is very beautiful) with a picture above it. This seemed to me to do honor to Cézanne and could not upset anyone, but not a soul would listen to me. I think a painter ought to be represented by his work. I simply can't imagine a large nude woman and no pictures." [16]

One of the first to go, after Manet and Berthe Morisot, had been Chocquet; he and his wife died just before the opening of the new century. Renoir had not forgotten the man who had done so much for him and his fellow painters and did not forget him after his death. When he visited a Paris exhibition that included one of his portraits of Chocquet, he stood in front of it and murmured to himself, "Portrait of a madman by a madman." And when the friend with him, overhearing, looked astonished, he explained: "That good Chocquet, how wonderfully dotty he was! He wasn't exactly earning a fortune in those early days and used to pinch and scrape from that poor salary at the ministry to buy paintings without ever once thinking whether they would increase in value. For months on end he would search Paris for a drawing or a sketch by Delacroix. He broke with his friends because they had prevented him from going to our first exhibition." [17]

He went on: "As for me, my craziness has consisted in putting color on a canvas all my life." He concluded: "Truly I can't see how any of this has harmed a single person." [18]

3

The year 1908 began badly. In January his efforts of the past three years recoiled on him; he had a hernia, followed, because of his enforced inaction, by a long bout of extreme arthritis. He had no sooner recovered from this than, in April, he went down with bronchitis. By June he was in Paris, at the apartment in rue Caulaincourt the Renoirs had occupied in snatches since 1902, but though spirited as ever he could no longer walk with a stick; he had to use crutches. He began to paint right away, portraits mostly, in Paris, at Essoyes that summer, and in Cagnes again throughout the winter. Rivière visited him again, Maillol sculpted a bust of him, collectors were forever trying to pick up a new Renoir canvas. He was busy, optimistic, and carried off the hindrance of the crutches gaily. He even branched for a moment into writing. A new edition of Cennini was being prepared, and after protests—"I'm a painter not a writer" [19]—he agreed to write a preface. He wrote from long and hard experience. "If it is necessary to take care that we don't get stuck in the forms we have inherited it is equally necessary to make sure that, simply for love of progress, we don't detach ourselves completely from the centuries before us. This tendency, particularly obvious among us today, is very understandable. So many marvelous discoveries have been made in the past hundred years that men seem to forget that others have lived before them. So it's a good thing that a man like Cennini comes to remind us of ancestors we must not despise.

"For them [the artists of Cennini's time] the glory of making a beautiful thing took the place of a salary; they worked to ensure themselves a place in heaven, not to make a fortune on earth. Besides, in Cennini's time men decorated churches, today they decorate railway stations; it is just as well to remember that, as far as their source of inspiration goes, our contemporaries are less well off than their ancestors.

"Above all they then had what to them was an essential condition of making collective works, a condition which gave them their sense of unity; all painters had the same training, a training that we shall never entirely comprehend because we have emancipated ourselves from our traditions. The training of the Renaissance painters was the same as their predecessors. If the Greeks had left a treatise on painting it would have been identical with this of Cennini. All painting, from Pompeii, made by the Greeks, as far as Corot, passing by way of Poussin, has the feeling of coming from the same palette. All were taught this manner of painting by their master; their genius, if they had it, did the rest. The severe apprenticeship imposed on young painters then did not prevent their originality from blossoming. Raphael, who was the studious pupil of Perugino, nevertheless became the divine Raphael.

"But to understand the general value of the art of the past it is necessary to recall that beyond the teachings of their master the painters had something else, something which has disappeared from modern life, something which filled the soul of the contemporaries of Cennini—a religious faith, the most fecund source of their inspiration. It is this which gives their work the character of nobility and artlessness which we now find so charming. In short, there then existed between men and the craft they practiced a harmony which came from a common belief." [20]

Renoir was not a man who spoke much about himself at any time of his life. His few comments on religion show his usual disposition to live and let live. If the sermon preached by the Curé of Cagnes [21] at his funeral has any meaning beyond the conventional panegyric to the famous dead it means that Renoir was a believer. Certainly he lived the second half of his life in the spirit of one; his wish was to spread joy through his painting.

At this time, in 1908, he was following the ancients in another way; he had moved into his last manner of painting, which is known as his red period; he began to specialize in the use of every conceivable nuance of red, a color used more than any other in the old masters he worshipped. He spoke about this to one of his more intelligent visitors, the American painter Walter Pach, who called on him at Cagnes. "When you are plunged in silence," Renoir told him, "and you suddenly hear the small sound of the small bell at the front door, you have the impression that the noise is louder than it really is. Well, I try to make a certain color vibrate as intensely as that small bell in the middle of silence." [22]

When asked how he set about it, he replied: "I arrange my subject the way I want it, then I go ahead and paint like a child. I want a red to be sonorous like a bell; if it doesn't turn out that way I apply more reds or other colors until I do get it. I am no cleverer than that. I have no rules and no methods; anyone can look at my materials and watch my painting—he will see that I have no secrets." [23]

He chose a special example, one of his favorites. "I look at a nude, I see myriads of tints. I must find the ones that will make the flesh come alive and quiver on my canvas. Nowadays they want to explain everything, but if they could explain a picture it wouldn't be art. Shall I tell you what I think are the two qualities of art? It must be indescribable and inimitable." [24]

4

Many times during the next three years, 1909 to 1911, he was to demonstrate this gift of painting like a child with a man's insight. His health was growing steadily worse, but no one could have guessed it from his letters or his paintings. He made a number of excellent portraits of friends, particularly of Vollard, of Durand-Ruel, and of his wife. The contrast between the two men is cleverly brought out: on the one hand the smooth, handsome Durand-Ruel with his white hair and carefully clipped

white mustache, on the other the too obviously prospering
Vollard, fat, greasy, ingratiating. Yet of the two, Vollard inspired Renoir to greater heights. In the Durand-Ruel canvas
there are traces of conventional portraiture, in the Vollard
none whatever, and this was a true reading of the men; the
creole possessed the gift of the unexpected.

Renoir also painted outstandingly *Nu à la fontaine, Jeune
pâtre au repos,* and two magnificent studies of Gabrielle, who
never failed to bring out the best in him—*Gabrielle assise sur
une chaise* and the already mentioned *Coco et les deux servantes,* which is a portrait of Gabrielle in everything but name.
It would be impossible to suspect from these vital canvases, full
of life, color, and movement, that they were painted by a man
with a right hand almost bent double by rheumatism. They
breathe a technical assurance which successfully carries the old
painter, now on the verge of his seventieth birthday, through
the hazards of physical handicap.

These years of much work, increasing illness which he refused to recognize, and growing fame throughout the world had
their material reward. In October, 1910, Renoir asked Durand-
Ruel (only the most important of his many dealers, it has to be
remembered) if he would bank forty thousand francs for him in
Paris.[25] That was then a small fortune.

Renoir's still sunny nature prevented him from becoming
hopelessly cynical at the sight of this money pouring in when
he could not buy the one thing he wanted; it would not
straighten his legs or fingers; it could not give him one painless
day. He did the next best thing with it, ensured the future of
all dear to him and, finally, in 1911, made—how wryly one can
imagine—his final concession to the modernity he loathed; he
bought an automobile. He had long since been obliged to
abandon his bicycle and had been confined to the garden of
Les Collettes, the new house he had built up on the Cagnes hill;
an automobile was the only possibility of movement, to see
friends and the inevitable doctors at Nice and Cannes.[26]

His answer to this increased immobility was characteristically
defiant. He talked of another visit to the Italian museums and,

dissuaded from this, managed to get himself even further, to friends near Munich, whose museum was one of the many to possess Renoirs.

5

This was to be his last journey outside France. He had driven himself too hard—as in 1908, after a heroic bout of work, so in 1912. Early in January he was telling Durand-Ruel that he was going to Nice for a time; his rheumatism was so bad that he could not even climb the stairs to his studio. Jean and Coco were at school in Nice; the doctors and hospitals were there.

He was not quick enough; before he could reach Nice under his own steam the rheumatism came to a head, as long ago in Essoyes; a ferocious attack paralyzed him. Not the face this time—that was already partly fixed for life—but arms and legs. He could not move hand or foot. He was taken to Nice in an ambulance.

In March he recovered sufficiently to scribble a few lines. They were as plucky and free from self-pity as ever. They avoided the truth, and in June his wife wrote to Durand-Ruel: "My husband is a little better. He is beginning to be able to move his arms but the legs remain just the same. It is impossible for him to stand up but he is much less discouraged than he was. He is getting used to his immobility but it is really heartbreaking to see him in this state." [27]

His martyrdom was not yet over. In August he was taken back to Nice. He was operated on—foot, knee, and hand. Not until January of the new year, 1913, did he write another line. By that time he had forced himself—with what a struggle only the crippled know—to accept the fact that he would never walk again. He reorganized his life always with the one object. He painted on. He sat in a wheelchair and was carried up to his studio every day. He faced the future with the perky gallantry which made him so much loved. "Now I'll *have* to paint all the time," [28] he said, turning a disaster into a blessing. And when commiserated with, he would say, "Ah, but I'm a lucky beggar all the same; I can still paint!" [29]

Durand-Ruel was shocked by the change when he came down in December, 1912, to see his old friend, but his horror quickly changed to admiration. "Renoir is in the same sad state," he wrote, "but his strength of character is simply amazing. He can neither walk nor lift himself from his chair. Two people have to carry him everywhere. What torture! Yet in spite of all this he shows the same sunny humor and happiness when he is able to paint. He has made a number of things already, and yesterday he made in the one day an entire torso he had begun that morning. It is not much worked on, but superb just the same." [30]

He was probably referring to a piece of sculpture—Vollard had persuaded Renoir to sculpt in odd moments—but the example holds good for everything the artist did; in painting as in sculpture he worked fast, sure of his aim, aware of time running out.

Durand-Ruel had to go back to Paris, but André provides a more detailed picture of Renoir at work during the years following the complete paralysis of 1912. This Cannes painter had become one of Renoir's most devoted friends and admirers; as his voluntary disciple he relieved him of many little tasks, kept at bay the worst of the increasing hordes of bores and sycophants milling around Les Collettes in the season. They used to come up from Cannes and Nice in droves, hoping for an interview or, failing this, snooping around trying to catch a sight of the crippled man at work. They were a pest, and the faithful André had no mercy on them, driving them off.

As for Renoir: "He sits in his chair, his thin legs crossed, his poor feet shod in woolen slippers, his body enveloped in shawls, his palid, delicate head covered up to the ears by a peaked cap or white linen cap according to the time of year. Between his fingers is the eternal cigarette which he relights unceasingly."

His impish spirit has survived all misfortunes, all pain. " 'Listen,' he says, his eyes twinkling, while he puffs away at his cigarette, 'I'll tell you my secret. No-one else knows it. Yes, I tell you that I discovered the secret of painting—in the tobacconist! One day, thinking only of this blessed painting, I asked for cigars by mistake. The tobacconist held out two boxes. 'Colorado or claro?' he asked. 'Colorado! Claro!' I said to myself. 'But that's painting!' I took both boxes.' " [31]

André used to watch the change in him when the daily batch of admirers and celebrity hunters had been dismissed. "When he got in front of the easel again he was transfigured. He whistled, hummed the songs his models taught him. . . . He had the habit, when wheeling himself up and down before the canvas, of staring at the picture, then looking down at his left hand to try to find the same tone on the palette. He always seemed astonished not to find it there."

Very soon the left hand, curled up with arthritis, would no longer hold the palette, then he kept it either on his knees or on the ledge of the easel. "This palette was amazingly clean and bright even when he had finished his day's work. 'A painter's palette,' he used to say, 'is of no significance, the eye does everything. There are colors one uses more happily than others; one ends by adopting them. I used to employ chrome, a superb color but which plays one some wicked tricks. I tried cadmium but found that it landed me in all sorts of difficulties, it made me paint heavily. Then I wanted to make myself into a little Rubens. I began to paint with Naples yellow. It gave me all the éclat I wanted but it's pretty dull. And it's always the same story; it depends what one puts round about it.' "

So he came to his reds in his old age, and André watched him begin from the beginning, building up from the white canvas. "When the subject was simple he drew an outline with the brush, generally using red-brown, sketched very roughly so that he could see the elements making up his picture. 'The volumes,' he used to say with his bantering air.

"Immediately afterwards he quickly scumbled the canvas with pure tones thinned in spirit as if he was going to make a water color, and one saw something indefinite and iridescent, the tones running into one another, something which quite ravished you even before you grasped the meaning of the picture."

This was as far as Renoir could go for the moment. Then "when the spirit had partly evaporated, he repeated the preparation, using almost exactly the same method but with a little more coloring matter mixed with the oil and spirit.

"He lightened the parts he wanted to be luminous by putting pure white directly onto the canvas. He reinforced the shadows and half tints in the same way, directly onto the canvas. He practically never mixed tones on the palette which was covered by tiny oily spots of virtually pure tones.

"Little by little he detailed the forms, always allowing them to merge into one another, however.

"A few more touches and from the colored mist of the first state one saw sweet, rounded forms loom out which shone with the glitter of precious stones and enveloped the golden and transparent shadows. He had discovered blues and reds never seen before he painted."

When he was attacking a more complicated composition "he didn't make a sketch in the usual meaning of the word. Once he had made up his mind on the subject he made small pictures of it, sometimes an isolated figure, sometimes many figures. For him this work was a kind of practice for the definitive work. Then he drew his composition in red chalk and traced it on the canvas. Drawing with a pencil didn't please him even though he had made some admirable things with it, he wanted a softer material than lead and more tinted to realize the large masses. He preferred charcoal or red-brown pastel." [32]

By the time André had made notes of Renoir's methods of painting, the old man's infirmity had moved into its last stage; not only was he unable to hold the palette in his left hand, he could no longer hold the brush in his right. It had to be strapped to his hand by strips of plaster. "My thumb," [33] he called it, gay to the end. This meant that he could not change brushes during a sitting—or at least it was so difficult and distracting to do so that he did not attempt it—and was forced to wash it in spirit repeatedly.

André cannot conceal his admiration, and no wonder. Renoir's feats with the brush were remarkable enough before his paralysis, when he could still manage to grasp it. Now, from 1913 onward, he was unable to feel the brush or direct it with his fingers. Most painters will tell you that the fingers are the essential interpreters of the mind's directions. Renoir was to comment before he died on this common and natural belief, which he had been driven to disprove, but long before he did so the astonished André was watching him in action, fingerless yet painting with a dash he had not shown when physically free.

He did not play the martyr or the grand old man. "When he became too tired to go on, the brush had to be unfastened from the fingers which could not open. He took a cigarette, rolled his wheeled chair round about the picture, screwed up an eye, growled that he wasn't satisfied. 'How difficult it is to find the point at which one should stop imitating nature!' he would sigh. 'A picture mustn't smell of the model, yet one must feel nature. A picture isn't an official report. For my part I love paintings that make me want to walk inside them, when they are landscapes, or to stroke a breast or back if they are studies of women. As for whether painting should be subjective or objective, I couldn't care less. I am always alarmed when young painters come to see me and question me about the aim of a painter. Who can explain to me why I put a red or a blue on such and such a part of my canvas? Obviously our trade is difficult and complicated and I understand all these worries, but all the same a little simplicity and frankness is needed too.' " 34

To end this account of Renoir the painter just before the war years, a letter of early 1913 to one of his favorites in Paris, Berthe Morisot's niece Paule Gobillard, about the Rouart sale in December, 1912, shows his courage and generosity. He lived for his painting, but no crowds of young admirers at Cagnes could persuade him that he was the great painter of the day.

"I'm not too bad," he wrote, "when you think that at my age one must expect anything. The moment I don't feel pain I ask nothing better. My wife is in fine health, we have superb weather and more roses than in spring." 35

Then he dismissed himself and turned to a greater. With the death of Henri Rouart, Degas had lost his best friend, his eyesight had become so poor that he was compelled to stop painting and try to console himself with sculpture, but the sale of the Rouart collection, mostly Degas canvases, had been a triumphant vindication of his position as one of the finest living painters.

Renoir was not sentimental and did not indulge in sentimentality now; Degas in trouble and triumph remained the Degas of old; his reception of the honors poured on him was in character, and so was Renoir's comment to a correspondent who expected, as so many young people do, the sudden emergence of a new and mellow man. "Degas must go on grumbling as a matter of principle, he wouldn't be Degas without it. But I have the happiness of seeing in my lifetime the apotheosis of this unique and magnificent artist." [36]

6

In 1914 he made two of his most famous portraits, of his wife with a little dog and of the actress Tilla Durieux. These portraits are at opposite poles. The portrait of Mme. Renoir conveys the essence of the domesticity her husband loved and of the naturalness he had known since childhood. There is no impression of a model taking up a pose, rather of a photograph taken without warning, but a photograph beautifully and honestly painted and full of character.

The portrait of the actress could not be more different. Here Renoir is adopting the grand manner in conformity with the conscious pose of his model. And how well he does it! Two points strike the onlooker at once, color and composition. It would be difficult to fault either in any particular, even the minutest. This is Renoir's red manner par excellence; his reds are deployed with the utmost generosity to re-create the florid personality of the sitter with its hint of exoticism. As for composition, one has only to note the painter's use of the rose in the model's hair and the scarf draping her shoulders and falling along her arms to see the hand of the master. His emphasis on the wide, parted mouth is no less sure. The whole effect is rich and right.

These two portraits painted, his life clouded; war broke out and his elder sons went off to the front. Early in 1915 both boys were wounded seriously. In March, the day Pierre was to be operated on, Renoir told Durand-Ruel, "As for me, I get older as tranquilly as I can when I can forget the anguish of this stupid war. I work a little and try not to think of it." [37]

His fears for the boys were slightly eased after a few weeks; both were recovering. Then a new sorrow loomed; his wife, unknown to him, was diabetic, and diabetes at that time was considered incurable. She insisted on going to see the wounded Pierre at Gérardmer. When she came back, late in June, she was very ill. On the twenty-eighth, Renoir wrote to Durand-Ruel, "My wife, ill already, came back from Gérardmer even worse and did not recover. She died yesterday, happily without knowing it." [38]

So there he was, ill and lonely—Coco was at school in Cannes, Gabrielle had gone away to marry an American painter, he was left with the Italian chauffeur (soon to be called up), the large cook imported from Essoyes, Louise, and the ever-faithful La Boulangère—and it must have seemed to him that his life was finished. That December he was laid up for six weeks with rheumatism and bronchitis, could not touch a paint brush, and cried to Durand-Ruel, "When will all this end! The inaction is maddening." [39]

As soon as he could make the journey he went up to Paris. Both elder sons were there, Pierre married and invalided out of the army, Jean in hospital. When Jean was discharged he joined his father at the family apartment. It was then that father and son held the conversations, in which Renoir spoke of his past life, which were to form the basis of his son's fascinating book.[40]

Then Jean, fit again, volunteered for the Air Force, and Renoir went back to Cagnes.

When Rivière saw him early the next year, 1916, he found him greatly changed. "He was thinner than ever—which I should have thought impossible—and his voice had become so feeble that I often could not hear what he said." But Renoir made no doubt that Rivière should hear what he thought of the war. "What stupidity! Instead of killing young men in holes they ought to use the old and infirm; we are the ones to be there." He despaired of the men who were leading the European countries: "Everything is in La Fontaine; why don't the idiotic politicians read him?" [41]

Of his illness during the winter he said, "Another bout like that and I'm done for." [42] This was the only reference he made to his state of health. He knew how bad he was, Rivière said, but did not speak about it. He was not afraid of death but hated the thought of it. He loved life as much as ever. He loved work, too, which was his life, and Rivière watched him with amazement: "He still painted all day but with frequent rests, he suffered so much." [43]

He was a pathetic sight by this time, bones sticking out of a parchment-like skin, his fingers bent so tightly that he had to wear bandages to prevent the nails from digging into the skin of his palms. He weighed so little that he could be carried everywhere like a child by Louise. Yet he would not give up; in face of this caricature of a life, with bronchitis almost chronic, scarcely ever free from rheumatic pains, his body a mockery of what a body should be, this man who loved activity struggled on, working every possible, and for most people impossible, minute of the day. "I have seen Renoir paint," wrote one of his disciples. "I have seen him disgusted with painting on certain evenings when bronchitis has driven him frantic. This was when the evening was just beginning, during the last three years of his life. If I asked, 'Are you feeling better?' he would screw up his left eye and growl through a twisted mouth, 'I'm fed up to the teeth,' which meant 'Leave me alone.' [44]

"Then: 'I'm not interested by anything. I'm quite indifferent to the thought of making a green face or a blue orange.' He would close his eyes as though to sleep. 'This sun is a curse. It gets on my nerves, why doesn't it clear off!' [45]

"Of course he was dreading the night, the inaction until

dinner, the certitude that when gripped by rheumatism he would spend the time until next morning, whether he stayed in his rocking chair or was laid on the bed, trying to find the position that gave him the least pain. 'I've never felt so old,' he would say and he sometimes even spoke of being too old to go on painting." [46]

That was Renoir at his lowest ebb. He was then seventy-five years old. Yet at this moment when everyone about him must have feared that even his gallant spirit would break, there came an astonishing rebirth. He was introduced to a new model. She was Andrée, a sixteen-year-old girl from Nice. She had red hair, the full figure he loved, and was the acme of youthful high spirits, cheeky like the Angèle of old, with a cheerful grin and forever singing Niceois ditties. Best of all, her skin reflected the light better than any model he could remember.[47]

He was transformed. The same disciple, Georges Besson, who had seen him so low, saw him rise to incredible heights. "When his young model arrived from Nice all his troubles were forgotten even though he still suffered as much as ever. Before ten in the morning he would be in his garden studio examining his work of the previous day and exclaiming at the quality of the light on the olive trees glowing in the morning sunshine. He would crack jokes: 'It's a great pity that someone can't recount later on that I used to paint surrounded by nymphs and crowned with roses, or even better with a beautiful girl on my knees like the *Raphael* of Ingres—though she must have been a little cumbersome!' " [48]

Figures speak better than words. From this time until his death in 1919, this pain-ridden and disabled man made more than one hundred sketches and paintings of Andrée; responding to her youth, he re-created it on canvas as though he too were young—as indeed he was in everything but years and body. Portraits, nudes, and heads were made with rapidity and decision. Most of them showed his favorite red used in an extraordinary variety of nuances. The best of these have been described as hymns to light and color and what, with Renoir, they stand for, youth and life. There were innumerable bathing studies, particularly *Deux baigneuses, Le repos après le bain, Danseuse nue au tambourin,* and *Femme à la guitare.* Impossible, looking at these works, to believe that the painter was tied to a chair.

The new spirit flowed into everything he did. Perhaps the finest canvas of all was painted in 1917 when Vollard came down to see him. Renoir never failed with Vollard—his "blue suit" portrait of 1915 is masterly—and this last portrait was the best of all. It came about by chance, as so many of Renoir's finest canvases did. Vollard decided to go to Spain, and Renoir asked if he would do him a favor: "I have a model just about as stout as you and I should like to paint him in a toreador's costume." [49]

Vollard duly bought the costume. At the customs on the French frontier he said, to avoid paying the heavy duty, that the costume was his working clothes.

"Ah! You're a toreador!" exclaimed the customs officer. "Let's see you in it." [50]

Vollard was obliged to change into the costume or pay the duty. He changed and, having no time to change back before the train left for Nice, got into the compartment as he was. At Nice the glittering costume and pink stockings attracted such a crowd outside the station that he jumped into a taxi and drove straight to Cagnes, again without changing.[51]

The moment Renoir saw him he forgot all about the plump model and demanded that Vollard pose immediately.[52] The resulting portrait was a triumph; the colors blaze and glitter and, possibly the most surprising success, Vollard, that most unimaginable of toreadors, is given such dignity and poise that the canvas, far from being the joke it so easily might have been, is extraordinarily impressive.

As ever, Vollard watched him at work, fascinated. As far as he could see, "Renoir always attacked his canvases without the slightest hint of a plan. First patches appeared on the canvas then, suddenly, the painter would make a few strokes of the brush and the subject 'came out.' Even with his crippled hand he could do a head in one sitting as easily as when he was young." [53]

Vollard could not take his eyes off this right hand with its "thumb" sticking between crooked first finger and palm. Renoir followed his eyes and smiled. "You see, Vollard," he said, "one doesn't need hands to paint. They are quite superfluous." [54]

7

These years from 1916 to 1919 were a triumph of mind over matter. By all rights Renoir should have been dead or a hopeless invalid. But he painted on day after day, and never had he painted better. There were technical weaknesses, certain roughnesses inevitable in a man whose freedom of action was so circumscribed, but these fade into insignificance before the life he put onto canvas; these late works glow with it.

Of course, there were periods of discouragement but always and only when even he could not work. He would then write painful letters. "For five weeks I haven't left my bedroom," he told Durand-Ruel in November, 1916. "That's not funny." [55] And in February, 1917: "I am very tired and work less and less. I can't move my arms." [56] But even in this extremity he could laugh at himself. In May, 1918, he tells Jeanne Baudot, "For months I have suffered day and night and up to the present without hope of it ever coming to an end. As my feet are so swollen it is impossible to sleep. That's why I have neglected my friends so badly. And all this for a big toe which will certainly make an end of me one of these days!" [57]

But the true man comes out even in these records of suffering. Three months later he is writing Durand-Ruel, "Heat, mosquitoes, flies, pain in my foot—I suffer enough. But apart from these things all goes well." [58] He was working again, and when he could paint, nothing else really mattered: "All goes well." [59]

All went well because he forced it to go well. He went on painting. The days he was clamped to his bed grew more frequent, but the moment he could get up he was in the studio again.

In August, 1919, he was invited to inspect the Louvre (closed to the public that summer) by the Director of the Beaux-Arts, Paul Léon. The museum was opened specially for him, and he was taken through the galleries—like "the pope of painting," said André, who wheeled his chair—to see the rehanging that had been carried out during the vacation. His portrait of the Charpentier family had been bought by the state and was hanging in the midst of the new acquisitions. It may be doubted whether he particularly wished to see it unless to smile at his commission days, but its presence there must have brought home to him the amazing change he had seen in half a lifetime. There were he and his friends, some living still, honored, respectable painters, nothing spared in the way of superlatives, the prides of the nation. Had they changed, or had Monet proved his point, that point he and Pissarro had belabored so often forty, fifty years earlier? One thing was certain, he and his friends had won a great victory; never again would French painting deny its heritage.

Yet it could be that Renoir thought little of this, for he was in the presence of men before whom he believed himself to be a mere dauber. It is significant that the picture he stopped longest in front of was Veronese's *Marriage at Cana*. For years he had loved it, for years he had raged at its treatment by the Louvre authorities, hung almost out of sight. This time he saw it as he had imagined it for so long. When he was back in Cagnes for fall and winter, the remark he made most often about this pilgrimage was, "I have seen the *Marriage at Cana* properly hung!" [60]

Almost all vestige of the past had disappeared. Symbolically, a German bomb hit the rue Saint Georges studio and demolished it. The tragic figure of Degas, friendless, practically blind, forced to leave his old home, had at last ceased to wander wretchedly round the darkened streets of wartime Paris. He died in 1917. "Rather any imaginable kind of death than to live on like that," Renoir told Durand-Ruel when he heard the news.[61] To him, as his life had shown, a painter is better dead when he cannot paint.

Monet lived on alone, famous but solitary, in his house at

Giverny. He had lost his second wife, his much-loved son Jean had been killed in the war in 1914, his second son was in the army. The last meeting between the two old friends was in 1916 soon after Renoir's last letter to Monet, congratulating him on the completion of twenty years' work on *Les Nymphéas*, "one of the masterpieces of the future." He arranged to meet Monet in Paris: "It will be a great joy to eat a cutlet with you." [62]

Then Monet retired to his silent life, fighting with failing eyesight like Degas but, like Renoir, forcing himself to paint on.

At Cagnes in 1919 the indomitable Renoir, so unlike his friend in all but spirit, was painting, painting, defying common sense, incessant pain, all the laws of nature. He should have been bedridden, dead, anything but at work, yet at work he was. In November he was brought to bed with pneumonia. This was the end. There was little or no hope that he would recover; he knew it as well as those around him; but the moment he felt a glimmer of strength he insisted on sitting up and making a study of anemones the maid had picked for him. [63]

This was his final gesture. Whether he realized it, we shall never know, for when he had made the picture he lay down and whispered, Renoir to the last, "I think I am beginning to understand something about it." [64]

That was on the afternoon of December third. And with that wonderfully characteristic remark he died.

BIBLIOGRAPHY

Autograph letters, documents, drawings, are to be found in Musée du Louvre, Bibliothèque Nationale, Bibliothèque de l'Institut de France, and Bibliothèque Doucet, Paris. Documents and records are to be found in Archives de la Seine, Paris, and the Mairies of Limoges, Saintes and Cagnes-sur-Mare.

No complete catalogue of Renoir's paintings exists. Professor Venturi was engaged on such a catalogue but died before he could complete it.

Books on or about Renoir

André, A.   *Renoir,* Paris, 1919, 1928.

André, A., and Elder, M.   *L'Atelier de Renoir,* Paris, 1931.

Barnes, A. C., and De Maza, V.   *The Art of Renoir,* New York, 1935.

Baudot, J.   *Renoir: ses amis et ses modèles,* Paris, 1930.

Bérard, M.   *Renoir à Wargemont,* Paris, 1938.

Besson, G.   *Auguste Renoir,* Paris, 1929.

Besson, G.   *Renoir,* Paris, 1938.

Coquiot, G.   *Renoir,* Paris, 1925.

Drucker, M.   *Renoir,* Paris, 1955.

Duret, T.   (A).   *Renoir,* Paris, 1924.

Hugon, H.   *Les aieux de Renoir et sa maison natale,* Limoges n.d.

Meier-Graefe, J.   *Auguste Renoir,* Munich, 1911.

Mirbeau, O., and Forthuny, P.   *Renoir: catalogue de l'exposition de mars, 1913,* Paris, 1913.

Renoir, J.   *Renoir My Father,* New York, London, 1962; Paris, 1962.

Rivière, G. (A). *Renoir et ses amis,* Paris, 1921.

Roger-Marx, C. (A). *Les lithographies de Renoir,* Monte Carlo, 1951; *Renoir,* Paris, 1933.

Venturi, L. *Les Archives de l'Impressionisme,* Paris, 1939.

Vollard, A. (A). *La vie et l'oeuvre de Pierre-Auguste Renoir,* Paris, 1919.

—— (B). *Renoir,* Paris, 1920.

—— (C). *Souvenirs d'un marchand de tableaux,* Paris, 1937.

—— (D). *En écoutant Cézanne, Degas, Renoir,* Paris, 1938.

—— (E). *Tableaux, Pastels et Dessins de Pierre-Auguste Renoir,* 2 Vols., Paris, 1918, n.d.

Articles on or about Renoir

Alexandre, A. (A). "Renoir sans phrases," *Les Arts,* 1919.

—— (B). *Preface au Catalogue de l'Exposition particulière de Renoir de mai 1892 chez Durand-Ruel.*

Baum (Abbé). "Oraison funèbre prononcée en l'Église de Cagnes," *La Vie,* 1920.

Bérard, M. "Renoir en Normandie et la famille Bérard," *L'Amour de l'Art,* 1938.

Besson, G. "Renoir à Cagnes," *Gazette des Beaux-Arts,* 1933.

Blanche, J,-E. "La technique de Renoir," *L'Amour de l'Art,* 1921. "Renoir portraitiste, *L'Art vivant,* 1933. "Sur les routes de la Provence, de Cézanne et Renoir," *Revue de Paris,* 1915.

Burty, P. Preface to the auction catalog, 24, March, 1875.

Cahen-Hayem, M.-L. "Renoir portraitiste," *L'Art et les Artistes,* 1938.

Cogniat, R., and Vollard, A. *Catalogue de l'exposition L'Oeuvre gravé, l'oeuvre sculpté, aquarelles et dessins de Renoir,* Galerie des Beaux-Arts, 1924.

Diole, Ph. "Les dix dernières années de Renoir," *Gazette des Beaux-Arts,* 1934.

Elias, J. "Paul Durand-Ruel," *Kunst und Kunstler,* 1911.

Florisoone, M. "Renoir et la famille Charpentier," *L'Amour de l'Art,* 1938.

Fontainas, A. "Renoir," *Mercure de France,* 1898. "La rencontre d'Ingres et de Renoir," *Formes,* 1931.

Fosca, F. "Triomphe de Renoir," *Gazette des Beaux-Arts,* 1933.

Geffroy, G. "Renoir, peintre de la femme," *L'Art et les Artistes,* 1920.

Houssaye, A. "Renoir," *L'Artiste,* 1877.

Jamot, P. "Renoir," *Gazette des Beaux-Arts,* 1923.

Joëts, J. "Les impressionistes et M. Chocquet," *L'Amour de l'Art,* 1935.

Jourdain, F. *Les décorés et ceux qui ne le sont pas,* Paris, 1895.

Moncade, C. L. de. *Le peintre Renoir et le Salon d'Automne, La Liberté,* Oct. 15, 1904.

Natanson, T. "Renoir," *La Revue Blanche,* 1896. "De Monsieur Renoir et de la beauté," *La Revue bleue,* 1900.

Renoir, E. Letter to Émile Bergerat, *La Vie Moderne,* June 11, 1879.

Rey, R. (A). *Renoir à l'école des Beaux-Arts, Société d'Histoire de l'Art,* 1926. Chapter on Renoir in *La peinture française a la fin du XIX siècle,* Paris, Brussels, 1932.

Rivière, G. *Renoir, L'Art vivant,* 1925. Five numbers of *L'Impressionniste* published between April 5 and 28, 1877.

Roger-Marx, C. "Renoir," *Mercure de France,* 1933. "Les eaux-fortes et les lithographies de Renoir, Byblis," 1930; *Arts et Métiers graphiques,* 1933.

Silvestre, A. "Demi-dieux et simples mortels au Salon de 1879," *La Vie Moderne,* 1879.

Valéry, P. "Souvenir de Renoir," *L'Amour de l'Art,* 1921.

Vollard, A. "Renoir et l'impressionisme," L'Amour de l'Art, 1921. "Dans l'atelier de Renoir," *L'Art vivant,* 1933.

Waldémar, G. "Cézanne et Renoir," *L'Amour de l'Art,* 1921. "L'Oeuvre sculpté de Renoir," *L'Amour de l'Art,* 1924.

Books and Articles on or about People and Events Concerning Renoir

Alexandre, A. *J. F. Raffaelli,* Paris, 1909.

Aubry, G. Jean-. *Eugène Boudin,* Paris, 1922.

Baudelaire. *Correspondance générale,* Paris, 1947–53. *Salon de 1859,* Paris, 1859.

Bazin, G. *L'époque impressionniste,* Paris, 1953. "Julien Tanguy," *Mercure de France,* 1908.

Besson, G. *L'impressionisme et quelques precurseurs,* Paris, 1932.

Blanche, J.-E. *Les Arts plastiques,* Paris, 1931.

Burger, W. *Salons 1861–1868,* Paris, 1870.

Cahen, G. *Eugène Boudin, sa vie et son oeuvre,* Paris, 1900.

Castagnary. *Salons,* Paris, 1892.

Cézanne. *Correspondance,* Paris, 1937.

Claretie, J. *Peintres et sculpteurs contemporains,* Paris, 1873.

Clément, C. *Gleyre,* Paris, 1878.

Daulte, F. *Frédéric Bazille et son temps,* Geneva, 1952.

Degas. *Lettres de Degas,* Paris, 1931, 1945.

Doiteau, V. "La curieuse figure du Dr. Gachet," *Aesculape,* 1923.

Duranty, E. *La nouvelle peinture,* Paris, 1876.

Duret, T. (B). *Les peintres impressionistes,* Paris, 1878.

—— (C). *Histoire des peintres impressionistes,* Paris, 1906.

——— (D). *Histoire d'Edouard Manet et son oeuvre,* Paris, 1902.

——— (E). *Manet and the French Impressionists,* London, 1910.

Elder, M. *Á Giverny chez Claude Monet,* Paris, 1924.

Faure, É. "Renoir," *Revue Hebdomaire,* April, 1920.

Fels, M. de. *Vie de Claude Monet,* Paris, 1929.

Fénéon, F. *Les Impressionnistes en 1886.* Paris, 1886.

Gachet, Dr. *Lettres des peintres impressionnistes à Dr. Gachet,* Paris, 1959.

Geffroy, G. "Paul Cézanne," *Le Journal,* 1894. *Claude Monet,* Paris, 1922. *Histoire de l'Impressionnisme, Paris,* 1894.

Hanson, L. and E. *Golden Decade: the Story of Impressionism,* London, 1961. *The Post Impressionists,* London, 1963.

Julien, A. *Fantin-Latour, Sa Vie, Ses Amitiés,* Paris, 1909.

Lecomte, G. *Guillaumin,* Paris, 1921.

Mallarmé, S. *Autobiographie,* Paris, 1924. *Poèmes et lettres,* Paris, 1948. *Correspondance inédite de Stéphane Mallarmé,* Geneva, 1949.

Manet. *Lettres du Siège de Paris,* Paris, 1935.

Mauclair, C. *L'Impressionnisme, son histoire, son esthétique, ses maîtres,* Paris, 1904.

Mondor, H. *Vie de Mallarmé,* Paris, 1939.

Montegut, E. *Nos morts contemporains,* Paris, 1884.

Moore, G. *Reminiscences of the Impressionist Painters,* Dublin, 1906.

Moreau-Nelaton, E. *Manet raconté par lui-même,* Paris, 1926.

Morisot, B. *Correspondance de Berthe Morisot,* Paris, 1950.

Pach, W. "Interview with Renoir," *Scribner's Magazine,* 1912.

Pascal, J. *Le Salon d'Automne,* Paris, 1904.

Pissarro. *Lettres à son fils Lucien,* Paris, 1950.

Poulain, G. *Bazille et ses amis,* Paris, 1932.

Proust, A. *Edouard Manet,* Paris, 1913.

Raynal, M. *Cézanne,* Paris, 1936.

Regamey, R. "La Formation de Claude Monet," *Gazette des Beaux-Arts,* 1927.

Renoir, C. *Souvenirs sur mon père,* Paris, 1948.

Rewald, J. (A). *Cézanne, sa Vie, son Oeuvre, son Amitié pour Zola,* Paris, 1939.

——— (B) *History of Impressionism,* New York, 1946.

Rey, R. *La peinture française à la fin du XIX siècle,* Brussels, 1932.

Rouault, G. *Souvenirs intimes,* Paris, 1927.

Signac, P. *D'Eugène Delacroix au néo-impressionnisme,* Paris, 1899.

Silvestre, T. *Histoire des artistes vivants,* Paris, 1856.

Sisley. *Lettres à Duret,* Paris, 1899. *Lettres inédités,* Paris, 1931. *Lettres à Duret, Monet et au Dr. Viau,* Paris, 1933.

Stevens, A. *Le Salon de 1863,* Paris, 1866.

Tabarant, A. *Pissarro,* Paris, 1924.

Thiebault-Sisson, C. *Claude Monet,* Paris, 1900.

Van Gogh. *Verzameldè Brieven van Vincent van Gogh,* Amsterdam, 1952–54.

Villiers, G. B. de. *Petites histoires sur les grands artistes,* Paris, 1941.

Vollard, A. (C). *Cézanne,* Paris, 1914. *Degas,* Paris, 1927.

Wheelwright, E. "Recollections of Jean François Millet," Atlantic *Monthly,* 1876.

Zola. *Correspondance, les Lettres et les Arts,* Paris, 1936–38.

NOTES

Unless otherwise stated references are to items listed in the Bibliography and identified by letters in parentheses.

CHAPTER 1

1. Vollard. See "La jeunesse de Renoir" by A. Vollard, *La Renaissance*, May, 1918.
2. Hugon.
3. Jean Renoir.
4. Hugon.
5. Jean Renoir.
6. Vollard (A, B).
7. Jean Renoir.
8. Rivière (A).
9. Jean Renoir.
10. Renoir told Vollard that he was reprimanded by his teachers for scribbling in his lesson books.
11. Jean Renoir.
12. *Ibid.*
13. This was *Sapho*.
14. Renoir told Vollard that he was twelve at the time, Jean Renoir says he was thirteen, Edmond Renoir says he was fifteen.
15. Vollard (A, B).
16. *Ibid.*

CHAPTER 2

1. Rivière (A).
2. Vollard. See "La jeunesse de Renoir" by A. Vollard, *La Renaissance*, May, 1918.
3. Rivière (A); Vollard (A, B).
4. Jean Renoir.

5. Vollard (A, B); Jean Renoir.
6. Jean Renoir.
7. Vollard (A, B); Jean Renoir.
8. Vollard (A, B).
9. *Ibid.*
10. Rivière (A).
11. Vollard (A, B).
12. *Ibid.*
13. *Ibid.*
14. Jean Renoir.
15. Vollard (A, B).
16. *Ibid.*
17. Jean Renoir.
18. Vollard (A, B).
19. *Ibid.*
20. *Ibid.*
21. *Ibid.*
22. *Ibid.*
23. Jean Renoir.
24. *Ibid.*
25. Vollard (A, B); Jean Renoir.
26. Jean Renoir.
27. Vollard (A, B).
28. *Ibid.*
29. *Ibid.*
30. Jean Renoir.
31. Vollard (A, B).
32. The relationship differs in the accounts of Vollard and Jean Renoir.
33. Vollard (A, B).
34. *Ibid.*
35. Jean Renoir.
36. *Ibid.*
37. Vollard (A, B).
38. *Ibid.*
39. *Ibid.*
40. Edmond Renoir in *La Vie Moderne,* June 19, 1879.
41. *Jean Renoir.*
42. Edmond Renoir, *op. cit.*

CHAPTER 3

1. Bazille to his parents, Nov. 10, 1862. *Cf.* Alexandre on Raffaelli.
2. Vollard (A, B).
3. Jean Renoir.
4. Faure. *Cf.* Moncade: "I was an extremely assiduous student; I swotted at the Academy, I studied the classic, but I never obtained the slightest good word, and my teachers were unanimous in finding my painting execrable.

5. Poulain.
6. Clément.
7. Montegut.
8. Clément.
9. André; Baudelaire.
10. Vollard (A, B); Moncade.
11. Vollard (A, B).
12. Rey (A).
13. Rivière (A).
14. André. The full text is: "Today, when I look back at my past life, I compare it to one of those corks thrown into a river. It slips along, then is caught by an eddy, is drawn backwards, plunges, comes to the surface again, is held by a weed, makes desperate efforts to free itself and ends up by going off I don't know where."
15. Jean Renoir.
16. Duret (C, E).
17. Duret (A, E); Tabarant.
18. Rey (A).
19. Jean Renoir.
20. Bazille to his parents, Nov., 1862.
21. Bazille to his mother, Dec., 1862.
22. Thiebault-Sisson.
23. Jean Renoir.
24. Bazille to his family, Jan., 1863.
25. Bazille to his mother, Dec. 28, 1862.
26. But see letter to Toulmouche, May 23, 1863. *Cf.* Regamey.
27. Thiebault-Sisson; Jean-Aubry; Montegut.
28. Thiebault-Sisson; Jean-Aubry; Cahen; Geffroy; Fels; Poulain.
29. André.
30. *Mary Cassatt,* by A. Segard, Paris, 1913.
31. Rewald.
32. Jean Renoir.
33. Duret (A); Moreau-Nelaton.
34. Duret (A).
35. Poulain.
36. Baudelaire; Rivière; Vollard; Poulain; Daulte.
37. Vollard (A, B).
38. Vollard (A, B); Rivière.
39. Tabarant; Geffroy; Fels.
40. Vollard (A, B).
41. Vollard (C); Raynal.
42. Bazille to his father, Spring 1863.
43. Rey (A).
44. Vollard (A, B).
45. Bazille to his father, April 5, 1863.
46. Geffroy; Poulain; Jean Renoir.
47. Baudelaire.
48. Stevens; Wheelwright.

49. Geffroy; Fels.
50. Duret (B, C, E).
51. André.

CHAPTER 4
1. Rey (A).
2. Poulain.
3. Jean Renoir.
4. *Ibid.*
5. *Ibid.*
6. Vollard (A, B).
7. Jean Renoir.
8. Vollard (A, B).
9. Thiebault-Sisson; Jean-Aubry; Geffroy; Bazille to his parents, Spring 1864.
10. Bazille to his father, July 31, 1864.
11. Vollard (A, B).
12. *Ibid.*
13. *Ibid.*
14. André.
15. Silvestre; Claretie.
16. Vollard (A, B); Duret.
17. Tabarant; Duret.
18. Vollard. In Moncade, Renoir is quoted as saying that he was refused by the Salon jury this year and the two years following. This statement, made to Moncade in 1904, is not borne out by the Salon catalogues of these years, which list the Renoir canvases mentioned above and following.
19. 6, rue Furstenberg.
20. Vollard (A, B); Rivière.
21. Paul Mantz and Astruc; Bazille to his parents, Spring 1865.
22. Monet to Bazille, Spring 1865: "I think of nothing but my picture."
23. Monet to Bazille, July 15, 1864: "You don't work hard enough or in the right way. You'll never get anywhere if you see too much of pleasure-mongers like Villa."
24. Vollard (A, B); Rivière (A).
25. Vollard (A, B).
26. Jean Renoir.
27. Letter of July 3, 1865; Daulte.
28. Bazille to his parents, Aug. 23, 1865.
29. Thiebault-Sisson; Geffroy; Fels; Poulain.

CHAPTER 5
1. Vollard (A, B).
2. See Moncade; Zola, *Correspondance*, Paris, 1907–8; Zola article in *Le Voltaire*, June, 1880; *Cézanne*, by J. Rewald (A), Paris, 1939.
3. See Note 2, Chapter 7.

4. The Paris winter of 1865–66 was one of the coldest and wettest for many years; *Archives de la Seine.*

5. Letter of March 29, 1866, *Cahiers d'Aujourd'hui,* Jan. 1921.

6. Accounts are to be found in *Le pèlerinage de Giverny,* by Duc de Trevise, *Revue de l'art ancien et modern,* Jan.-Feb., 1927; *The Invincible Monet,* by C. P. Weekes, New York, 1960 (*Camille,* London, 1962); Geffroy; Fels; Poulain.

7. Letter of June 6, 1866, from Mlle. Lecoeur, *Cahiers d'Aujourd'hui,* Jan., 1921.

8. Vollard (A, B).

9. *Ibid.*

10. See Weekes, *op. cit.*

11. Beginning with the 1863 Salon des Refusés. *Cf. Cézanne;* Zola, *Correspondance;* Rewald (A).

12. Courbet's aim was "to interpret the manners, ideas and appearance of my age in terms of my own experience—to produce, in a word, art that lives." *Le Réalisme* by Courbet. *Cf. Gustave Courbet,* by G. Riat, Paris, 1906.

13. *Op. cit. Cf.* Vollard (A, B).

14. This is corroborated by a host of eyewitnesses, from Edmond Renoir and Rivière to Vollard, André and Besson. *Cf.* Jean Renoir.

15. Vollard (A, B).

16. See letter of Feb. 12, 1866, from Bazille to his brother Marc: "I'm not sorry to live alone for a while; the ménage à deux has plenty of inconveniences even when both get on well." *Cf.* Weekes, *op. cit.;* Jean-Aubry; Poulain; Fels; Geffroy.

17. *Cf.* Jean-Aubry; Poulain; Fels; Weekes, *op. cit.*

18. No. 20. They took possession July first.

19. He often suffered from "indigestion of walls and streets." Letter of Nov., 1862, to his parents.

20. "Monet is fine company while painting," Renoir was to tell Bazille in a letter of Sept., 1869. *Cf.* Fels; Geffroy; Weekes, *op. cit.*

21. See also the treatment of the chestnut trees in Monet's *Saint-Germain l'Auxerrois* painted during this period.

22. See Edmond Renoir on his brother in *La Vie Moderne,* June 19, 1879. *Cf.* Jean Renoir; Vollard.

23. *Ibid.*

24. *Ibid. Cf.* "Auguste Renoir et son frère," by J. Rewald, *Gazette des Beaux-Arts,* March, 1943.

25. Vollard (A, B).

26. *Ibid.*

CHAPTER 6

1. Jean Renoir.

2. Geffroy; Fels; Vollard (A, B).

3. Vollard (A, B).

4. *Ibid.*

5. *Ibid.;* Duret. *Cf.* letter of Monet to Bazille, May 26, 1867.

6. Bazille to his parents, April, 1867.
7. Bazille to his father, May, 1867.
8. Letter of Aug. 23, 1867.
9. Vollard (A, B).
10. *Ibid.*
11. *Ibid.*
12. *Ibid.*
13. Letter of Maître to Bazille, Aug. 23, 1867.
14. Letters of June 25, July 9 and 16, 1867.
15. Jean-Aubry; Geffroy; Fels; Duret.
16. Bazille to his sisters, Autumn, 1867.
17. l'rue Pigalle.
18. For descriptions of the Guerbois gatherings, see Duret (B, C, D, E) and Tabarant.
19. First known use of the phrase by Solari, the sculptor from Aix, to Zola in Spring, 1868. See *Cézanne,* by Rewald (A).
20. He had no wish "to play the martyr," he told André later.
21. Elder; Raynal.
22. Monet to Bazille, Spring, 1868.
23. Moncade.
24. But see Burger; Boudin to Martin, May 4, 1868; Jean-Aubry.
25. Jean Renoir.
26. In *Le Salon de 1863.*
27. In *La femme de Paul.*
28. *Ibid.*
29. *Ibid.*
30. Vollard.
31. *Ibid.*
32. *Ibid.*
33. *Ibid.*
34. *Ibid.*
35. Letter of June 29, 1868.
36. Letter of August, 1868.
37. *Ibid.*
38. *Ibid.*
39. *Ibid.*
40. Vollard (A, B).
41. Stevens to Bazille, May, 1869: "You have been defended [between ourselves] by Bonnat and—can you guess—by Cabanal!"
42. Bazille to his parents, May, 1869.
43. *Ibid.*
44. See letter of Monet to Houssaye, June 2, 1869; "Claude Monet," by R. Chavance, *Le Figaro illustré,* Dec. 16, 1926; *cf.* letters to Zola, Bibliothèque Nationale; "Autour de Manet," by A. Tabarant, *L'Art Vivant,* May 4, 1928; *Claude Monet,* by G. Clemenceau, Paris, 1928.

CHAPTER 7

1. *Cf.* Monet to Duret (C). See *La grande misère des impressionnistes* in *Le Populaire,* March 1, 1924: "I must ask, virtually beg for my life, not having a sou left to buy colors or canvases."
2. Renoir's remark in full was: "I have always abandoned myself to my destiny. I've never had a fighter's temperament and would often have broken away from our association if my old Monet, who certainly had the temperament of a fighter, hadn't given me a leg up." André.
3. Letter of August 9.
4. Poulain; Daulte.
5. Letter of Sept. 25.
6. Vollard (A, B); André.
7. Letter of Sep.; Poulain.
8. *Ibid.*
9. *Ibid.*
10. *Souvenirs,* Paris, 1922.
11. The evidence against it is formidable; see later text. The origin of the phrase was a caricature by Bertell in *Journal amusant* when Fantin's picture was hung in the 1870 Salon. The caricature was titled "Jesus painting in the midst of his disciples, or the Divine School of Manet." See *Jullien; Nelaton.*
12. See Jullien.
13. Of the six figures shown, only three—Manet holding the brush, Bazille leaning on the easel, and Maître playing the piano—have been firmly identified. Of the rest, the man standing behind Manet is variously identified as Monet and Astruc, the man on the staircase as Zola, Astruc, Sisley and Monet, the man sitting on the table as Sisley, Renoir and Zola. Moreau-Nelaton, who quotes Manet, places them as Manet, Bazille and Astruc by the easel and Monet and Sisley by the stairs.
14. May, 1870; Daulte.
15. Letter to his mother, May 26, 1870; Daulte.
16. *Claude Monet,* by A. Alexandre, Paris, 1921.

CHAPTER 8

1. Vollard (A, B).
2. See Alexandre, *op. cit.;* Weekes; Fels; Geffroy; Poulain.
3. Vollard (A, B).
4. Mme. Morisot to a daughter, Oct. 18, 1870.
5. Letter of Aug. 2, 1870; Daulte.
6. Jean Renoir.
7. Vollard (A, B); Jean Renoir.
8. Manet to his wife, Dec., 1870; Moreau-Nelaton. *Cf. Lettres du siège de Paris,* Paris, 1935. Writing to Bazille's father from Paris on Oct. 31, 1870, Maître says: "In spite of all the optimists say, famine will seize Paris before the end of January."
9. Letter of May 30, 1871; Rewald.

10. Vollard (A, B).

11. Jean Renoir.

12. Rivière (A).

13. *Ibid.;* and see *Confessions of a Young Man,* by George Moore, London, 1888.

14. Vollard (A, B).

15. *Ibid.*

16. Edmond Renoir.

17. Letter of Jan. 2, 1872; Jean-Aubry.

18. Venturi.

19. *Ibid.*

20. *Ibid.*

21. Vollard (A, B); Duret (A). *Cf.* "Souvenirs sur Degas," by G. Jeanniot, *La Revue Universelle,* Oct. 15, 1933, and Nov. 1, 1933; *Les mots de Degas,* by F. Charles, Paris, 1918.

22. Tabarant.

23. Florisoone. *Cf.* Duret (A).

24. André.

25. Rivière (A); Vollard (A, B).

CHAPTER 9

1. On Montmartre at this time and later, see *Montmartre à vingt ans,* by F. Carco, Paris, 1938; *La vie à Montmartre,* by G. Montorgueil, Paris, 1899; *La Vieux Montmartre,* by A. Warnod, Paris, 1914, and *Les Peintres de Montmartre,* by A. Warnod, Paris, 1928.

2. Rivière (A).

3. *Ibid.*

4. *Ibid.*

5. *Cf.* Renoir's remarks in André; Maître's note in his *Livre de Raison,* April 9, 1875; Daulte; Moncade. See also Renoir's statement to Moncade: "It is a great mistake to believe that I am opposed to exhibitions. On the contrary there isn't a greater supporter of exhibitions than I, for in my opinion painting is made to be shown."

6. *Recueil d'estampes, Galerie Durand-Ruel,* Paris, 1873, Introduction to Vol. 1.

7. "Un après-midi chez Claude Monet," by L. Vauxelles, *L'Art et les Artistes,* Dec., 1905; Tabarant; "Degas," by J. Elias, *Neue Rundschau,* Nov., 1917. Duret (D, E).

8. Rivière (A). *Cf.* letter of Degas to Bracquemond, 1874; Degas.

9. Vollard (A, B). *Cf.* Moncade: "It is the most comical thing in the world that I should be represented as a revolutionary, I who am certainly the greatest old fogey among painters."

10. *Cf.* Duret (D, E) on Manet.

11. See Duret (B, C), Moncade to Pissarro, Feb. 15, 1874; Tabarant. *Cf.* Venturi; Moncade.

12. Tabarant. *Cf.* Degas to Bracquemond, 1886; Degas.

13. Durand-Ruel Memoirs; Venturi.

14. See *Notes et Souvenirs,* by J. de Nittis, Paris, 1895; Degas to Bracquemond, March, 1875; Degas.
15. Vollard (A, B).
16. *Ibid.*
17. Joëts.
18. Venturi.
19. Tabarant. See also *La grande misère des impressionnistes, Le Populaire,* March 1, 1924.
20. Duret (C).
21. Geffroy.
22. Morisot.
23. Elder.
24. See *Le peintre Caillebotte et sa collection,* by A. Tabarant, Paris, 1921.
25. Elder.
26. Rivière (A); Vollard (A, B). *Cf. Emmanuel Chabrier d'après ses lettres,* ed. J. Desaymand, Paris, 1934.
27. Vollard (A, B); Rivière (A); Moore, *op. cit.*
28. See Rivière (A); *La curieuse vie de Marcellin Desboutin,* by Clément-Janin, Paris, 1922.
29. Rivière (A).
30. *Ibid.*
31. *Ibid. Cf.* Desaymand, *op. cit.*
32. Rivière (A).
33. *Ibid.*
34. Tabarant; Duret (C); Fels; Geffroy.

CHAPTER 10
1. Degas; Tabarant; Morisot.
2. Memoirs; Venturi.
3. Vollard (A, B).
4. Morisot.
5. She had married Eugène Manet late the previous year.
6. Vollard (A, B).
7. Durand-Ruel Memoirs; Venturi.
8. Ibid.; Duret (A, C).
9. *Ibid.*
10. Letter of March 19, 1875; Moreau-Nelaton.
11. Masque de Fer in *Le Figaro,* March 23, 1875.
12. By P. Girard, March, 1875.
13. *Le Rappel,* probably by E. d'Hervilly.
14. Introduction to catalogue: *Vente du 24 mars 1875. Tableaux et aquarelles par Cl. Monet, B. Morrisot, A. Renoir, A. Sisley.*
15. *Ibid.*
16. Memoirs; Venturi.
17. *Ibid.*
18. Vollard (A, B).
19. Joëts; Tabarant; Vollard (A, B); Duret (C, E).

20. *Ibid.*
21. Vollard (A, B).
22. *Ibid.*
23. *Ibid.*
24. *Ibid.*
25. For details of Tanguy see: "Julien Tanguy," by E. Bernard, *Mercure de France,* Dec. 16, 1908; *Des Artistes,* by O. Mirbeau, Paris, 1922; *Van Gogh,* by T. Duret, Paris, 1919; *Vincent van Gogh,* by G. Coquiot, Paris, 1923. One of Tanguy's most prized feats was his ability to grind a particularly attractive lapis-lazuli which was in much demand.
26. Vollard (A, B).
27. *Ibid.*
28. *Ibid.*
29. *Ibid.*
30. Joëts; Fels.
31. Rivière (A); Florisoone.
32. Jean Renoir places the painting before the war but this would appear unlikely.
33. Rivière (A).
34. Degas; Morisot.
35. Venturi.
36. Tabarant. *Cf.* "Souvenirs sur Degas," *op. cit.;* "Degas," by W. Sickert, *Burlington Magazine,* Nov., 1917; *Impressions and Opinions,* by G. Moore, New York, 1891.
37. *Le Figaro,* April 3, 1876.
38. Morisot.
39. Quoted in Venturi.
40. *Ibid.*
41. *Ibid.*
42. *Ibid.*
43. *Ibid.*
44. Rivière (A).
45. See *Notes et souvenirs,* op. cit.; "Souvenirs sur Manet," by F.F. (énéon), *Bulletin de la vie artistique,* Oct. 15, 1920, and (with caution) *Reminiscences of the Impressionist Painters,* Dublin, 1906, and *Modern Painting,* by G. Moore, New York, 1898. Moore was by no means so intimate with the Impressionist painters or with Manet as he afterward claimed.
46. Rivière (A).
47. *Confessions of a Young Man, op. cit.*
48. Rivière (A); Florisoone.
49. Rivière (A).
50. *Ibid.*
51. *Ibid.*
52. One of them can be seen, for instance, in Sisley's *Vue de Montmartre* of 1869, now in the Musée de Grenoble.
53. Rivière (A).

54. *Ibid. Cf.* "Les bals de Paris: Le Moulin de Galette," by E. Patrick, *Le Courrier Français*, Sept., 1896; *Bals, Cafés et Cabarets*, by A. Warnod, Paris, 1913.
55. Rivière (A).
56. *Ibid.* See also *Le Salon de Madame Charpentier*, by A. Vollard, *L'Art et les Artistes*, 1920.
57. Florisoone.
58. Rivière (A).

CHAPTER 11

1. See Degas; Morisot; Jeanniot, *op. cit.*
2. See letter to Faure, March, 1877; Degas. *Cf. Impressions and Opinions, op. cit.*
3. See letter to Pissarro, Jan. 24, 1877; Rewald.
4. Venturi.
5. *L'Impressionniste.*
6. Rivière (A).
7. *Ibid.*
8. Drucker.
9. Rivière (A).
10. *Ibid.*
11. *Le Radical* (A. Lepelletier).
12. *La Presse.*
13. *Petit Parisien* (A. Pothey).
14. *Le Courrier Français* (O'Squarr).
15. Rivière (A).
16. *Ibid.;* Vollard.
17. Rivière (A).
18. Wolff in *Le Figaro* was excessively violent; the critic of *Le Pays* cried, "This is madness, this deliberate accentuation of the horrible and execrable"; the critic of *Le Sportsman* complained that he "felt seasick" every time he looked at the canvases; Roger Ballu in *Le Chronique des Arts* said, "I can't understand the portrait of Mlle. S at all," and, after tearing it to pieces, ended with, "Nothing, it seems to me, could be further removed from life." The same critic was extravagantly harsh with *Le Balancoire* and *Le Moulin de la Galette,* which, he declared," are speckled with round blobs and spots . . . intended to represent the shadows cast by leaves . . . but which only make the pictures ridiculous."
19. *Le Charivari.*
20. A. Legrand, a former employee of Durand-Ruel's, is now remembered chiefly, if at all, for his invention of what he strangely named Maclean cement. This cement, which Renoir used extensively, proved useless, cracking when dry. Caillebotte, persuaded to back the invention, lost 30,000 francs over it. See Fels.
21. See Pissarro to Murer and Duret in Tabarant, and Monet to Chocquet in Joëts.
22. Rivière (A).

23. Musée du Louvre; Florisoone.
24. Rivière (A). *Cf.* Durand-Ruel (Venturi), Vollard, Jean Renoir.
25. Tabarant.
26. *Ibid. Cf.* Pissarro; Rewald (B).
27. Rivière (A).
28. Tabarant.
29. *Ibid.*
30. *Ibid.*
31. *Ibid.*
32. Pissarro to Murer, Summer, 1878; Tabarant.
33. Morisot.
34. Degas; Jeanniot, *op. cit.*
35. Baudot.
36. To Murer; Tabarant.
37. Letter to Chocquet, Fall, 1877; Joëts.
38. Duret; Tabarant.
39. Duret; *La Revue Blanche.*
40. See Degas to Bracquemond, May 13, 1879; Caillebotte to Monet, Degas; Geffroy.
41. Moncade.
42. Alexandre (A). See also Castagnary, quoted in "Mme. Charpentier and her children by Auguste Renoir," by L. Benedite, *Burlington Magazine,* May, 1907.

CHAPTER 12

1. Rivière (A). See also *Le Salon de Madame Charpentier,* by A. Vollard, *L'Art et les Artistes,* 1920.
2. Venturi.
3. To Theo van Gogh, May, 1888.
4. Bérard; Vollard (A, B) says that this year Renoir spent several weeks in Algeria, painting with Lestringuez, but this is not confirmed by any existing letters.
5. Rivière (A).
6. See Monet to Durer, Spring, 1880, quoted in *Pissarro, Sisley, Monet nach eigenen und fremden Zeughissen,* by H. Graber, Basle, 1943.
7. Letter to Murer, May 25, 1879; Tabarant.
8. Caillebotte to Pissarro, Jan., 1881; Rewald (B).
9. *Ibid. Cf.* letter of Sisley to Charpentier, March 28, 1879; Huyghe.
10. Venturi.
11. *Ibid.*
12. *Ibid.;* Rivière (A).
13. Rivière (A).
14. *Le Voltaire,* June, 1880.
15. Preface to the catalogue.
16. Geffroy.
17. Letter of July 4, 1880; Cézanne.
18. Letter of Sept. 26, 1874; Cézanne.
19. *L'Impressionnisme;* Venturi.

20. Elder.
21. Vollard (A, B). *Cf.* letter to C. Camion, 1902; Cézanne.
22. Letter of March, 1881. Musée du Louvre; Florisoone. *Cf.* Letter to Duret from Algiers, March 4, 1881. *Bulletin des Expositions* No. 3. Galerie d'Art, Braun et Cie. Paris, 1932.
23. Letter of March, 1881; Venturi.

CHAPTER 13

1. Jean Renoir.
2. Rivière (A).
3. Jean Renoir.
4. *Ibid.*
5. Letter of Easter, 1881; Musée du Louvre; Florisoone.
6. Morisot; Vollard (A, B).
7. Jean Renoir.
8. *Ibid.*
9. Letter of Autumn, 1881; Musée du Louvre; Florisoone.
10. *Ibid.*
11. *Ibid.*
12. Morisot.
13. Venturi.
14. Letter of Dec. 28, 1881; Joëts.
15. Venturi.
16. Letter of Dec. 28, 1881; Moreau-Nelaton.
17. *L'Amateur d'Autographes,* Paris, 1913.
18. *Ibid. Cf.* Vollard. See also *The Renoir Portrait of Wagner,* by E. Lockspeiser, *Music and Letters,* Jan., 1937.
19. Letter of Jan., 1882; Musée du Louvre; Florisoone.
20. Letter of March 2, 1882 to Chocquet; Joëts.
21. Moreau-Nelaton.
22. Baudot; Duret (E).
23. Venturi.
24. *Ibid.*
25. Geffroy.
26. Venturi.
27. *Ibid.*
28. *Ibid.*
29. *Ibid.*
30. Morisot.
31. *Ibid.*
32. Venturi.

CHAPTER 14

1. Vollard (A, B).
2. Rivière (A).
3. Tabarant. *Cf.* notes of Louis le Bail; Rewald (B).
4. Vollard (A, B). *Cf.* André.
5. *Ibid.*

6. *Degas, Danse, Dessin,* by Paul Valéry (including *Souvenirs de Berthe Morisot, notes par elle sur un carnet*), Paris, 1936. *Cf. Théories,* by M. Denis, Paris, 1912; "Deux heures avec Degas," by Moreau-Nelaton, *L'Amour de l'Art,* July, 1931.
7. *Ibid.*
8. Venturi.
9. *Ibid.*
10. *Ibid.*
11. André.
12. *L'Impressionniste.*
13. Letter of May, 1884; Venturi.
14. *Ibid.*
15. Rivière (A).
16. *Baudot.*
17. Morisot.
18. To Monet; Baudot.
19. Letter of Aug., 1885; Venturi.
20. Letter of Sept., 1885; Venturi.
21. Valéry, *op. cit.*
22. *Ibid.*
23. See *Trente Années de Lutte pour l'Art,* by M. O. Maus, Brussels, 1926.
24. Venturi.
25. Letter to Durand-Ruel; Venturi.
26. Letter of May 14, 1887; Pissarro.
27. *Ibid.*
28. Letter of May, 1888; Van Gogh.
29. Letter of May, 1887; Venturi.
30. *Ibid.*

CHAPTER 15

1. "I was simply plastered with makeup," Valadon told Coquiot later. "Pretty severe, eh? That's what collectors and critics call the Ingres period." Coquiot.
2. Morisot.
3. *Ibid.*
4. See letter of Oct. 15, 1887; Pissarro.
5. Vollard (A, B).
6. *Ibid.*
7. Baudot.
8. *Ibid.*
9. Venturi.
10. Letters of Feb. and March; Venturi.
11. Letter of Aug. 11, 1889; Geffroy.
12. Letter of Sept., 1888; Morisot.
13. Letter of Oct. 1, 1888; Pissarro.

14. *Cf.* a typical discussion: Renoir, "You have abandoned the dot but won't admit it." Pissarro, "You follow your caprice, I know where I'm going." Letter of Aug. 28, 1889; Pissarro.
15. Letter of Oct. 1, 1888; Pissarro.
16. *Ibid.*
17. Letter of Oct., 1888; Morisot.
18. Letter of Dec., 1888; Morisot.
19. Letter of Dec., 1888; Venturi.
20. Letter of Oct. 20, 1896; Pissarro.
21. Roger-Marx.
22. Letter of July, 1902, to J. Gasquet: *Paul Cézanne,* by J. Gasquet, Paris, 1921. *Cf. Le dimanche avec Paul Cézanne,* by L. Larguier, Paris, 1925; Vollard (C); Cézanne.
23. Morisot.
24. *Ibid.*
25. Preface to *Renoir peintre du Nu,* Paris, 1923.
26. Morisot. Renoir, as always, said what he thought, and owing to the manner in which he said it, his frankness was appreciated. One farewell to Berthe Morisot, after an evening at which Mallarmé had read some of his poems, has become well known. "It's such a pleasure seeing you! For if I don't understand the meaning of what he writes, what a treat it is to hear it recited!" Vollard (A, B).
27. *Ibid.*
28. Morisot; Vollard (A, B).
29. Morisot.
30. *Ibid.*
31. *P. A. Renoir,* by T. de Wyzewa, *L'art dans les deux mondes,* December 26, 1890 (reprinted in *Peintres d'hier et d'aujourd'hui,* Paris, 1930.
32. Venturi.
33. *Ibid.*
34. *Ibid.*
35. *Ibid.*
36. Morisot.
37. *Ibid.*
38. Vollard (A, B).
39. *Ibid.*
40. *Ibid.*
41. *Ibid.*
42. *Ibid.*
43. *Ibid.*
44. Morisot.
45. *Ibid.*
46. *Ibid.*
47. Vollard (A, B).
48. Morisot.
49. Venturi.
50. *Ibid.*

51. *Ibid.*
52. Geffroy.
53. See *Histoire de la peinture française 1800–1933,* by A. Leroy, Paris, 1934.
54. *Ibid.*
55. *L'Artiste,* April, 1894.
56. See Leroy, *op. cit. Cf.* "La peintre Caillebotte et sa collection," by A. Tabarant, *Bulletin de la vie artistique,* Aug., 1921; "Enquête," by H. Bataille, *Journal des Artistes,* 1894; "Le legs Caillebotte et l'État," by Octave Mirbeau, *Le Journal,* Dec., 1894; Vollard (A, B); Geffroy.
57. Letter of March 10, 1897; Pissarro.
58. Leroy, *op. cit.;* Vollard (A, B).
59. *Ibid.*
60. Vollard (A, B).
61. Morisot.
62. Jean Renoir.
63. Morisot.
64. *Ibid.*
65. *Ibid.*
66. *Ibid. Cf.* Baudot; *Mon Oncle Degas,* by J. Fèvre, Geneva, 1949.
67. Baudot.
68. Morisot.
69. Jean Renoir.
70. *Ibid.*

CHAPTER 16

1. Letter of Jan. 21, 1894; Pissarro. See Vollard (D) for an account of his beginnings.
2. Besson, in a review of Vollard (B) (*Renoir par Ambroise Vollard,* in *Les Cahiers d'Aujourd'hui,* July, 1921) claims that Renoir told him and other friends that in joke he often misled Vollard by stating views that he did not really hold. This may be true. But it could also be the fact that Renoir was exercising his sense of humor at the expense of Besson. Renoir had considerable experience of the jealousies and bickerings between followers of great men, and he had his own way of commenting on the weakness.
3. Jean Renoir.
4. Vollard (A, B).
5. *Ibid.*
6. *Ibid.*
7. *Ibid.*
8. *Ibid.*
9. Letter of Nov. 21, 1895; Pissarro.
10. Letter of Dec. 4, 1895; Pissarro.
11. Vollard (A, B).
12. *Ibid.*
13. *Ibid.*

14. *Ibid.*
15. *Ibid.*
16. *Ibid.*

CHAPTER 17

1. Letter to Durand-Ruel, Dec., 1881; Venturi.
2. Jean Renoir.
3. *Ibid.*
4. Baudot.
5. Jean Renoir.
6. Letter of Jan. 22, 1899; Pissarro.
7. Jean Renoir.
8. *Ibid.* Vollard (A, B, D, E). See also *Dans l'atelier de Renoir,* by A. Vollard, *L'Art vivant,* 1933.
9. Venturi.
10. *Ibid.*
11. *Ibid.*
12. *Ibid.*
13. *Ibid.*
14. Baudot.
15. Jean Renoir.
16. Baudot.
17. *Ibid.*
18. Venturi.
19. Geffroy; Fels.
20. Letter of Aug. 20, 1900; Geffroy; *Cf.* Baudot.
21. Letter of Aug. 23, 1900; Geffroy; *Cf.* Baudot.
22. Baudot.
23. Venturi.
24. Jean Renoir.
25. *Ibid.*
26. *Ibid.*
27. Venturi.
28. See *Bulletin des Expositions,* Nov., Dec., 1932, Galerie d'Art, Braun et Cie., Paris for letters from Renoir to André.

CHAPTER 18

1. Baudot.
2. *Ibid.*
3. *Ibid.*
4. *Ibid.*
5. Rivière (A).
6. Vollard (A, B).
7. Venturi.
8. *Ibid.*
9. *Ibid.*
10. *Ibid.*

11. *Ibid.*
12. *Ibid.*
13. André.
14. *Ibid. Cf.* Vollard (A, B).
15. Renoir's last sight of Cézanne seems to have been at Giverny in Nov., 1894, when Cézanne unexpectedly arrived at the inn for a few days' painting. Monet persuaded him with difficulty to lunch at his house, and Degas' protégée, Mary Cassatt, has given an account of one of these lunches when she, Mirbeau, Rodin, Clemenceau, and Geffroy were all present (quoted in Weekes, *op. cit.,* and in *Paul Cézanne,* by Gerstle Mack, New York, 1935). See also Segard, *op. cit.;* Vollard (C). Geffroy has also commented at length on this visit of Cézanne's to Giverny. Monet's efforts to do honor to Cézanne by arranging a dinner of old friends—Renoir and Sisley were invited especially for the occasion—ended in the now well-known scene. Monet's attempt to express the high regard all felt for him was taken in the wrong sense by Cézanne, who, with bowed head and, "Ah, Monet! Even you make fun of me!" at once left both house and village—left so hastily that Monet had afterward to pack up and send after him to Aix all his canvases and painting gear. Cézanne regretted his misreading of the situation and wrote to Monet thanking him for "the moral support I found beside you which served as a stimulant for my painting" (letter of July 6, 1895; Cézanne). He also told Geffroy of Monet, "He is the strongest of us all" (Geffroy). Later still he told Gasquet, as already quoted in the text, "I despise all living painters except Monet and Renoir" (Gasquet, *op. cit.*).
16. Letter of Dec. 6, 1909; Geffroy.
17. André.
18. *Ibid.*
19. Vollard (A, B).
20. From the preface (in the form of a letter to the translator's son) to *Livre de l'Art,* by Cennino Cennini, trans. V. Mottez, Paris, 1911.
21. Baume.
22. Pach.
23. *Ibid.*
24. *Ibid.*
25. Venturi.
26. Jean Renoir.
27. Venturi.
28. Vollard (A, B). *Cf.* Rivière (A).
29. *Ibid.*
30. Venturi.
31. André.
32. *Ibid.*
33. *Ibid. Cf.* Vollard (A, B).
34. *Ibid.*

35. Baudot.
36. *Ibid.*
37. Venturi.
38. *Ibid.*
39. *Ibid.*
40. Jean Renoir.
41. Rivière (A).
42. *Ibid.*
43. *Ibid.*
44. Besson.
45. *Ibid.*
46. *Ibid.*
47. Jean Renoir.
48. Besson.
49. Vollard (A, B).
50. *Ibid.*
51. *Ibid.*
52. *Ibid.*
53. *Ibid.*
54. *Ibid.*
55. Venturi.
56. *Ibid.*
57. Baudot.
58. Venturi.
59. *Ibid.*
60. André.
61. Venturi.
62. Baudot. *Cf.* Geffroy.
63. Jean Renoir.
64. More than one version of this remark has been handed down, but
the sense of all is identical. *Cf.* Jean Renoir; André; Venturi. One
account of Renoir's last illness, written by an eyewitness to Durand-
Ruel, gives the chief cause as congestion of the lungs. This account
does not mention Renoir's final remark, and says that his last attempt to work—to draw a vase—failed because a pencil could not
be found. His final remark given here, on the day before his death,
is "Je suis foutu" (I'm finished) but, as the writer comments, Renoir
had been saying this every time he fell ill during the past three
years. The letter is quoted in Vollard (B). See also *Sur le mort de
Renoir, Nouvelles Théories*, 1914–1921; *Diary of an Art Dealer*, by
René Gimpel, New York, 1966.

WORKS OF RENOIR
MENTIONED IN THE TEXT

INDEX

BR418H

Hanson.

Renoir: the man,
the painter, and
his world.

BR418H

Hanson.

Renoir: the man, the painter, and

his world.

September 1969